D0934231

Romanticism in Perspective: Texts, Cultures, Histories

General Editors: **Marilyn Gaull**, Professor of English, Temple University/New York University; **Stephen Prickett**, Regius Professor of English Language and Literature, University of Glasgow

This series aims to offer a fresh assessment of Romanticism by looking at it from a wide variety of perspectives. Both comparative and interdisciplinary, it will bring together cognate themes from architecture, art history, landscape gardening, linguistics, literature, philosophy, politics, science, social and political history and theology to deal with original, contentious or as yet unexplored aspects of Romanticism as a Europe-wide phenomenon.

Titles include:

Jeffrey C. Robinson
RECEPTION AND POETICS IN KEATS
'My Ended Poet'

Anya Taylor
BACCHUS IN ROMANTIC ENGLAND
Writers and Drink, 1780–1830

Nicola Trott and Seamus Perry (*editors*)
1800: THE NEW *LYRICAL BALLADS*

Michael Wiley
ROMANTIC GEOGRAPHY
Wordsworth and Anglo-European Spaces

Eric Wilson
EMERSON'S SUBLIME SCIENCE

John Wyatt
WORDSWORTH'S POEMS OF TRAVEL, 1819–42
'Such Sweet Wayfaring'

Romanticism in Perspective
Series Standing Order ISBN 0–333–71490–3
(*outside North America only*)

You can receive future titles in this series as they are published by placing a standing order.
Please contact your bookseller or, in case of difficulty, write to us at the address below with
your name and address, the title of the series and the ISBN quoted above.

Customer Services Department, Macmillan Distribution Ltd, Houndmills, Basingstoke,
Hampshire RG21 6XS, England

1800: The New *Lyrical Ballads*

Edited by

Nicola Trott
Lecturer in English Literature
University of Glasgow

and

Seamus Perry
Reader in English Literature
University of Glasgow

palgrave

First published 2001 by
PALGRAVE
Houndmills, Basingstoke, Hampshire RG21 6XS and
175 Fifth Avenue, New York, N. Y. 10010
Companies and representatives throughout the world

PALGRAVE is the new global academic imprint of
St. Martin's Press LLC Scholarly and Reference Division and
Palgrave Publishers Ltd (formerly Macmillan Press Ltd).

ISBN 0–333–77398–5

This book is printed on paper suitable for recycling and
made from fully managed and sustained forest sources.

A catalogue record for this book is available
from the British Library.

Library of Congress Cataloging-in-Publication Data
1800 : the new Lyrical ballads / edited by Nicola Trott and Seamus Perry.
        p. cm.
    Includes bibliographical references and index.
    ISBN 0–333–77398–5
    1. Wordsworth, William, 1770–1850. Lyrical ballads. I. Trott, Nicola,
    1962– II. Perry, Seamus.
    PR5869.L93 A617 2000
    821'.7—dc21
                                                                00–055672

10   9   8   7   6   5   4   3   2   1
10   09   08   07   06   05   04   03   02   01

Printed and bound in Great Britain by
Antony Rowe Ltd, Chippenham, Wiltshire

Contents

Notes on the Contributors

John Beer is Emeritus Professor of English Literature at Cambridge University, and Fellow of Peterhouse. He is author of *Coleridge the Visionary* (1959; 1971), *Milton, Lost and Regained* (British Academy Chatterton Lecture, 1964), *Blake's Humanism* (1968), *Blake's Visionary Universe* (1969), *Coleridge's Poetic Intelligence* (1977), *Wordsworth and the Human Heart* (1978), *Wordsworth in Time* (1979), *Romantic Influences: Contemporary—Victorian—Modern* (1993), *Providence and Love: Studies in Wordsworth, Channing, Myers, George Eliot, and Ruskin* (1998), and many other works on romantic, Victorian, and modern writers. He has edited several collections of essays, including *Coleridge's Variety: Bicentenary Studies* (1974) and *Questioning Romanticism* (1995); and he is editor of a number of standard texts, including Coleridge's *Poems* (Everyman, 1963; new edn, 1999), and *Aids to Reflection* (1993) for the Bollingen *Collected Works* of Coleridge.

Tim Fulford is Professor of English at Nottingham Trent University. He is author of *Coleridge's Figurative Language* (1991), *Landscape, Liberty and Authority: Poetry, Criticism and Politics from Thomson to Wordsworth* (1996), and *Romanticism and Masculinity: Gender, Politics and Poetics in the Writing of Burke, Coleridge, Cobbett, Wordsworth, De Quincey and Hazlitt* (1999). He is editor, with Morton D. Paley, of *Coleridge's Visionary Languages: Essays in Honour of J.B. Beer* (1993), and, with Peter J. Kitson, of *Romanticism and Colonialism: Writing and Empire, 1780–1830* (1998).

Marilyn Gaull is Professor of English at New York University and Temple University. She is author of *English Romanticism: the Human Context* (1988) and of many essays and articles on romantic literature, cultural history, and science. She has been editor of a number of series, including *Romanticism in Perspective*, and is founding editor of *The Wordsworth Circle*. She is also co-founder and American Director of the Wordsworth Summer Conference, held annually in Grasmere.

Kenneth R. Johnston is Professor of English at Indiana University. He is author of *Wordsworth and* The Recluse (1984) and *The Hidden Wordsworth: Poet, Lover, Rebel, Spy* (1998). He is editor of *Romantic*

Revolutions: Criticism and Theory (1990), and, with Gene W. Ruoff, of *The Age of William Wordsworth: Critical Essays on the Romantic Tradition* (1987).

Zachary Leader is Professor of English Literature at the University of Surrey, Roehampton. He is author of *Reading Blake's Songs* (1981), *Writer's Block* (1991), and *Revision and Romantic Authorship* (1996). He is also editor of *The Letters of Kingsley Amis* (2000), and, with Ian Haywood, of *Romantic Period Writings 1798–1832: an Anthology* (1998).

Lucy Newlyn is Fellow and Tutor in English, St Edmund Hall, and a Lecturer in the English Faculty at the University of Oxford. She is author of *Coleridge, Wordsworth and the Language of Allusion* (1986), and *'Paradise Lost' and the Romantic Reader* (1993), and editor, with Richard Gravil and Nicholas Roe, of *Coleridge's Imagination: Essays in Memory of Pete Laver* (1985).

Michael O'Neill is Professor of English at the University of Durham. He is author of *The Human Mind's Imaginings: Conflict and Achievement in Shelley's Poetry* (1989), *Percy Bysshe Shelley: a Literary Life* (1989), *Auden, MacNeice, Spender: the Thirties Poetry* (with Gareth Reeves; 1992), and *Romanticism and the Self-Conscious Poem* (1997). He is editor of *Shelley* (a *Longman Critical Reader*; 1993), *Keats: Bicentenary Readings* (1997), and *Literature of the Romantic Period: a Bibliographical Guide* (1998). For the *Manuscripts of the Younger Romantics* series he has edited, with Donald H. Reiman, volume 8 (*Fair-copy Manuscripts of Shelley's Poems in European and American Libraries* (1997)); and, for *The Bodleian Shelley Manuscripts* series, vol. 20 (*'The Defence of Poetry' Fair Copies* (1994)). A volume of his poems, *The Stripped Bed*, appeared in 1990.

Seamus Perry is Reader in English Literature at the University of Glasgow. He is author of *Coleridge and the Uses of Division* (1999) and editor of *Coleridge: Interviews and Recollections* (2000).

Nicholas Roe is Professor of English at the University of St Andrews. He is author of *Wordsworth and Coleridge: the Radical Years* (1988), *The Politics of Nature: Wordsworth and some Contemporaries* (1992), and *John Keats and the Culture of Dissent* (1997). He is editor of *Keats and History* (1995), and, with Richard Gravil and Lucy Newlyn, of *Coleridge's Imagination: Essays in Memory of Pete Laver* (1985). He has edited

William Wordsworth: Selected Poetry for the Penguin Poetry Library (1992) and *John Keats: Selected Poems* for the Everyman Library (1995). He is Director of the biennial Coleridge Summer Conference at Cannington, and founding editor of the journal *Romanticism*.

Nicola Trott is Lecturer in English Literature at the University of Glasgow. She is editor of the *Blackwell Annotated Anthology of the Gothic Novel*, and has published essays on Wordsworth and Milton, romantic aesthetics, Wollstonecraft, and many other romantic subjects, in several critical collections and journals.

A Note on Texts

Quoting from poets who revised their own work as persistently as did Wordsworth and Coleridge is bound to present problems of consistency, especially in a volume of diverse essays by several hands. Our policy attempts to combine a more or less coherent position on texts with the more practical consideration of which texts readers will find it most easy to track down and convenient to use. Poems from both editions of *Lyrical Ballads* are quoted (unless otherwise specified) in their first versions of 1798 and 1800, which are readily available in many modern texts and facsimiles. Other Coleridge poems are quoted from the Oxford *Complete Poetical Works*. For other Wordsworth poems, we have preferred the (early) versions printed in Stephen Gill's widely used *Oxford Authors* volume; and where Gill does not include the work in question, we turn to the five-volume complete Oxford edition of De Selincourt and Darbishire. (The Oxford edition bases itself on late texts, but earlier readings can usually be reconstructed from the extensive *app. crit.*) Thus, a line-number for 'The Ancient Mariner' will normally refer to the 1798 text; for 'Elegaic Stanzas' to the version printed by Gill; and for *The Excursion* to the text printed by De Selincourt and Darbishire. All references to *The Prelude* follow the Norton edition, and are made to the 1805 text unless explicitly acknowledged otherwise (e.g., '*Prelude* (1799)'). Ellipses are marked '...' and are the work of the several essayists, unless explicitly marked as originally authorial; emphases, contrariwise, are all originally authorial, unless declared editorial. Non-standard spellings have been allowed to stand without benefit of a '[sic]'.

The following abbreviations are used throughout:

BL: S.T. Coleridge, *Biographia Literaria or Biographical Sketches of My Literary Life and Opinions*, ed. James Engell and W. Jackson Bate (2 vols; London/Princeton, NJ: Routledge and Kegan Paul/Princeton University Press, 1983)
CL: *The Collected Letters of Samuel Taylor Coleridge*, ed. Earl Leslie Griggs (6 vols; Oxford: Oxford University Press, 1956–71)
CPW: The Complete Poetical Works of Samuel Taylor Coleridge ..., ed. Ernest Hartley Coleridge (2 vols; Oxford: Clarendon Press, 1912)

DWJ: *Journals of Dorothy Wordsworth*, ed. E. de Selincourt (2 vols; London: Macmillan, 1941)
ELH: *English Literary History*
ELN: English Language Notes
EY: The Letters of William and Dorothy Wordsworth: The Early Years, 1787–1805, ed. Ernest de Selincourt, rev. Chester L. Shaver (Oxford: Clarendon Press, 1967)
Gill: *William Wordsworth. The Oxford Authors*, ed. Stephen Gill (Oxford: Oxford University Press, 1984)
Hazlitt: *The Complete Works of William Hazlitt*, ed. P.P. Howe (21 vols; London: Dent, 1930–4)
JEGP: *Journal of English and Germanic Philology*
LBB: William Wordsworth and S.T. Coleridge, *Lyrical Ballads. The Text of the 1798 Edition with the Additional 1800 Poems and the Prefaces*, ed. R.L. Brett and A. R. Jones (2nd edn; London: Routledge, 1991)
LBM: Lyrical Ballads, ed. Michael Mason (London: Longman, 1992)
N&Q: Notes and Queries
NB: The Notebooks of Samuel Taylor Coleridge, Kathleen Coburn *et al.* (4 double volumes to date; London/Princeton, NJ: Routledge/Princeton University Press, 1957–)
Norton Prelude: William Wordsworth, *The Prelude 1799, 1805, 1850 . . .,* ed. Jonathan Wordsworth, M.H. Abrams and Stephen Gill (NY/ London: Norton, 1979)
PMLA: Publication of the Modern Language Association of America
PQ: Philological Quarterly
SiR: Studies in Romanticism
TWC: The Wordsworth Circle
WPW: The Poetical Works of William Wordsworth, ed. E. de Selincourt, rev. Helen Darbishire (5 vols; Oxford: Clarendon Press, 1952–9)
WPrW: The Prose Works of William Wordsworth, ed. W.J.B. Owen and Jane Worthington Smyser (3 vols; Oxford: Clarendon Press, 1974)

Introduction: the New *Lyrical Ballads*

Nicola Trott and Seamus Perry

> I have no other motive for soliciting your friendship than what (I should think) every man, who has read and felt the 'Lyrical Ballads,' must have in common with me. ... I may say in general, without the smallest exaggeration, that the whole aggregate of pleasure I have received from some eight or nine other poets that I have been able to find since the world began – falls infinitely short of what those two enchanting volumes have singly afforded me; – that your name is with me for ever linked to the lovely scenes of nature; – and that not yourself only but that each place and object you have mentioned – and all the souls in that delightful community of your's – to me 'Are dearer than the sun!'
>
> Thomas De Quincey, to Wordsworth[1]

The 'two enchanting volumes' responsible for turning the head of the young De Quincey are the second edition of *Lyrical Ballads* of 1800 (as it says on the title page, though in fact it did not appear until January 1801) – the bicentenary of whose publication this volume of essays commemorates.

'1800' is not one of the most famous dates in English literary history, but it should be: indeed, there is a good case for elevating it above the more celebrated rival of 1798. For it is the 1800 edition of *Lyrical Ballads* that sees into print much of Wordsworth's most innovative and lasting poetry: not only 'Michael', 'The Brothers', and the 'Lucy' poems, but also the first public glimpse of what will later become *The Prelude* ('There was a Boy'), and some of the earliest and most memorable appearances of one of the period's greatest creations – Wordsworth's Lake District (pre-eminently in the 'Poems on the

Naming of Places'), the 'lovely scenes of nature' that so stirred the young De Quincey. It is the 1800 edition, also, that first introduces the famous 'Preface', one of the defining documents of British romanticism – even though (perhaps, especially because) its definitions are so contradictory and paradoxical. There was more to Wordsworth's 1800 than the second edition of *Lyrical Ballads*, of course: it was a crucial year in his imaginative life, particularly in the relationship with Coleridge, and, in many ways, it defined the kind of poet that Wordsworth was to remain, and as which he would be remembered – a Lake Poet. 'Home at Grasmere' at last, back among the scenes of his childhood after turbulent years of exile, and intent on his philosophical masterwork, he embarked upon an extraordinary act of willed self-creation, evidences of which can repeatedly be found in the *Ballads*. And, besides all this, and in an exemplarily Wordsworthian way, the 1800 volumes acknowledged continuity with a past identity, as well as announcing the brave innovations of the recreated self: by reprinting the 1798 *Ballads* (rearranged and revised) as volume one of the 1800 edition, Wordsworth implicitly recorded a sense of growth and development, a moving on which was not a renunciation of what he had been. The 'new' *Lyrical Ballads*, that is to say, contain an implicit invitation to reconsider the achievements of the old.

All of these several aspects of the book, and its moment, appear in the essays collected in this volume. The first, by John Beer, returns to the original 1798 collection and describes the kind of underlying unity of purpose that it possessed, reconstructing the speculations about human benevolence and natural energies in which Coleridge was involving Wordsworth in the Alfoxden year. The expanded edition of 1800, in Beer's reading, represents a dissipation of the original focus, as Wordsworth moves away from the Coleridgean territory of the 'One Life' and towards a more humanistic poetry of the 'heart': Wordsworth's displacing of 'The Ancient Mariner' from the pole position it had occupied in 1798 eloquently implies the shift in imaginative interest that the composite text of 1800 embodies. Zachary Leader's essay also addresses the question of the volumes' conceptual unity, but from a generic perspective. Leader finds a kind of imaginative oxymoron within the phrase, 'Lyrical Ballads' – a mixture of dramatic objectivity and self-questioning subjectivity, reminiscent of the hybrid genre 'Lyrical Drama' devised by Shelley for his intensely internal anti-drama, *Prometheus Unbound*. A good deal of recent criticism has regarded such moves towards the 'internal' as bad politics; but, as Leader argues, the kinds of obstacle which this brand of lyricism places in the path of balladic simplicity can work positively to enrich our sense of the social and human realities which underlie the poems.

The simplicity of the 'ballad' which excited so many literary commentators in the later eighteenth century chimed with a much wider cultural obsession with the primitive, and Tim Fulford's essay relates some of the *Lyrical Ballads* – including 'Ruth', 'The Complaint of a forsaken Indian Woman', and Coleridge's 'Foster-Mother's Tale' – to the often exotic travel literature that was contemporaneously reporting back on the indigenous peoples of North America. These 'Indian'-influenced poems by Wordsworth and Coleridge, in turn, influenced other poets, and an unexpected relationship emerges between the aesthetic preferences of the young Romantic poets and a later nineteenth-century history of colonial expansion. The 'primitive' and 'original' are also the subject of Marilyn Gaull's essay – not as the Romantic age thought it discovered them in mysterious cultures buried deep in dark continents, but as it heard their lingering voice, in the tales that antiquarians and folklorists were beginning to collect all across Europe. Wordsworth reflects upon this tradition, and upon his place within it, in the 1805 *Prelude*; and traces of his close imaginative kinship to the rich, fearful realm of the folktale can be detected in the intensely original poetry of childhood which he was writing in and about 1800: the *Lyrical Ballads* themselves, 'Home at Grasmere', and other works. Together, these poems offer us a Wordsworthian 'child' very different from the sanitized and civilized figure embraced by the nineteenth century – a creature altogether more rebellious, difficult, and savage.

The next group of essays addresses the contents of the 1800 volumes more directly. Kenneth Johnston's contribution places the new *Ballads* within the context of Wordsworth's colossal attempts at self-invention as he prepared himself for the life-long task of *The Recluse*. Read in this way, we can see many of the poems anew, as variously coded accounts of Wordsworth's own experience, returning to his home ground and beginning work on his vindicating epic. The sense of frustration and anxiety that overcame him, as 1800 went on and 'Home at Grasmere' came to a halt, is registered in the boisterous exuberance of the 'Preface', a fundamental and self-defining statement (as Johnston argues) of much wider reference than to the collection of poems – most of them, in 1800, *mis*named *Lyrical Ballads* anyway – that follow it. Michael O'Neill's essay also seeks to characterize the special temper of the poems, not by placing them within their biographical moment, but by teasing out the distinctive mixture of apparent lucidity and complicating subtext that features in so many of them. The poems often set about unsettling received opinions or overturning literary norms (as indeed the famous 'Preface', and its brief forerunner, the 'Advertisement' of 1798, had polemically promised); but it is a more subtle interpenetration of the expected and the unpredicted that moves them at their most characteristic – a play between the common and the singular, the communal and the individual, the monistic and the particular, with neither giving ground. Nicola Trott also finds dissension and disquiet at work in Wordsworth's poems of 1800, which she describes by setting them against their Coleridgean background. Coleridge's optimistic beliefs in nature's goodness and its proximity to the divine were supposed to underwrite Wordsworth's career as a philosophical poet; but while traces of that creed of natural piety certainly persist in the new *Lyrical Ballads*, so too does a very different rhetoric of nature, one drawing instead on the tradition of eighteenth-century natural philosophy which Coleridge had sought to overturn. This tradition stresses, not nature's blessedness and implicit wisdom, but her sexuality and organic instincts of desire; and its Wordsworthian voice challenges the Coleridgean orthodoxies, in tones ranging from the subtle to the disturbingly brutal. Finally in this group of essays, Seamus Perry takes up the context of *The Recluse* (that Johnston describes), the idiosyncratic formal qualities of the poems (finding, rather as does O'Neill, a characteristic pattern of frustrations and self-checkings in the verse), and Wordsworth's Coleridgean inheritance (as discussed by Trott), and tries to relate them to one another. Wordsworth's failure to pull off the Coleridgean commission of *The Recluse* is the failure of a millennial and inevitabilist vision; and, implicitly recording that defeat, the *Ballads* which emerged in the epic's place explore, not inevitability, but accidence and contingency. These remain the terms in which Coleridge expresses his disappointment with Wordsworth's failure to fulfil his epic destiny in the *Biographia Literaria* of 1817, a book with its deepest roots in the 1800 moment.

Our last two essays lead on from Wordsworth's appearances in Coleridge's later prose to discuss the uses to which the famous collection and its poems were subsequently put by other writers and critics. Lucy Newlyn shows how we may read 'My First Acquaintance with Poets' (1823), Hazlitt's celebrated memoir of meeting Wordsworth and Coleridge in 1798, as a coded expression of Hazlitt's scepticism about the democratic credentials of poetry. Focusing upon the essay's vivid description of Coleridge's chanting voice, Newlyn teases out the cultural significance of Hazlitt's portrait by placing it in the context of the surprisingly large, and often heavily politicized, eighteenth-century dispute about the rival merits of chanting and 'plain speaking'. Once alerted to the nuances of that debate, we can find in Hazlitt's account of Coleridge's supposedly radical youth seeds of the conservative Anglican that he was later to become, much to Hazlitt's disgust and dismay. In Newlyn's reading, 'My First Acquaintance' re-imagines *Lyrical Ballads*, and its moment, to describe subsequent ideological disappointments – which may look a peculiarly Hazlittian manoeuvre. But such acts of interpretative re-creation have been central to the poems' afterlife; and our last essay, by Nicholas Roe, shows how they have been successively re-figured by generations of literary historians. Tracing the protracted reception of the *Lyrical Ballads* in the later nineteenth century, Roe recovers what he calls the 'low tradition' of Wordsworth commentary. This rich and diverse critical legacy, although largely the work of writers now forgotten or unread, was the basis upon which Wordsworth's canonical status came to be established, and with it the powerful and tenacious mythology of the *Lyrical Ballads* as an 'epoch-making' event: the birth of a new poetry, a reinvigorating spring-time of the imagination. Attending to the strong voice of the low tradition, Roe argues, brings back to mind a poet rather different to the Wordsworth we normally meet: we encounter once again the 'popular' poet praised by Hazlitt, whose nineteenth-century admirers produced the enormous body of biographies, memoirs, and editions which the academy now largely ignores.

The wide variety of nineteenth-century voices gathered in Roe's piece eloquently implies the power which these extraordinary poems seemingly possess to re-make themselves as new *Lyrical Ballads* in the eyes of successive generations of readers. We hope very much that the essays we have gathered in this volume, with all their diversity of approach and method, may work to something of the same effect.

Note

1 31 May, 1803; quoted in John E. Jordan, *De Quincey to Wordsworth: A Biography of a Relationship* ... (Berkeley/Los Angeles: University of California Press, 1962), p. 30.

1
The Unity of *Lyrical Ballads*

John Beer

One of the most surprising things that has ever been said about the 1798 *Lyrical Ballads* collection was also one of the earliest. Writing to their publisher, Joseph Cottle, in May 1798, Coleridge said:

> We deem that the volumes offered to you are to a certain degree *one work*, in *kind tho' not in degree*, as an Ode is one work – & that our different poems are as stanzas, good relatively rather than absolutely: – Mark you, I say *in kind* tho' not in degree. (*CL*, i.412)

To the general reader who is familiar with the finished volume this must appear an extraordinary statement. Here we have a collection which begins with a long ballad, ends with a long meditative poem, and in the interspace comprises a range of various shorter works in different modes, some written in the poet's own voice, one or two not: and yet the authors can apparently agree in regarding it as '*one work*, in *kind tho' not in degree*'.

One reason why this must seem strange is that readers of the 1798 edition, then as now, tended to approach new work in terms of what was familiar. An early reviewer commented, for instance, that 'The Ancient Mariner' did not read like any ballad in the English tradition. He was evidently unaware of the new German ballads that were currently being translated into English – though those reviewers who were did not treat the poem much better, regarding it as a failed attempt to imitate a currently fashionable mode.

Some years ago, however, an important article appeared, entitled 'The Contemporaneity of the *Lyrical Ballads*', written by Robert Mayo, who had made a special study of the magazines of the 1790s.[1] Many of these made a habit of publishing a few poems in each number.

What he found, rather to his surprise, was that many of the poems which might strike the present-day reader as unusual turned out not to seem out of the ordinary once one turned the pages of the contemporary magazines.

Mayo quoted surveys from a number of respected critics and scholars, each asserting that Wordsworth had broken new ground by being the first to write about the real outcasts of society such as beggars, convicts, and forsaken women. As he pointed out, however, this was simply a received opinion, passed from one critic to the next: for each of these categories, he showed, there were at least twenty poems that could be cited from the magazines of the time. If one thought of the *Lyrical Ballads* poem title 'The Mad Mother' as unusual in its choice of subject, one might turn to the contemporary magazines and find 'Crazy Kate', 'Mad Peg', 'Crazy Luke', 'Bess of Bedlam', 'Ellen, or the Fair Insane' or 'Moll Pot, the Mad Woman of Gloucester-Street'.

If readers thought Coleridge's poem on the nightingale was distinctive in its subject, similarly, Robert Mayo could disillusion them with the titles of a dozen poems on nightingales in the 1790s and the assurance that there were many more. And it was not only the subjects that could be duplicated over and over again. If one was intrigued by the way in which the ballads sometimes reply to one another one might consider 'The Wish, by a Bachelor' in the *Weekly Magazine*, followed by 'The Reply to the Bachelor's Wish, by a Husband'. And if the title 'Lines written at a small distance from my House, and sent by my little Boy to the Person to whom they are addressed' seemed a little verbose, one might turn to the *Universal Magazine* in 1796 and find 'Lines, Written by Sir Richard Hill, Bart, at Hawkestone, his Elegant Seat in Shropshire, When Contemplating the Scenes around Him in his own Park, and to be Seen in a Natural Cavern of a Vast Rock, from the Top of which is a Very Diversified and Romantic Prospect'. Many of the titles contained terms that were also common – 'Complaints', 'Sketches', 'Inscriptions', and 'Verses' (which latter might be verses 'found under a Yew-Tree', 'Made at Sea during a Heavy Gale', or 'Left in a Summer-house'). Most striking, in view of what has come to be said about this Romantic mode, is the very large number of poems in the collection styled 'Fragments'.

Not only would the first readers of *Lyrical Ballads* have been conversant with all these features of the collection, but editors recognized them with a similar sense of familiarity: fifteen out of the twenty shorter items in it were reprinted within a year or so of publication in these very same magazines.

By the time one has finished looking at all the features of *Lyrical Ballads* that were common to the magazines of the time, indeed, one is left asking what exactly *was* original about them. Mayo insists on their superiority, but does not say very much about wherein it consists. Even the forms adopted for the ballads, he points out, are not particularly original: only 'Goody Blake and Harry Gill' could be said to be. He also reminds the reader that Wordsworth and Coleridge never claimed to be drawing on new subjects; they simply spoke of experiments in language. And even these claims are not altogether convincing. They do not apply to 'The Ancient Mariner', for example, nor for that matter to 'Lines written ... above Tintern Abbey', which was simply developing the meditative mode in terms already familiar from the work of poets such as Cowper. Both poems, in any case, stand away from the nature of the shorter pieces.

So where is the 'unity' of the collection to be found? The assumption that such a unity existed was always a somewhat fragile one, certainly: so fragile that by 1800 Wordsworth had changed the order of the poems, claiming that 'The Ancient Mariner' had been an injury to the volume. He also wanted to change the title, preferring that it should be called simply *Poems* (*EY*, p. 297) – which suggests that he thought the very conception of the original volume had proved unsatisfactory. In the event, his publishers would not allow him to change it, presumably thinking the earlier one had proved more saleable (and also perhaps that it would confuse readers to find that they were getting much of the same work under a new title), so the two-volume edition, also, bore it. As Kenneth Johnston has pointed out, this was rather a pity in view of the firm direction exhibited by Wordsworth's poetry in the second edition. For when one looks at what he was adding one finds that the second volume was dominated by poems such as the third piece, 'The Brothers', and the last, 'Michael' – each of which demonstrates the new way in which his poetry was developing – poems, often extended, about the pathos of the tragedies that can beset very ordinary human beings.[2]

It is nevertheless clear that many of the early readers and reviewers were taken aback by the disparate nature of the collection when it first appeared and did not know what to make of it, so that Wordsworth may well have been justified in feeling that it in some way *affronted* the reader more than was necessary. Yet it should also be borne in mind that for some readers the collection, whether in its 1798 or 1800 form, had all the excitement of a new departure in poetry. John Wilson, writing to Wordsworth in 1802 at the age of seventeen, claimed that *Lyrical Ballads* was 'the book which I value next to my Bible';[3] and the following year De Quincey, who was also seventeen, wrote saying 'from the wreck of all earthly things which belong to me, I should endeavour to save that work by an impulse second to none but that of self-preservation'.[4] Young men who could say that were evidently responding to something they felt to be important in the collection as a whole; they seem to have detected immediately some kind of unity to which they could readily respond.

In pursuing this puzzle it is natural to turn for enlightenment to the 'Preface' which Wordsworth wrote for the 1800 edition, and many later readers have done so. The statement there about the language chosen for the poems is the one that has aroused most interest, since it raises a number of important questions about its social basis:

> Low and rustic life was generally chosen because in that situation the essential passions of the heart find a better soil in which they can attain their maturity, are less under restraint, and speak a plainer and more emphatic language; because in that situation our elementary feelings exist in a state of greater simplicity and conse-quently may be more accurately contemplated and more forcibly communicated; because the manners of rural life germinate from those elementary feelings; and from the necessary character of rural occupations are more easily comprehended; and are more durable; and lastly, because in that situation the passions of men are incorporated with the beautiful and permanent forms of nature. (*WPrW*, i.124)

Such statements have been given attention because they suggest in Wordsworth a view of language that anticipates the idea, sometimes loosely associated with Marxism, that the language of the proletariat is more 'real' than that of other classes. Yet as soon as one turns back to the poems themselves, it is clear that their achievement is a long way from realizing any hopes that they might embody such a sharp social critique. Many of them contain no new departures in language or (in the case of 'The Ancient Mariner') experiments of a quite differ-ent kind, while those that do are often using language in a way that half-smiles at its own usage: 'For very cold to go to bed, / And then for cold not sleep a wink' ('Goody Blake and Harry Gill', ll.47–8), or the notorious 'His poor old ancles swell' ('Simon Lee', l.68). The radical claims of the 'Preface' do not seem to be well supported by such uses.

In directing his readers specifically to points such as the diction of 'low and rustic life', Wordsworth was in any case not necessarily doing these poems a service, since what they require for a full understanding is a kind of double reading, which will at one and the same time attend to the line of the verse and maintain an awareness of undercurrents in the authors' minds. Hazlitt is a good guide here: of Wordsworth's achievement in *Lyrical Ballads* he wrote

> Fools have laughed at, wise men scarcely understand them. He takes a subject or a story merely as pegs or loops to hang thought and feeling on; the incidents are trifling, in proportion to his contempt for imposing appearances; the reflections are profound, according to the gravity and the aspiring pretensions of his mind. (Hazlitt, xi:87)

We have to see the texts of these poems as more complex, in other words, and be ready to give them a double reading before they will make sense, attending both to what is being said directly, and to the underlying meditation or questioning.

One other point should be made, again surprising in terms of Hazlitt's assertion. Wordsworth himself claimed almost immediately afterwards that the poems had been written simply to make money and should not have been criticized so sharply by friends such as Southey, who knew that (*EY*, pp. 267–8); and after Coleridge criticized the theory of poetic language many years later, Wordsworth said, 'I never cared a straw about the theory – & the Preface was written at the request of Coleridge out of sheer good nature.'[5] Again, this seems at first sight to go against Hazlitt's sensing of a profundity in the poems. If they were being written fast, simply to make money, are we not taking the whole issue too seriously?

I believe that this is only a part of the truth, however. Clearly the ballads were written quite fast, over a few months, but there is evidence to suggest that they were written during a time of considerable intellectual excitement on the part of both poets. There is also a difference between the successive collections: in the 1800 volume Wordsworthian profundity plays an increasing part, giving it a corresponding unity. In 1798 the situation was different. A whole range of ideas had come to the surface in their minds simultaneously, and were fermenting together – ideas which they were ready to explore further. In due course they hoped to produce more ambitious works of poetry from them; in the meantime, however, whether presented in a raw form or, more often, working just behind the presented text, the ideas could occasion poem after poem.

One reason why the 1798 volume of *Lyrical Ballads* should have taken the form it did, and why the authors should have seen a continuous thread running through them, has to do with the political situation of the time. These were, after all, men who had seen the extraordinary excitement which accompanied the French Revolution and who had lived for the previous five years under the weight of contending emotions. On the one hand, they had felt a growing disillusionment concerning the course of the revolution itself: whatever their feelings about the aspirations involved they could not wish to see the bloodshed and mass executions reduplicated in England. On the other hand, they were forced to recognize the great wave of idealism that had been released among young men by those same events. Was that all now to be discounted and forgotten? Did it have no significance at all?[6] They could hardly believe that, either; what they were looking for was a line of inquiry and prospect that they could cling to and transmit to their fellows as an explanation of what had happened and a promise of hope for the future. Such a line they had found in their growing conviction that the world was not, as often assumed in contemporary thinking, simply a great machine, pursuing its way without regard for human beings. Against such a view they could find evidence to suggest that in ordinary life charities and bonds of affection between human beings existed which were not called for if human behaviour was dictated simply by mechanical and impersonal factors.

This was in no way equivalent to a sentimental belief that the universe was always working for the benefit of humanity: on the contrary, they were all too aware of the current argument that the universe was *not* on the side of human beings, and that the natural behaviour of those human beings was to fight one another rather than work co-operatively. Shortly after concluding the first edition of *Lyrical Ballads* Wordsworth was to write a number of poems now commonly grouped together as the 'Lucy' poems, in which he explored the implications of the fact of human death in face of any sense that nature was benevolent. But in the year or two immediately before, the evidence they were finding gave them a sense of relief.

We do not properly understand the 1798 *Lyrical Ballads*, then, unless we see that the starting-point of the whole enterprise had been a previous state of disillusionment and hopelessness, the poems in the collection representing successive attempts to build from that hopelessness towards some kind of positive stance. This helps to explain why 'The Ancient Mariner' should in the first edition have been chosen to open the volume: it can be seen as intended to initiate the reader into an understanding of the state of mind in which the poems that follow had been written. For these are poems written by poets who, like the Mariner, have entered upon an experience of despair and desolation in the world, and yet who – like him again – have passed through into an appreciation of the blessings of ordinary existence that suggests something important about the positive forces at work in the world. And these are supplemented by poems in which nature itself is seen at times to radiate a simpler and more happy sense – as if the birds and the flowers on a spring morning are acting and growing out of a joy, interwoven at some level with all the processes of creation, that is far from mechanical, just as the Mariner's utterance is at times blessed with images from the pleasures of the natural world: the jargoning of birds, the melody of a hidden brook (ll.347–51, 358–61).

Approaching the collection from this point of view, one can begin to trace a thread which begins from the Mariner's bewildered appreciation of ordinary life – passing from place to place as a haunted and tormented being, yet also celebrating its simple ceremonies – and moves through other poems which look at human life and find special virtues in its ordinariness. Simple incidents are presented: an old man has lost the strength to perform a straightforward operation on a tree-root; a shepherd is carrying his last surviving sheep. Most tellingly of all, perhaps, a mother is not repelled by the behaviour of her idiot son but can appreciate and even enjoy it. And side by side with these are poems which celebrate the pleasures of nature: Coleridge's 'The Nightingale', Wordsworth's 'Lines written at a small distance from my House', 'Expostulation and Reply', and 'The Tables Turned'.

The two threads – enjoyment of the beauty of nature and appreciation of the ordinary life of human beings – which both spring from an appreciation, like the Mariner's, of the interdependence and linking of all life, can eventually be seen to come together and interweave in the last poem, the 'Lines written ... above Tintern Abbey', which opens with appreciation of a quiet, unusually harmonic scene in nature and then proceeds into meditation on the relationship between appreciation of such scenes and an apprehension of the links that draw all human beings together.

'Lines left upon a Seat in a Yew-tree' is a 'scene-setting' poem of the same kind, suggesting what is lost to a man who is so disillusioned by civilization that he decides simply to live alone in nature. (The motif develops, of course, the tradition of the melancholy hermit of eighteenth-century verse.[7]) Yet this appeal to the link between a sympathetic view of nature and the possibility of taking a similar attitude to the needs of humanity is hardly enough to explain the extraordinary *diversity* of themes in the collection, which suggests that the poets were exploring more widely than my simple summary so far might suggest. If the ultimate concerns of Wordsworth and Coleridge ran together, with extraordinarily creative results, at this time, those concerns found their main centre in different areas of their human experience. From this point of view it is worth looking at the opening of the passage from which I quoted earlier – an opening which is often overlooked:

> The principal object ... which I proposed to myself in these Poems was to make the incidents of common life interesting by tracing in them, truly though not ostentatiously, the primary laws of our nature: chiefly as far as regards the manner in which we associate ideas in a state of excitement. (*WPrW*, i.122–4)

The ending of this sentence points us in a different direction from that involved in the question of language. It suggests some kind of psychological exploration; and here we may well suspect that the dominant presence was not Wordsworth's. It was Coleridge who had recently been giving most thought to questions of mental process; and in doing so had been concerned to find a complement to the theories of David Hartley. Hartley, as may be recalled, saw the whole of mental process as one of association between ideas based on sense experience. Such sense experiences, once imprinted in the human body, persisted as vibrations in the memory, which could allow them to be associated this way and that, to make up the various patterns which we think of as ideas. Coleridge, who had at first been very attracted by this system, had come to see that it offered a very simplistic account of mental process. For one thing it suggested the existence of 'simple sensations', a very doubtful concept; for another, it made mental process seem in itself blind and purposeless. In particular it paid too little attention to the sense of controlling currents in the mind, which might be thought at times to dominate associations and to some extent control them. Coleridge had thought at first that it might be possible to direct the associative process by educational methods so that in the end it would move irresistibly in the direction of the divine; but then the question arose – if all our thought processes were associative, how could they ever truly be changed?

Wordsworth's simple statement suggests that they had envisaged a clue as to how these processes might operate. If the human mind, when in a state of excitement, made associations of a different kind from those which occurred in a passive state of quiet meditation, then it might be claimed that the account offered by Locke and Hartley called for modification. *Their* work would suggest that we lived in a world of necessity, and that our only hope lay in manipulating social relationships in such a way that the patterns of association in the minds of all the members of society would be improved. But if there were other powers at work in the human mind then we could look to those for a more optimistic view. One might make an analogy with the physical universe: the ideas of Locke and Hartley were sometimes thought of as a psychological complement to the laws of Newton that had produced so simplified a view of the workings of the planetary universe; now in the same way a simple basic idea for the working of very complex factors could be proposed. Just as the fact of gravitation cannot explain other things in the universe, such as the existence of light, or for that matter the workings of life, so it could be argued that Locke and Hartley had provided one straightforward mechanism to explain the workings of the human mind, but had not explained the *life* of that mind, or for that matter its occasional experiences of 'illumination'. Coleridge, by contrast, continually thought of the mind in ways that allowed for such a possibility. There was always a touch of enthusiasm in everything he brushed with this idea, and its infectiousness can be traced in Wordsworth's writing. In 'The Ancient Mariner' it is to be seen as a controlling power, as the Mariner is stripped of all the normal conventional ways of thinking, or nonthinking, that allow him to shoot an albatross casually and without any real consideration of what he is doing, and is thus exposed to more primitive states of mind in which he experiences both the depth of human suffering (his shipmates' even more than his own) and, in due course, a sense of the link between all living things. He cannot understand the full significance of what has happened to him, nor indeed does the poet try to be explicit about it, but he returns to the world haunted by a sense that things are not what they are conventionally made to seem, coupled with a new feeling for the simple charities of human existence represented by such events as weddings and assemblies of human beings to pray together.

If we think of the collection in these terms, our attention is directed to different matters: to those poems that show the human mind in unusual states – poems such as 'The Thorn', 'The Mad Mother', 'The Complaint of a forsaken Indian Woman', that present human beings in extremity and suggest how in such states the human being might seem to be acting according to a quite different sense of the world: the bereaved mother, simply clinging to the spot where her baby's grave is, the mad mother, resting everything on her relationship to her child, the Indian Woman who finds it easier to relate herself to the Northern Lights than to the companions who have abandoned her. The constant suggestion is that in such extreme states the human being discovers where the true bondings of existence lie.

When Wordsworth comes to write about this last poem, he describes it as one of his attempts to 'follow the fluxes and refluxes of the mind when agitated by the great and simple affections of our nature' (*WPrW*, i:126). The phrase 'fluxes and refluxes' is again significant, suggesting as it does the mystery involved in the gravitational influence of the moon on the tides. And although, as Wordsworth says, the poem is a picture of the mind in extremity, 'the last struggles of a human being at the approach of death, cleaving in solitude to life and society' (*WPrW*, i.126), there is something more to it than this might suggest. The woman's factual sense of her own weakness is dominated by primary yearnings that are not directed simply towards her companions. It might be truer to say that her condition has set up alternating magnetisms. Alone in the snowy wastes, devoid of all normal contact with the world, her basic magnetization is to the energies of the universe, as manifested in the cracklings of the aurora borealis: it is as real in her dreams as in her waking perceptions, so that she is even surprised to wake and find herself still surviving:

> In sleep I heard the northern gleams;
> The stars they were among my dreams;
> In sleep did I behold the skies,
> I saw the crackling flashes drive;
> And yet they are upon my eyes,
> And yet I am alive.

> ('The Complaint of a forsaken Indian Woman', ll.3–8)

Her first wish, therefore, is to die: in this magnetized solitude she has no fear of death, which will simply confirm her, in the waste under the stars, as a part of the living universe at large. Yet the thought of her fellow human beings, initiated by a feeling of reproach towards the companions who refused to take her further, attracts her back to her child – and this thought reminds her of the moment when they were separated:

> Through his whole body something ran,
> A most strange something did I see;
> – As if he strove to be a man,
> That he might pull the sledge for me.
> And then he stretched his arms, how wild
> Oh mercy! like a little child.

(ll.35–40)

There is here a suggestion that at the moment when the filial bond was being severed the child's primal consciousness was not only excited into action but stirred to operate at its extremes: first expanding with its own growth-impulse, trying to assume manhood in a moment in order to help her, before contracting to the helplessness of the baby in its plight and its separation. The mother's own adult consciousness extends the process. The urge to be with her child relapses towards a more general impulse to be with her people, and then to recognition that she cannot even lift a limb, which gives place to a final yearning that she could have her child with her at the moment of death and so die happily, the two great magnetisms in her consciousness finally reconciled.

The same sense of a kind of double magnetism is to be found in the preceding poem – at least as it existed before Wordsworth excised its ending. In 'Old Man Travelling; Animal Tranquillity and Decay, a Sketch' he depicts an old man who in his age has become so much a part of nature that even the birds do not notice him (ll.1–2). Yet when the man speaks, it is to reveal the undertaking of a journey dominated by a quite different kind of attraction: the need to visit his dying son, if at all possible, while he is still alive (ll.17–20).

The poem 'Goody Blake and Harry Gill' seems in turn to reflect with a very particular intensity and directness the excitement of Wordsworth's exposure to Coleridge's ideas, since it stands very close to Coleridge's belief in a connection between the primary consciousness of human beings and the warmth-sense of the body. The story from which it is derived appeared in Erasmus Darwin's *Zoönomia*, a work which (I have elsewhere argued)[8] stimulated Coleridge strongly. Wordsworth's anxiety to obtain it is evident from a note in the early spring of 1798 in the course of which he says,

> I write merely to request (which I have very particular reasons for doing) that you would contrive to send me Dr Darwin's Zoönomia *by the first carrier.* (*EY*, p. 199)

The urgency of the emphasized words suggests that Coleridge had already told him of the story and made him eager to read the original. It earned its particular Wordsworthian significance, in turn, both by its support for his sense that the common link between human beings was recognized best by those in a village community and by Darwin's firm claim that it was true. Harry Gill, by his mean attitude to his neighbour, depriving her of the fuel which was vital to her life but of little use to himself, had broken the bond of natural affection; it was therefore appropriate (and in this instance, it seemed, an established physical fact) that the coldness of his heart should become physically manifest in the uncontrollable coldness of his body. Wordsworth himself commented on the peculiar significance of the story in view of Darwin's assertion:

> I wished to draw attention to the truth that the power of the human imagination is sufficient to produce such changes even in our physical nature as might almost appear miraculous. The truth is an important one; the fact (for it is a *fact*) is a valuable illustration of it. (*WPrW*, i.150)

The emphasis, characteristically, is on the *factual* nature of the episode.

Wordsworth was, I have suggested, strongly affected by Coleridge's ideas in the writing of such poems, and also in those which display his quite unusual enthusiasm for nature – though he also guards his position continually with elements of scepticism: 'And I must think, do all I can', 'If I these thoughts may not prevent' ('Lines written in early spring', ll.19, 21), 'for such loss, I would believe, / Abundant recompense' ('Lines written ... above Tintern Abbey', ll.88–9). And when we look at the direction in which his mind had been moving before this time we find that although it had recently been lightened by the presence of Coleridge and Dorothy, his chief poetic preoccupation had previously been not with the undercurrent of life and pleasure in nature but the facts of solitude and suffering. In various poetic drafts of that time he returns again and again to the same situation, of a single figure, often in a landscape, who is eloquent of the disparate human condition: the discharged soldier, the old man travelling, the woman of 'The Ruined Cottage'. There is even a suggestion that such individuals may be gifted with special insight. One of his most characteristic observations, assigned to a character in *The Borderers* and used again later more directly as an epigraph for *The White Doe of Rylstone*, occurs in the lines:

> Action is transitory – a step, a blow,
> The motion of a muscle – this way or that—
> 'Tis done, and in the after-vacancy
> We wonder at ourselves like men betrayed:
> Suffering is permanent, obscure and dark,
> And shares the nature of infinity.
>
> (*The Borderers*, ll.1539–44; *WPW*, i.188)[9]

It is evidently a crucial statement, enshrining his belief that more is sometimes disclosed in suffering than in action, and that what is revealed may be closer to the central truth of things. That sense too has its part to play in what Hazlitt thought of as the 'profundity' of these poems.

There are, it must be acknowledged, contradictions in some of them – most notably in 'The Ancient Mariner'. Had the two poets given themselves more time to think they would have wished, no doubt, to remove some of these contradictory patterns and make their work more homogeneous – as Wordsworth did when he abridged 'Old Man Travelling' (see *WPW*, iv.247, *app. crit.*), and as Coleridge did when he wrote in the explanatory marginal glosses for his poem nearly twenty years later. But the fact that they allowed some of the contradictorinesses of actual life to be there in these poems actually adds to their value as texts to think with and argue about. As we enter into the poets' minds we can re-experience the current excitement that made them explore in a variety of ways the possible links between certain elements in nature and the workings of the human heart, and as we attend more closely to the text itself it will be found to reflect some of the obliquities, cross-currents and contradictions that we recognize in our own attempts to understand other people and find a proper language to describe our more puzzling human encounters. The very differences between them – Coleridge responding to the signs of life, Wordsworth standing back and contemplating the significance of isolated organisms in the context of those signs – convey to us the varying strands of emotion and reason at work in these poems, with all their possibilities for varying interpretation.

It may be concluded, then, that there *was* a unity to the 1798 poems, but it was a unity provided by the mutual stimulus at work between Wordsworth and Coleridge – and to some extent Dorothy Wordsworth also – during those months. It was not a unity that would have been evident to the first readers, since to appreciate it truly they would have needed to share in that underlying interplay. In 1798 it would have been far from most people's apprehension; they would not, like the original protagonists, have been led to it step by step. Hence the bewilderment of many of the first readers, coupled with the excitement of a few young men who sensed that in English poetry something new was afoot.

If, even now, we have some difficulty in thinking ourselves back into their shared state of mind at the time, that is, I think, because even while the collection was in the process of formation, a difference of emphasis was at work which was to become steadily more pronounced over the succeeding years. Four years later Coleridge remarked,

> I rather suspect that some where or other there is a radical Difference in our theoretical opinions respecting Poetry – / this I shall endeavor to go to the Bottom of (*CL*, ii.830; and cf. ii.812)

— so laying the first foundation for what was to be his extended discussion of their difference in *Biographia Literaria*. But although that later discussion was probing and extensive it can be suggested that it still did not go sufficiently deeply – that the differences of concern went further than a simple disagreement about poetry. I can best indicate what I mean by pointing to the respective formulae which each poet developed in the subsequent period to indicate their fundamental positions. For Coleridge it crystallized into the saying that 'every Thing has a Life of it's own, & that we are all *one Life*' (*CL*, ii.864). The twin affirmation provided a keynote for his view of life generally, indicating why he was so deeply interested in mental phenomena – including the way in which we associate ideas in a state of excitement. It also gave him the cue for affirmations and investigations concerning the difference beween saying 'It is' and saying 'I am': a distinction about which Thomas McFarland has written eloquently.[10] And it was a good reason for his coming to think that he might, after all, be more of a metaphysician than a poet.

At one level Wordsworth would not have disagreed. After all, in the account of the young boy in the poem of his that became 'The Pedlar' one of the firmest statements was

> ... in all things
> He saw one life, and felt that it was joy.

('The Ruined Cottage', ll.251–2; *WPW*, v.385)

But the most central belief of Wordsworth's came to be his sense not that 'we are all one Life' but that 'we have all of us one human heart', the statement explicitly formulated so in 'The Old Cumberland Beggar' (l.146). Even while he was composing the lyrics described earlier, in which his awareness of the pathos of the individual figures about whom they are written is deepened and extended by his contact with Coleridge's psychological speculations, the true weight of his concern lay with what those figures told the reader about the human heart, and this shifting emphasis gained momentum during the years after 1798. It seems as if Wordsworth could no longer see why 'The Ancient Mariner' had deserved such prominence in the original collection. The Mariner, it now seemed to him, was not a human being with whom we could readily identify ourselves at a human level. He should have had some leading characteristic – a profession, for instance – which would arouse the reader's recognition. So he concluded that the poem had been an injury to the volume and resolved to downgrade it in the order of presentation when the next edition came out.[11]

The poems he then contributed were much more firmly devoted to the theme of the 'one human heart': 'The Brothers', 'Michael', 'Hart-Leap Well', 'Ruth', 'The Old Cumberland Beggar'. Although he included features of strong psychological interest in some, as for example the accounts of the 'calenture' and of somnambulism in 'The Brothers', these were no longer partly speculative but now based on firmly-attested phenomena. Coleridge's ideas had taken a hard knock when they visited Germany and he discovered not only that theories of animal magnetism were not currently in favour among German intellectuals but that the distinguished physiologist Blumenbach did not even believe in the existence of hypnotic power – prompting, no doubt, the omission of references to 'the power that comes out of thine eyes' that is a notable feature in the 1800 reworking of 'The Ancient Mariner'. The balance of his concern had swung firmly toward development of the philosophy of the mind and heart that was to be laid out in much of his future writing.

If this is so, it follows that the unity that has been traced here in the 1798 *Ballads* was not matched in the 1800 collection. It had been the effect of an association between Wordsworth's and Coleridge's ideas that flourished during their conversations together, particularly during the year 1798–9, when Coleridge's psychological speculations, working together with Dorothy Wordsworth's sensitive observations and William's reflections on the solitary human condition, had combined to produce a state of excitement and mutual stimulus highly favourable to the creative process. That excitement had already begun to diminish by 1800, with the visit to Germany and the scepticism concerning 'magnetic' phenomena among intellectuals there. Previously it had seemed for a time as if their views were more or less identical, Coleridge's vision of the beautiful interweaving energies of the water-snakes as an emblem of the dynamic harmony at the heart of the 'one Life', and so of all living things, being matched by that which prompted Wordsworth's less active, more meditative account of the mood in which

> ... with an eye made quiet by the power
> Of harmony, and the deep power of joy,
> We see into the life of things.

('Lines written ... above Tintern Abbey', ll.48–50)

It was the production of lines such as those that convinced Coleridge that he was in the presence of a great poet whom he could never hope to emulate: he was still quoting from the poem a quarter of a century later.[12] Wordsworth, meanwhile, who was to affirm after Coleridge's death that despite their lack of recent contact Coleridge's mind had been constantly present to him during the intervening period, had developed strong reservations, nevertheless, concerning his vitalist assertions and the fuller implications of his speculations about the unconscious.

The further staking out of his own territory of the human heart for the 1800 collection and the concomitant downplaying of Coleridge's offerings may not have been intended as a personal slight, but they certainly marked the end to a *concordat* that had seemed at times more like the adoption of a dual identity. It would gradually become evident that there *was* a difference between them, involving not only their theoretical opinions respecting poetry but much else besides. For a short period, however, they had been so successful in believing that the heart of life and the life of the heart were one and the same that they had been able to regard their respective contributions to the 1798 volume as more like stanzas of a common ode to joy. In that sense, as in others, Hazlitt's analysis proves to have been strictly correct: fools have laughed at them, while wise men scarcely understand them.

Notes

1 Robert Mayo, 'The Contemporaneity of the *Lyrical Ballads*,' *PMLA* 69 (1954), pp. 486–522.
2 See Kenneth Johnston's essay below, pp. 98–100. Johnston also remarks on the facility with which Wordsworth was producing new short poems in the 1798 period, by comparison with the struggles he had endured to produce anything at all during his time at Racedown. For a discussion of the implications of this sudden fluency, see below, p. 95.
3 Letter to Wordsworth, 24 May, 1802; quoted in Mary Gordon, *'Christopher North': A Memoir of John Wilson* ... (2 vols; Edinburgh: Edmonston and Douglas, 1862), i.38–48.
4 Letter to Wordsworth, 6 August, 1803; quoted in John E. Jordan, *De Quincey to Wordsworth: A Biography of a Relationship* ... (Berkeley and Los Angeles: University of California Press, 1962), pp. 33–4.
5 Annotation to Barron Field's *Memoir* of Wordsworth (BL Add MS 41325, f111^v); quoted in *WPrW*, i.167, in commentary upon ll.27–33 of the 1800 'Preface'.
6 Compare Hazlitt's similar questions in his essay 'William Godwin'; in *The Spirit of the Age* (1825): Hazlitt, xi.17–18.
7 See Mary Jacobus, *Tradition and Experiment in Wordsworth's Lyrical Ballads (1798)* (Oxford: Clarendon Press, 1976), pp. 16–21, 31–7.
8 *Coleridge's Poetic Intelligence* (London: Macmillan, 1977), esp. pp. 50–7, 74–7.
9 For the lines' use as epigraph to *The White Doe of Rylstone* (pub. 1815), see *WPW*, iii.283.
10 See his *Coleridge and the Pantheist Tradition* (Oxford: Clarendon Press, 1969), esp. chapter 4.
11 See, e.g., the account given by Stephen Gill, *William Wordsworth: A Life* (Oxford: Clarendon Press, 1989), pp. 186–8.
12 See *Aids to Reflection*, ed. John Beer (London/Princeton, NJ: Routledge/ Princeton University Press, 1993), p. 404, and n.

2
Lyrical Ballads: the Title Revisited

Zachary Leader

(i)

When in 1821 the Northamptonshire poet John Clare suggested 'Village Minstrelsy' as an alternative to 'The Village Minstrel', one of several projected titles for his second collection of poems, he received the following response from his publisher, John Taylor:

> 'Village Minstrelsy' is not free from the same Charge which comes against the other Titles. It is too like 'English Minstrelsy' – a Compilation of Walter Scott's which *did not sell*, & that is another bad sign. I have preferred your old Title The Peasant Boy after duly Considering all Circumstances. – For some time I thought favourably of 'The Village Minstrel' – & also of 'The Village Muse' – but unless you recommend either of them I cannot trust to adopting either.[1]

This advice Clare takes to heart, declaring he has 'had my dose' of 'Village Minstrelsy':

> *woud not sell* is plenty to abandon anything of that nature so I am content but 'Minstrel Villager' & 'Village Muse' are very poor & very bad – the 'Peasant Boy' is but middling while your 'Village Minstrel' still sticks in my memory as best of all.[2]

That no such exchange survives between Wordsworth, Coleridge, and Joseph Cottle, the publisher of *Lyrical Ballads with a Few Other Poems* (1798), a title retained for the 1800 second edition (minus 'a Few') is a pity. For the title *Lyrical Ballads*, though no less market-savvy than

The Village Minstrel (ballads were as much in vogue in 1798 as peasant poets were in 1821, though both soon fell from fashion), is also problematic. 'The title of the Poems is in some degree, objectionable', wrote Francis Wrangham of the 1800 second edition in the *British Critic*, 'for what Ballads are not *lyrical*?'[3]

Redundancy has a proud history in titling, especially in generic titles; consider 'Sonnet', which John Hollander calls 'the completely redundant title'.[4] Wordsworth and Coleridge are capable of 'Sonnet', but more frequently make an effort (even with titles they wish to be nondescript).[5] It is hard to imagine them either missing or seeking out the tautology to which the *British Critic* objects (as opposed to tolerating it for the sake of other meanings). But what little they say about the lyrical (the more problematic term in *Lyrical Ballads*) settles nothing. That Wordsworth considered abandoning the title for the much-expanded 1800 edition (Dorothy reports that '[h]e intends to give them the title of "Poems by W. Wordsworth"': *EY*, p. 297) has been taken by John E. Jordan, the critic who has thought most fully about these matters, to imply that 'the title seems not to have been of very great importance to [him]'.[6] But this conclusion need not follow. Though, as Robert Mayo claims, '[b]y 1798 almost anything might be called a "ballad"'[7] even poems that did not tell stories, the form's traditional associations were clear: ballads were associated with the folk, the non-literary classes (in 1797 the *Encyclopaedia Britannica* defined ballad as a form 'adapted to the capacity of the lower class of people');[8] they were originally sung; they told simple stories (often of a popular or sensational nature, involving extreme emotions); their authors or speakers were impersonal, anonymous, 'objective' (and thus invested with an authority later imitators, including Wordsworth and Coleridge, seek to appropriate through a variety of distancing devices); and they were divided into stanzas.[9]

With these criteria, or at least some of them, in mind, it is possible to identify twelve of the twenty-three poems in the 1798 edition (eleven by Wordsworth, one by Coleridge) as ballads.[10] For the 1800 edition, though, the situation is quite different. As Kenneth R. Johnston points out, 'only twelve of [Wordsworth's] much larger number of new poems (forty-one) were ballads at all'.[11] 'Lyrical Ballads' might be an apt title for the first edition but not the second. Hence Wordsworth's letter of c.2 October, 1800, to Biggs and Cottle (*EY*, p. 303), who were printing the second edition in Bristol (having given up the publishing part of their business to Thomas Longman in the autumn of 1799), begging Longman, through them, to omit the words '*Second Edition*' from the title-page to 'the 2nd Volume' (consisting of forty-one new poems by Wordsworth). In other words, the newness of the volume must be signalled, as it would have been by a new title.

In the 'Preface' to *Poems* (1815), his first collected edition, Wordsworth enumerates six 'moulds' into which '[t]he materials of Poetry ... are cast'. These are: The Narrative, The Dramatic, The Lyrical, The Idyllium, Didactic, and 'philosophical Satire'. Lyrical poems are of several sorts: 'the Hymn, the Ode, the Elegy, the Song, and the Ballad; in all which, for the production of their *full* effect, an accompaniment of music is indispensable' (*WPrW*, iii.27–28, 27). Yet ballads were traditionally thought of as songs (making 'Lyrical' redundant, as is also the case with 'Song' in Wordsworth's list). Hence the objection of the reviewer from the *British Critic*. Ballads, moreover, were usually thought of as stories (unlike Hymns, Odes, and Elegies, the non-narrative forms with which they are grouped by Wordsworth). Jordan points to the previously-quoted letter by Dorothy Wordsworth of 10 and 12 September, 1800, which seems to confirm the connection between ballad and narrative. Dorothy explains to her friend Jane Marshall that one of the reasons William wants *Lyrical Ballads* changed to 'Poems by W. Wordsworth' is that 'Mrs. Robinson has claimed the title and is about publishing a volume of *Lyrical Tales*', a remark implicitly identifying ballads and tales (*EY*, p. 297).[12]

To be more than merely redundant, lyrical must mean something aside from song-like. Jordan thinks it means metrically sophisticated, or, more generally, superior, adducing a passage from the 'Preface' and one from the 'Note' to 'The Thorn', also first printed in the 1800 edition, as supporting evidence.[13] In the 'Preface' Wordsworth describes 'Goody Blake and Harry Gill' as 'one of the rudest of this collection', but also as narrated 'in a more impressive metre than is usual in Ballads' (*WPrW*, i.150). 'The Thorn' is similarly mixed: its narrator is variously described in the 'Note' as 'credulous and talkative', 'of slow faculties and deep feelings', 'utterly destitute of fancy', but its metre is 'Lyrical and rapid', of necessity, given that readers 'are not accustomed to sympathize with men feeling in that manner or using such language'. As Wordsworth explains: 'It was necessary that the Poem, to be natural, should in reality move slowly; yet I hoped that, by the aid of the metre, to those who should at all enter into the spirit of the Poem, it would appear to move quickly' (*LBB*, p. 288; *WPW*, ii.512–13). Here, the lyrical and the rapid are used to counter the dull (the narrator is 'slow' in several senses); lyrical metre is more sophisticated or impressive than common ballad metre, leavening or cutting the 'rudeness' of ballad materials.

This impression is reinforced, Jordan argues, by the omission of 'The Three Graves' from the *Lyrical Ballads*. 'The Three Graves' was worked on in 1798 by both Wordsworth and Coleridge, though never finished by either partner (Wordsworth wrote the first two parts, Coleridge added parts III and IV, though more detailed aspects of the collaboration are unclear).[14] It has thematic links with a number of other poems in the 1798 collection, in particular through the motif of the curse. When Coleridge published parts III and IV of the poem in *Sibylline Leaves* (1817), he apologized for the crudeness or simplicity of the metre (the manuscript reads, 'in the common ballad metre'): 'The language was intended to be dramatic; that is, suited to the narrator; and the metre corresponds to the homeliness of the diction' (*CPW*, i.268n., 267).[15] Had the metre countered rather than corresponded to this homeliness, Jordan implies, 'The Three Graves' would have been a 'lyrical' ballad, and included in the volume, a view Jordan bolsters with several citations from other writers and critics of the period, for all of whom 'lyrical' means distinguished or sophisticated. As Jordan concludes: 'by "lyrical" ballads, therefore, Wordsworth and Coleridge probably meant "superior" ballads',[16] a view shared by their first reviewers, as in Charles Burney's praise in the June 1799 *Monthly Review*: 'The style and versification are those of our antient ditties: but much polished, and more constantly excellent' (quoted in *LBB*, p. 326).

The advantage this explanation has over 'lyrical' as song-like is that it replaces tautology with paradox or oxymoron, ballads being as commonly associated with simplicity as they are with song, or as they are narrative. When Jordan suggests yet another meaning for lyrical – emotionally charged[17] – tautology returns, since strong feeling is also a hallmark of the ballad, whether traditional, broadside, or magazine. It is only when strong feeling is associated with the speaker, as in Ruskin's '[l]yric poetry is the expression by the poet of his own feelings',[18] that tension or paradox returns to the title. Jordan balks at the appeal to 'his own feelings' when applied to *Lyrical Ballads* since so many of their speakers are dramatic characters (the mad mother, the 'credulous and talkative' sea-captain Wordsworth identifies as the speaker of 'The Thorn'), yet Jordan's distinction obscures a key link between Ruskin's sense of the lyrical and those poems in the volume usually thought of as ballads: that the feelings in question are mostly those of the poems' speakers. The speakers of the *Lyrical Ballads* are not Wordsworth or Coleridge, but the feelings they express are as much our concern as the stories they tell, as in conventional lyric. 'The Thorn' is as much about its speaker as about Martha Ray (or should have been, according to the 'Note'), just as 'Ode to a Nightingale' or 'Ode to the West Wind' are as much about the thoughts and feelings the nightingale's song and the west wind provoke in their speakers as about the song and the wind themselves. The experimental nature of *Lyrical Ballads* – clearly announced in the 'Advertisement' – may thus be suggested by its title, in which a traditionally objective and anonymous form, the ballad, is associated with subjectivity (the speaker's or dramatic narrator's feelings) and self-interrogation.

Nor is this understanding of the lyrical as internal a mere reading back, or ahistorical imposition.[19] In 1798 the young Hazlitt visited Wordsworth and Coleridge at Alfoxden and Nether Stowey, visits memorialized in 'My First Acquaintance with Poets' (1823). During these visits, both poets read from *Lyrical Ballads*, still in manuscript (and perhaps without its title, which Johnston thinks may have been proposed 'at or about this time'[20]), and Hazlitt noted their quite different reading styles: 'Coleridge's manner is more full, animated, and varied; Wordsworth's more equable, sustained, and internal. The one might be termed more *dramatic*, the other more *lyrical*' (Hazlitt, xvii.118–19). For Hazlitt the lyrical is the internal, and is opposed to the dramatic, a familiar distinction in the period, and one that recalls Shelley's *Prometheus Unbound: A Lyrical Drama in Four Acts* (1819). Shelley's 'Lyrical Drama' functions in the same way as *Lyrical Ballads*, and the tension or paradox it encodes may in part be an inheritance from the earlier volume; 'in part' because it is also likely to derive from a work of criticism, A.W. Schlegel's *Lectures on Dramatic Art and Literature* (1809), which Shelley was reading in March, 1818, six months or so before be began work on *Prometheus Unbound*.[21] One way to understand the tensions in the conjunction of 'lyrical' and 'ballads' is to trace comparable tensions in Shelley's 'Lyrical Drama', in particular those concerning time.

(ii)

In the second of his *Lectures* Schlegel declares that 'a dramatic work can ... be considered in a double point of view, how far it is *poetical*, and how far it is *theatrical*'. By 'poetical', in this context, Schlegel means lyrical, defined as 'the musical expression of mental emotions by language'; by 'theatrical' he means that species of the dramatic 'fitted to appear with advantage on the stage'.[22] These identifications Yeats echoes in 'The Tragic Theatre' (1910), in a passage protesting the supposed inevitability of the opposition between the poetical and the dramatic. 'In poetical drama', he writes, with critics like Schlegel in mind, 'there is, it is held, an antithesis between character and lyric poetry, for lyric poetry – however much it move you when read out of a book – can, as these critics think, but encumber the action'.[23] Yeats's assimilation of character and action in this passage, an inheritance from Aristotle, ought not to distract; what matters (for the purposes of this essay) is that lyrical and poetical are used as synonyms, as in Schlegel.

Throughout Schlegel's *Lectures* the lyrical aspect of drama is also associated with the sublime, as lyric and sublime are associated in Edward Young's 'A Discourse on Lyric Poetry', a work Coleridge alludes to in several *Notebook* entries prior to 1798.[24] In Lecture III, which deals in part with 'Tragical lyric poetry', Schlegel directs the reader to Kant's account of sublimity in the *Critique of Judgement* (1790).[25] For Kant the sublime is partly associated with limitless or formless sequences and objects, the sort that can only be conceived by what he calls 'a super-added thought of ... totality'. The initial experience of the sublime is one of discontinuity, of a lack of harmony or correspondence between the object or event (towering peaks, numberless stars) and our attempts to conceive or represent it. This initial stage of blockage Kant calls 'a momentary check to the vital forces'.[26] But blockage is only a part of the sublime experience, and paradoxically proves to be positive or propitious, for it instantly results in a sudden influx of power.

What makes this influx of power possible is the supra- or extra-analytic faculty, associated by Kant with 'Reason' as opposed to 'Understanding',[27] whereby the mind or imagination exults in its ability to apprehend the very totality its senses and understanding have just failed to take in. The analytic powers recede before a higher order of meaning; in the religious sublime, before an apprehension of divinity. The sublime and the lyrical oppose the dramatic and the theatrical, then, in part because sublime or lyrical insight takes the subject out of time. The thought of an endless succession of years or hours, for example, initially blocks or baffles, but in the sublime the moment of bafflement is immediately followed by an apprehension of Eternity or Infinity, of a *totality* of hours and years, a realm outside time.[28] The lyrical is drawn to the timeless, while the theatrical or dramatic is wholly involved in time.

Drama resembles narrative, the category to which the ballad might less confusingly have been consigned by Wordsworth in the 1815 'Preface', in that it unfolds over time. The protagonist's relation to time, it could even be argued, is the key to generic differentiation within both drama and narrative. In comedy, time is an ally, everything works out in the end. In tragedy, whether on stage or in story, time is the protagonist's enemy, gets him in the end; which is why tragic protagonists often think of themselves as at odds with time, and wish, like Macbeth, to 'trammel up the consequence' or 'jump the life to come',[29] or, like Antigone or Ajax or Coriolanus, refuse to change or be moved. This adversarial relation to time dooms the tragic protagonist, being a form of trespass on divine territory: by acting as if immune to time or change, the protagonist aspires to, approaches, the status of an immortal – and is cut down for his presumption. It is time – clock time, calendar time – that does the cutting; just as in comedy time heals all, repairing or stitching together lost or divided families, friends, and lovers.

Shelley's attraction both to Aeschylus and to the Prometheus myth reflects, or is connected to, his attraction to the lyrical and the sublime. Aeschylean drama is famously static. In the comic *agon* or contest between Aeschylus and Euripides in Aristophanes' *The Frogs* (405 BC), it is the inaction and sublime obscurity of Aeschylus's plays Euripides objects to at first (their political conservatism is a later target, one that anticipates comparable objections to Romantic lyric, or to the subsequent privileging of lyric over other literary forms in the Romantic period):

> The play would begin with a seated figure, all muffled up – Niobe, for example, or Achilles: face veiled, very dramatic, not a word uttered ... Then the Chorus would rattle off a string of odes – four of them, one after another: still not a syllable from the muffled figure ... Well, the whole thing was a swindle, of course. The audience sat there all tensed up, waiting for Niobe to say something. And she just didn't. The play went on, and Niobe sat and sat ... Well, eventually, after a lot more of this nonsense, about half-way through the play we get a speech. And what a speech! A dozen great galumphing phrases, fearsome things with crests and shaggy eyebrows. Magnificent! Nobody knew what they meant, of course.[30]

What the character of Euripides is objecting to here and elsewhere in *The Frogs* is how little happens in Aeschylus's plays and how opaque the verse is, all jagged and irregular lines, sentences left hanging, meaning conveyed in poetical flashes, sudden vivid images or metaphors, startling juxtapositions. Both style and structure privilege the moment and the evocation or delineation of internal states, rather than dramatic sequence or external enactment. As Schlegel puts it in the fourth of his *Lectures*:

> the lyrical part of the tragedy ... occupies too much space in his pieces ... he did not understand the art of enriching and varying an action, and dividing its developement and catastrophe into parts, bearing a due proportion to each other. Hence his action often stands still, and this circumstance becomes still more apparent, from the undue extension of his choral songs. But all his poetry betrays a sublime and serious mind.[31]

That such a dramatist should find himself drawn to the Prometheus story, with its immobile hero and internalized transformation, is hardly surprising.

Shelley's version of the story is, if anything, more static and inward than that of Aeschylus. The plot of *Prometheus Unbound* is weirdly compacted. Instead of beginning at the beginning, or even *in media res*, it begins at the end; the reversal and recognition, stages in a sequence for Aristotle, occur in the opening soliloquy, where pity supplants hatred, unity division. The soliloquy opens with an extended account of the misery Jupiter has visited upon the world; it is then followed by Prometheus's declaration of hope:

> And yet to me welcome is Day and Night,
> Whether one breaks the hoar frost of the morn,
> Or starry, dim, and slow, the other climbs
> The leaden-coloured East; for then they lead
> Their wingless, crawling Hours, one among whom
> – As some dark Priest hales the reluctant victim –
> Shall drag thee, cruel King, to kiss the blood
> From these pale feet, which then might trample thee
> If they disdained not such a prostrate slave.
> Disdain? Ah no! I pity thee. —

> (I, ll.44–53)

At which point, Prometheus revokes his curse, in lines rightly termed 'perfunctory':[32]

> I speak in grief,
> Not exultation, for I hate no more,
> As then, ere misery made me wise. – The Curse
> Once breathed on thee I would recall.
>
> (I, ll.56–9)[33]

Prometheus's crucial transformation in this first soliloquy is undramatic not only because it is matter-of-factly announced ('Ah no! I pity thee', 'I hate no more'), but because it bears no relation to a succession of enacted events, or to character development.

Two other crucial moments in the play are comparably abrupt and baffling. After the initial breakthrough the Furies arrive to torment Prometheus, and receive the following response: 'Thy words are like a cloud of winged snakes / And yet, I pity those they torture not' (I, ll.632–3) (that is, those unmoved by suffering). This response is as matter-of-fact as the line that follows: 'Thou pitiest them? I speak no more!' (l.634), or as the immediately ensuing stage direction: '*Vanishes*'. In Act II, Scene iv, when Asia at last learns of the world's renovation, she asks: 'When shall the destined hour arrive?' (l.128). Demogorgon replies: 'Behold!' It is characteristic of the play that Asia's response, 'The rocks are cloven' (l.129) suggests an event that has already occurred, the dramatic moment is elided;[34] as in Prometheus's initial soliloquy, the world's transformation is presented as a state or condition not an action. Moments like these, which leave the reader uncertain, recall Young on lyrical poetry: 'Its conduct should be rapturous, somewhat abrupt, and immethodical to a vulgar eye. That apparent order, and connexion, which gives form and life to some compositions, takes away the very soul of this'.[35]

(iii)

The ungrounded nature of the turning points in *Prometheus Unbound* marks them as lyrical. No theatrical explanation is provided; they derive from no succession of enacted events or causes. At such instances, as Goethe puts it, 'Der Augenblick ist Ewigkeit', the moment is eternal.[36] In Shelley's words, from *A Defence of Poetry*, they (our 'best and happiest moments') arise 'unforeseen', depart 'unbidden', explicable only, if at all, as 'the interpenetration of a diviner nature through our own'.[37] In the *Lyrical Ballads*, the atemporal quality of such moments is often suggested, but only sometimes do they signal 'a diviner nature' or Eternity. In 'The Ancient Mariner', notoriously, the sudden, inexplicable shooting of the albatross is transformative but hardly a mark of divine intervention, unlike the comparably uncontingent but redemptive upsurge of love for the watersnakes. Whatever their origins, though, these and other 'strange fits of passion' in Lyrical Ballads take the reader out of the story; or rather, evoke a realm outside story.

This is a point Wordsworth himself reflects on in his tragedy *The Borderers*, originally written just before *Lyrical Ballads*, and itself a sort of 'lyrical drama':[38]

> Action is transitory – a step, a blow,
> The motion of a muscle – this way or that –
> 'Tis done, and in the after-vacancy
> We wonder at ourselves like men betrayed:
> Suffering is permanent, obscure and dark,
> And shares the nature of infinity.

> (ll.1539–44; *WPW*, i.188)

The contrast Wordsworth's Oswald draws here between action and suffering, and the way he draws it, suggests a more general dichotomy between the dramatic and the lyrical. The two last lines of the passage lift the reader out of a time-soaked present (suggested by phrases like 'transitory', ''Tis done', 'after-vacancy') into a realm that 'shares the nature of infinity'. The contemplation of deeds ('a step, a blow / The motion of a muscle') gives way to that of consciousness, a mind disturbed by suffering in 'the after-vacancy' of action.

The shift from deeds to the contemplation of consciousness, from story to feeling, is a common feature of many of the ballad poems in *Lyrical Ballads*. In 'Strange fits of passion' itself, for example, in the 'after-vacancy' of the moon's sudden disappearance, the speaker imagines Lucy dead: '"O mercy!" to myself I cried, / "If Lucy should be dead!"' (ll.27–8). This thought he characterizes as 'fond and wayward', but it enters the poem like a sublime revelation, even for those who find something comical or 'absurd' about the moon's disappearance. To R.P. Draper, 'the "lyrical" essence (as against the "ballad" form) of the poem is the consciousness of mortality implicit in stanzas 2–6, but not articulated till the final brief speech'.[39] This articulation overrides

the knowing ironies of the story; the speaker no longer views his feelings *ab extra*, offering them instead, and for the first time in the poem,
through direct speech. Ballad objectivity – all sequence, causation,
contingency ('And now we reach'd the orchard plot, / And, as we
climb'd the hill': ll.13–14) – gives way to a moment of lyric subjectivity, sudden, ungrounded, as if from another dimension.

'The Idiot Boy' offers a comparable interaction of ballad and lyric
elements. Everything about Johnny undermines the narrative. He
disrupts Betty's plans by never engaging with them, by doing
nothing; it is Betty who pats the pony's side to set it moving, while
Johnny's 'head and heels are idle' (l.85), the bough in his left hand
'motionless and dead' (l.89). As Johnny's fate displaces Susan's in his
mother's mind, the poem's plot (the tracing of the mother's plan)
unravels with comic expedition: 'The piteous news so much it
shock'd her, / She quite forgot to send the Doctor, / To comfort poor
old Susan Gale' (ll.284–6), while Susan herself is miraculously cured
by anxieties for Betty and Johnny: 'And as her mind grew worse and
worse, / Her body it grew better' (ll.425–6). When Johnny is found,
his oddity takes centre-stage, crowding ballad concerns (including
that 'primary law of our nature' which is mother-love) to the margins
of the tale. It is Johnny the reader wonders at, not Betty; or rather,
Johnny's consciousness has about it a lyrical or sublime element (the
'glory' Betty ascribes to him in line 136 is not merely ironic) that
seems at odds with the demands of the story. This element
Wordsworth hints at in a letter to John Wilson of 7 June, 1802, when
he admits he has 'often applied to Idiots, in my own mind, that
sublime expression of scripture that, *"their life is hidden with God"'*
(*EY*, p. 357).

Johnny's obliviousness to time is reflected in his relation to
language as well as in his actions, or inaction. In Peter Manning's
words, Johnny's 'Burr, burr, burr' is '[l]ike the hooting of the owls ...
pure sound that repeats but does not connect, can be aggregated but
not synthesized'.[40] When asked by his mother to explain what he has
seen and heard, Johnny replies in a manner that again conflates
sequence and suggests a realm outside time:

> And thus to Betty's question, he
> Made answer, like a traveller bold,
> (His very words I give to you,)
> "The cocks did crow to-whoo, to-whoo,
> "And the sun did shine so cold."

> – Thus answered Johnny in his glory,
> And that was all his travel's story.

> (ll.457–63)

These lines, Wordsworth later told Isabella Fenwick, were 'the foundation of the whole' (*WPW*, ii.478). What they communicate, again in the 'after-vacancy' of action, is Johnny's consciousness; this is all his 'story', which is no story at all in ballad terms. In place of exotic incident (the sort conjectured in lines 327-46) the poem offers sublime strangeness; 'the sun did shine so cold' retains its mystery even for readers who identify the phrase, at Wordsworth's suggestion in the previous stanza, as a figure for the moon. As Mary Jacobus puts it, '[a] mysterious inner life sets [Johnny] apart, identifying him with the other-worldliness of the moon or the well-being of the curring owlets whose call he echoes with his burring'.[41] This other-worldliness has previously been presented as in conflict with narrative, as drawing us away from the theme of mother love, but it can also be seen as enriching it. As Johnny's words reverberate in the mind, the delusional intensity of Betty's love – its power to imagine away or reconfigure the boy's limitations – is fully revealed. The relation of ballad to lyrical elements, in other words, is shifting, unstable.

'The Idiot Boy' is one of several ballads in *Lyrical Ballads* ('Simon Lee' is another) which reflect directly on their experimental status. These reflections encourage the reader to make generic questions – the sort the title raises – a central concern in reading. The tensions between ballad and lyric elements are meant to be intriguing, as is the comparable mix of kinds (described by Geoffrey Hartman) in Wordsworth's generic experiments with 'Inscription', a venerable poetical form revived in the mid-eighteenth century by Akenside and Shenstone. According to Hartman, in poems like 'Lines left upon a Seat in a Yew-tree, which stands near the Lake of Esthwaite, on a desolate part of the shore, yet commanding a beautiful prospect' (the full title is part of the point in this context), '[t]here is a pleasure in not knowing, or not being able to discern, the traditional form; the lack becomes a positive virtue, and we begin to seek, not quite earnestly, for the proper formal description'.[42] In the case of the ballads in *Lyrical Ballads*, the formal description is given in the volume's title; what is sought is its meaning, in a comparably relaxed and pleasurable manner.

One place to look for this meaning is in the titles of individual poems. 'The Idiot Boy', for example, hints at the relative weighting of lyrical over ballad elements. In crude terms, Betty's hopes for Johnny set the poem's plot or story in motion, which is its ballad aspect; the delineation of Johnny's mentality is its lyrical aspect. The poem might well have been called 'Betty Foy' (this is how Hazlitt refers to it in 'My First Acquaintance with Poets': Hazlitt, xvii.117) or 'A Mother's Love'. Naming it after Johnny licenses or smoothes our entry into the boy's consciousness at the end; this is what the poem is about, the title implies. A similar weighting of lyrical and ballad elements is suggested in the title 'We Are Seven', which not only emphasizes the unshakeable faith of the 'simple child' who is its subject, but suggests the narrator's continuing reflection on that faith (he tells the poem in the past tense, the child using the present only). The title puts the reader inside the speaker's head in a way a third-person title ('A Simple Child', for example) would not. It also lifts the reader, like the speaker, out of a world of clock time, in several senses, since the child's vision is atemporal, like Johnny's, and the implied reflection on her words suggests the speaker's abstraction, his stepping out of time.

To some critics the mixture I have been tracing is seen as a form of usurpation: lyric supplants ballad in *Lyrical Ballads* as mind supplants nature in Romanticism in general (that is, in Wordsworthian or High Romanticism). Which is to say, as the personal supplants the social. For Alan Liu, for example, the lyric impulse in Wordsworth is 'an *émigré* flight from narrative', one in which 'collective loss can be imagined as the gain of the individual'.[43] This association of lyric with apostasy and withdrawal derives as much from Wordsworth's champions as from the poet himself, in particular from John Stuart Mill, whose essay 'What Is Poetry?' (1833) is cited by both M.H. Abrams and Northrop Frye, the most influential twentieth-century theorists of Romantic lyricism.[44] Mill's essay grew out of his first reading of Wordsworth in the autumn of 1828. In his *Autobiography* (1873) Mill describes the years immediately before this saving encounter as a period of depression, 'a crisis in my mental history', one brought on by doubts about his capacity 'to be a reformer of the world'. Reading Wordsworth cured him of this ambition 'as from a dream', offering in its place 'the internal culture of the individual', 'the very culture of feelings'. Wordsworth's poetry made him 'at once better and happier', promoting not only personal renewal but 'a greatly increased interest in the common feelings and common destiny of human beings'.[45]

In 'What Is Poetry?' Mill sees the virtues of Wordsworth's poems as those of poetry in general, by which he mostly means lyric poetry, the form, he declares in another essay, 'The Two Kinds of Poetry' (also 1833), 'more eminently and peculiarly poetry than any other'[46] (epic, for example, 'in so far as it is epic (i.e. narrative) ... is not poetry at all'). Poetry in Mill's sense is to be contrasted with eloquence:[47]

> eloquence is *heard*, poetry is *over*heard. Eloquence supposes an audience; the peculiarity of poetry appear[s] to us to lie in the poet's utter unconsciousness of a listener. Poetry is feeling, confessing itself to itself in moments of solitude ... Eloquence is feeling pouring itself out to other minds, courting their sympathy, or endeavouring to influence their belief, or move them to passsion or to action.[48]

This view of poetry as internal, private, expressionist, underlies the current suspicion of Wordsworthian lyric as escapist, a 'conversion of public to private property, history to poetry' (Marjorie Levinson), a 'denial of history' (Liu).[49] In the ballad poems of *Lyrical Ballads*, though, lyrical elements often serve communal or public as well as personal ends, as Mill in his *Autobiography* insists, and as Wordsworth insisted before him, in the 1800 'Preface' and elsewhere. For though the moment of lyric intrusion takes one out of the story, it hardly 'denies' (or represses, or occludes) the social or the communal, or history. On the contrary, halting or disrupting the story can be a way of facing social reality, a release from ballad or narrative simplification or distortion.

In 'The Idiot Boy', for example, the poem's lyrical elements bring us right into Johnny's consciousness, in all its strangeness. Wordsworth has a social purpose in effecting this meeting. As he tells Wilson: '[It] is not enough for me as a poet, to delineate merely such feelings as all men *do* sympathize with but, it is also highly desirable to add to these others, such as all men *may* sympathize with, and such as there is reason to believe they would be better and more moral beings if they did sympathize with' (*EY*, p. 358). What makes this broadening of sympathies desirable, Wordsworth elsewhere explains in the letter, is the effect it will have not only on oneself but on boys like Johnny: 'Poor people, seeing frequently among their neighbors such objects, easily forget what there is of natural disgust about them, and have therefore a sane state, so that without pain and suffering they perform their duties towards them'. The key to performing these duties – and the poor are not alone in having them, Wordsworth is implying – is 'seeing' the objects in question, which is precisely what the lyrical elements in 'The Idiot Boy' make readers do in respect to Johnny, even as they mock ballad conventions for drawing us away from them, by ignoring or smoothing over 'what there is of natural disgust' about their condition.

A similar function is performed by the lyric elements in 'Simon Lee', a poem in which the protagonist's situation is more directly or explicitly related to social conditions or 'history' than is Johnny's. 'Simon Lee' has been read as a paradigmatic instance of Romantic solipsism or evasion. As the description of Simon's financial and emotional crisis gathers to a head, the narrator interrupts his account to explain why what follows – his encounter with the old huntsman – does not constitute a 'tale'. In Stuart Curran's words: 'Simon Lee's inability to uproot a tree stump transforms the traditional objectivity of the ballad into a lyrical – which is to say, psychological – confrontation',[50] one which turns our attention to the narrator himself. 'This lyric turn into "silent thought,"' writes Sarah M. Zimmerman, paraphrasing new historicist objections to the poem, 'turns a profit from Simon Lee's suffering ... The shift from narration to effusion is accompanied by a change in perspective, from the broader contours of a social narrative to the interiority of reflection and emotion'.[51]

Zimmerman detects a counter-impulse in the lyrical turn, one similar to that I have identified in 'The Idiot Boy'. The disruption of Simon's story, with its interpolated 'incident' of the tree's uprooting, brings the reader face to face with Simon's condition. The reader hardly forgets the social or historical sources of that condition, which are related in the narrative of his life (in lines like 'This scrap of land he from the heath / Enclosed when he was stronger': ll.61–2); the incident merely makes the condition felt. Simon Lee ceases to be a figure in a story, his destitution is confronted directly by both reader and narrator. 'In "Simon Lee"', Zimmerman argues, in words which apply also to 'The Idiot Boy', 'lyricism demands engagement, while narrative is equated with entertainment. The poet refuses to turn this social history into a ballad, which would be to make a profit on it'.[52] What is often transcended by the stopping of time in the lyric intrusions in Wordsworth's ballads is not history but story.[53]

In the 1800 'Preface' Wordsworth, in a much-quoted passage, stresses the importance of a reader's first impressions and expectations: 'It is supposed, that by the act of writing in verse an Author makes a formal engagement that he will gratify certain known habits of association, that he not only thus apprizes the Reader that certain classes of ideas and expressions will be found in his book, but that others will be carefully excluded'. As the 'Preface' makes clear, Wordsworth expected a number of his readers to feel the verse in *Lyrical Ballads* had 'not fulfilled the terms of an engagement thus voluntarily contracted' (*WPrW*, i.122). What he expected them to feel about the volume's title – how he wished it to function – is less clear. The 'known habits of association' of the words 'lyrical' and 'ballad', I have been arguing, make their conjunction problematic. To those who think the title blandly descriptive, as unconcerned with tautology as 'Sonnet', the conjunction might function as a disguise or blind to the volume's experimental character, thus heightening subsequent sensations of strangeness or affront. William Carlos Williams sought just this effect in his first volume of poems, *Al Que Quiere!* (1917), when using the title 'Pastoral' for a poem 'admiring the houses / of the very poor', with their littered backyards, 'chicken wire', discarded objects, 'all, / if I am fortunate, / smeared a bluish green'.[54] To those who detect paradox rather than redundancy in Wordsworth and Coleridge's title, though, its function is more direct, offering the first of many puzzles for the reader of the volume. So considered, the title 'apprizes the Reader' of what is to come, in the process creating expectations (of defamiliarization) the volume will meet. In either case, though, the title, like the verse it introduces, is not as simple as it looks.

Notes

1   John Taylor to John Clare, 10 February, 1821; in *The Letters of John Clare*, ed. Mark Storey (Oxford: Clarendon Press, 1985), p. 148.
2   John Clare to John Taylor, 13 February, 1821; *Letters of John Clare*, p. 151.
3   *The British Critic* 17 (February, 1801), p. 131n.
4   John Hollander, '"Haddocks' Eyes": A Note on the Theory of Titles'; in *Vision and Resonance* (2nd edn; New Haven, Conn.: Yale University Press, 1985), p. 218. The title's complete redundancy is limited to the page; in a table of contents or an index it informs.
5   According to Anne Ferry in *The Title to the Poem* (Stanford: Stanford University Press, 1996), p. 4, Wordsworth belongs with Jonson, Browning, Whitman, Hardy, Frost, William Carlos Williams, Wallace Stevens, W.H. Auden, and John Ashbery, as poets who have 'thought in specially concentrated and sustained ways' about titling and 'have shaped titling practices'. Ferry pays special attention to Wordsworth's practice with generic titles, that is titles which 'focus on the poem as a formal entity' (see Chapter 5, 'What kind the poem belongs to', pp. 139–72), though she has relatively little to say about 'Lyrical Ballads' itself. See in particular her discussion of the title 'Lines', used five times in the first edition of *Lyrical Ballads*. This title, she argues, unlike other formal terms such as 'Verses' or 'Stanzas',

'does hint at the poet's individuality. It grants the freedom to follow natural, inner motions rather than the constraining dictates of man-made conventions, what Wordsworth in the "Advertisement" calls "pre-established codes of decision"' (p. 159; quoting *WPrW*, i.116). Ferry also discusses several of Coleridge's titles, including 'Rime of the Ancyent Marinere' (p. 85) and 'This Lime-Tree Bower My Prison' (pp. 218–19), which she sees as self-conscious and artful.

6 John E. Jordan, *Why the 'Lyrical Ballads'?* (Berkeley and Los Angeles: University of California Press, 1976), p. 173.

7 Robert Mayo, 'The Contemporaneity of the *Lyrical Ballads*', *PMLA* 69 (1954) 486–522, p. 507.

8 The *Encyclopaedia Britannica* is cited in *LBM*, p. 9.

9 Between 1882 and 1898, Francis James Child, the foremost authority on the subject of ballads, published his exhaustive *English and Scottish Popular Ballads*, a five-volume compilation containing 305 traditional ballads plus 1,000 variants. In the unfinished 'Introduction', appended to volume 5 of the collection, Child defines the ballad as 'a folk-song that tells a story'. In 1711, Joseph Addison, an early champion of the form, praised ballads for their 'majestick Simplicity' (*Spectator* 74; *The Spectator*, ed. Donald F. Bond (5 vols; Oxford: Clarendon Press, 1965), i.316). Thomas Percy, in the Introduction to his compilation, *Reliques of Ancient English Poetry* – a work Wordsworth praises in the 1815 'Essay, Supplementary to the Preface': 'I do not think that there is an able writer in verse of the present day who would not be proud to acknowledge his obligations to the Reliques' (*WPrW*, iii.78) – stressed their appeal to the emotions: 'I am sensible that many of these reliques of antiquity will require great allowances to be made for them. Yet they have, for the most part, a pleasing simplicity ... and if they do not dazzle the imagination, are frequently found to dazzle the heart' (*Reliques of Ancient English Poetry* (3 vols; London: Dodsley, 1765), i.x). For a discussion of the most famous of the distancing devices used by Wordsworth and Coleridge to appropriate the authority of ballad antiquity, see Ferry, *The Title to the Poem*, p. 85, on the pseudo-archaic spelling of the title 'The Rime of the Ancyent Marinere' in the first edition of *Lyrical Ballads*. For Ferry, '[t]he generic title of [*Lyrical Ballads*] may also have been designed in part to suggest anonymous origins in antiquity for the poems, and no authors' names appear on the title page' (p. 85).

10 According to Mayo, 'For Wordsworth and for most of his reviewers, the ballads seem to have been the narrative poems of the volume, of which there are about nine' ('The Contemporaneity of the *Lyrical Ballads*', p. 508). I make the number twelve, including, in the order they appear in the 1798 edition, Coleridge's 'The Rime of the Ancyent Marinere', 'Lines left upon a Seat in a Yew-tree' (the most problematic of my inclusions, being the only non-stanzaic poem on the list, and written in blank verse), 'The Female Vagrant' (also problematic, because in Spenserians), 'Goody Blake and Harry Gill', 'Simon Lee', 'Anecdote for Fathers', 'We Are Seven', 'The Thorn', 'The Last of the Flock', 'The Mad Mother', 'The Idiot Boy', and 'The Complaint of a Forsaken Indian Woman'. Mary Moorman's list, in *William Wordsworth: A Biography; The Early Years: 1770–1803* (Oxford: Clarendon Press, 1957), p. 369, includes not only 'Lines left upon a Seat in a Yew-tree',

but 'The Convict', 'The Dungeon' (an excerpt from Act V of Coleridge's *Osorio*, a blank verse tragedy), and, most puzzlingly of all, 'Remembrance of Collins', which appears as part of 'Lines Written near Richmond' in the 1798 edition, and only becomes a separate work in the 1800 edition, not as 'Remembrance of Collins', but as 'Lines Written Near Richmond, upon the Thames'. (The first part of the 1798 'Lines Written near Richmond' is also printed, separately, as 'Lines Written when Sailing in a Boat at Evening'.) Kenneth Johnston (below, p. 96), gives the number of Wordsworth's lyrical ballads for the first edition as ten, but does not list them.

11 Below, p. 96. Again, Johnston does not list the poems.

12 It is worth noting that Robinson's *Lyrical Tales* was also published in 1800 by Thomas Longman and printed by Biggs and Cottle. The volume contains no introduction or prefatory material, nor has it a sub-title or epigraph, nor do any of its poems refer to the title. See Stuart Curran, 'Mary Robinson's *Lyrical Tales* in Context'; in *Re-visioning Romanticism: British Women Writers, 1776–1837*, ed. Carol Shiner Wilson and Joel Haefner (Philadelphia: University of Pennsylvania Press, 1995), pp. 17–35.

13 See Jordan, *Why the 'Lyrical Ballads'?*, pp. 174–5. Jordan also mentions non-metrical forms of sophistication or superiority, including varied stanza lengths and combinations of rhymed and unrhymed lines. Anne Janowitz points to a related combination of simplicity and sophistication: 'What we now miss in the peculiarity of the term "lyrical ballad" is the extent to which it sews together the popular and demotic activity of the ballad with a classical heritage: the voices and choral collectivity of Greek tragedy' (*Lyric and Labour in the Romantic Tradition* (Cambridge: Cambridge University Press, 1998), p. 34).

14 For an account of 'The Three Graves', and of its relation to the 1798 edition of *Lyrical Ballads* as a whole, see Stephen Parrish, '"Leaping and Lingering": Coleridge's Lyrical Ballads'; in *Coleridge's Imagination*, ed. Richard Gravil, Lucy Newlyn, and Nicholas Roe (Cambridge: Cambridge University Press, 1985), pp. 102–16.

15 Quoted in Parrish, '"Leaping and Lingering": Coleridge's Lyrical Ballads', p. 109.

16 Jordan, *Why the 'Lyrical Ballads'?*, p. 178.

17 Jordan, *Why the 'Lyrical Ballads'?*, p. 178.

18 John Ruskin, *Fors Clavigera: Letters to the Workmen and Labourers of Great Britain*, III, letter xxxiv, section 4 (October, 1873); quoted in Jordan, *Why the 'Lyrical Ballads'?*, p. 178.

19 This is the implicit accusation of Paul D. Sheats, *The Making of Wordsworth's Poetry 1785–1798* (Cambridge, Mass.: Harvard University Press, 1973), who believes 'Wordsworth called these ballads "lyrical" not to stress their romantic subjectivity, but to alert the reader to their music. The function of the title is intensive; it emphasizes an aspect of the poems that the reader was likely to take for granted' (p. 185). This sense of lyrical as 'especially musical' is close both to Stephen Maxfield Parrish's account of the term in 'Dramatic Technique in the *Lyrical Ballads*', *PMLA* 74 (1959) 85–97, p. 87 (later incorporated in *The Art of the* Lyrical Ballads (Cambridge, Mass.: Harvard University Press, 1973), p. 86), and to Jordan,

Why the 'Lyrical Ballads'?, pp. 175–6 (as we have seen). Unlike Parrish and Jordan, though, Sheats would seem to deny the possibility of other associations. For an opposing view, see Albert B. Friedman on 'lyrical', in *The Ballad Revival: Studies in the Influence of Popular on Sophisticated Poetry* (Chicago: University of Chicago Press, 1961), p. 274: 'Contrary to the surface implications of the word, Wordsworth was not stressing the musical dimension of his ballads because they are just as tuneless and unsingable as the magazine ballads. By "lyrical" Wordsworth can only have meant that in his transmutation of the ballad, the emotional, subjective element predominates over the narrative'. Abrams, in chapter 4 of *The Mirror and the Lamp* (NY: Oxford University Press, 1953), pp. 70–99, offers numerous pre-Romantic instances of 'lyric' as subjective or internal.

20 Kenneth R. Johnston, *The Hidden Wordsworth: Poet, Lover, Rebel, Spy* (NY/London: Norton, 1993), p. 583.

21 For Shelley's reading of Schlegel see the entries of 16–21 March, 1818, in *The Journals of Mary Shelley*, ed. Paula R. Feldman and Diana Scott-Kilvert (2 vols; Oxford: Clarendon Press, 1987), i.198–9. The edition Shelley was reading was Augustus William Schlegel, *A Course of Lectures on Dramatic Art and Literature*, trans. John Black (2 vols; London: Baldwin, Craddock, and Joy, 1815). For Schlegel's distinction between the theatrical and the poetic (or lyrical) see i.30, 31; for his association of the poetical, the sublime, and Kant, see i.92.

22 Schlegel, *Lectures*, i.30, 39, 31.

23 W.B. Yeats, 'The Tragic Theatre' (1910); in *Essays and Introductions* (London: Macmillan, 1961), p. 240.

24 See Edward Young, 'A Discourse on Lyric Poetry'; in *The Complete Works, Poetry and Prose of the Rev. Edward Young, LL.D.* (2 vols; London: Tegg, 1854), i.416: 'as its subjects are sublime, its writer's genius should be so too'. For Coleridge's references to Young's 'Discourse', see *NB* i.33n. and 34n.

25 See Schlegel, *Lectures*, i.52, 77.

26 These quotations come from section 23 of 'The Critique of Aesthetic Judgement', the first part of Immanuel Kant's *Critique of Judgement* (1790), in the slightly modified version of James Creed Meredith's translation (Oxford: Clarendon Press, 1952) excerpted in David Simpson (ed.), *German Aesthetic and Literary Criticism: Kant, Fichte, Schopenhauer, Hegel* (Cambridge: Cambridge University Press, 1984), p. 47.

27 See 'Critique of Aesthetic Judgement', section 26 (Simpson, *German Aesthetic and Literary Criticism*, pp. 49–50) for the distinction between 'Reason' and 'Understanding'.

28 See 'Critique of Aesthetic Judgement', section 27 (Simpson, *German Aesthetic and Literary Criticism*, pp. 52–3).

29 *Macbeth*, I, vii, l.3; I, vii, l.7; William Shakespeare, *Macbeth*, ed. Kenneth Muir (London: Methuen (Arden Shakespeare), 1951; corr. repr., 1957), pp. 37, 38.

30 *The Frogs*, II; in Aristophanes, *The Wasps, The Poet and the Women, The Frogs*, trans. David Barrett (Harmondsworth: Penguin, 1964), p. 190.

31 Schlegel, *Lectures*, i.92.

32 Stuart Sperry, *Shelley's Major Poetry: The Narrative and Dramatic Verse* (Cambridge, Mass.: Harvard University Press, 1988), p. 76.

33   *Shelley's Poetry and Prose*, ed. Donald H. Reiman and Sharon B. Powers (NY: Norton, 1977), p. 137.
34   *Shelley's Poetry and Prose*, pp. 155, 175.
35   Young, 'A Discourse on Lyrical Poetry'; in *Complete Works*, i.415.
36   From the poem 'Vermächtnis' ('Testimony'); quoted in M.H. Abrams, *Natural Supernaturalism: Tradition and Revolution in Romantic Literature* (London: Oxford University Press, 1971), p. 387. The quotation is offered in the second section of chapter 7, entitled 'Moments' (pp. 385–90), which gathers together a number of accounts of, or allusions to, the 'intersection of eternity with time' (p. 385) in Romantic writing.
37   'A Defence of Poetry' (written 1821, published 1840); in *Shelley's Poetry and Prose*, p. 504.
38   As he said of the play, in one of the notes taken down by Isabella Fenwick: 'My care was almost exclusively given to the passions and the characters, and the position in which the persons in the Drama stood relatively to each other, that the reader (for I had then no thought of the Stage) might be moved, and to a degree instructed, by lights penetrating somewhat into the depths of our nature' (*WPW*, i.342).
39   R.P. Draper, *Lyric Tragedy* (London: Macmillan, 1985), p. 15.
40   Peter Manning, 'Troubling the Borders: *Lyrical Ballads* 1798 and 1998', *TWC* 30 (1999) 22–7, p. 26.
41   Mary Jacobus, *Tradition and Experiment in Wordsworth's 'Lyrical Ballads' (1798)* (Oxford: Clarendon Press, 1976), p. 260.
42   'Inscriptions and Romantic Nature Poetry'; in Geoffrey H. Hartman, *The Unremarkable Wordsworth* (Minneapolis: University of Minnesota Press, 1986), p. 31.
43   Alan Liu, *Wordsworth: The Sense of History* (Stanford: Stanford University Press, 1989), pp. 51, 455.
44   For a shrewd discussion of the relation of Mill to Abrams and Frye, and, more generally, of the politics of Romanticist and anti-Romanticist definitions of lyric, see chapter 1 of Sarah M. Zimmerman, *Romanticism, Lyricism, and History* (Albany, NY: SUNY Press, 1999). Mill's theory of poetry, and its relation to lyric, is cited by Abrams throughout *The Mirror and the Lamp*, but see particularly pp. 23–5. See also 'Structure and Style in the Greater Romantic Lyric' (1965); reprinted in M.H. Abrams, *The Correspondent Breeze: Essays on English Romanticism* (NY: Norton, 1984), pp. 76–108. Frye quotes Mill on the lyric in *The Anatomy of Criticism: Four Essays* (Princeton, NJ: Princeton University Press, 1957), p. 5. For his own theory of lyric see pp. 270–81; and also his 'Approaching the Lyric'; in *Lyric Poetry: Beyond New Criticism*, ed. Chaviva Hošek and Patricia Parker (Ithaca, NY: Cornell University Press, 1985), pp. 31–7.
45   John Stuart Mill, *Autobiography* (NY: New American Library, 1964), pp. 106, 107, 116.
46   'The Two Kinds of Poetry' (first published in the November issue of the *Monthly Repository*, 1833); in *Early Essays by John Stuart Mill*, ed. J.W.M. Gibbs (London: Bell, 1897), p. 228.
47   'What is Poetry?' (first published in the January issue of the *Monthly Repository*, 1833); in *Early Essays*, p. 213.
48   'What is Poetry?'; in *Early Essays*, pp. 208, 209.

49 See Marjorie Levinson, *Wordsworth's Great Period Poems* (Cambridge: Cambridge University Press, 1986), p. 37, and Liu, *Wordsworth: The Sense of History*, p. 35.
50 Stuart Curran, *Poetic Form and British Romanticism* (New York: Oxford University Press, 1986; repr., 1989), p. 182.
51 Zimmerman, *Romanticism, Lyricism, and History*, p. 90.
52 Zimmerman, *Romanticism, Lyricism, and History*, p. 92.
53 That lyricism is compatible with social engagement in other ways as well is suggested by Anne Janowitz, *Lyric and Labour in the Romantic Tradition*, pp. 50–6, which draws on George Dyer's essay 'Lyric Poetry' (1802) to connect what Dyer calls the 'liberality' of the genre with political and social liberty.
54 *The Collected Poems of William Carlos Williams*, ed. A. Walton Litz and Christopher MacGowan (2 vols; NY: New Directions, 1986–8), i.64.

3
Primitive Poets and Dying Indians

Tim Fulford

The *Five Nations* are a poor and, generally called, barbarous People bred under the darkest Ignorance; and yet a bright and noble Genius shines through these black Clouds. None of the greatest *Roman* Heroes have discovered a greater Love to their Country, or a greater Contempt of Death.

> Cadwallader Colden,
> *History of the Five Indian Nations of Canada*[1]

Low and rustic life was generally chosen because in that situation the essential passions of the heart find a better soil in which they can attain their maturity, are less under restraint, and speak a plainer and more emphatic language; because in that situation our elementary feelings exist in a state of greater simplicity and consequently may be more accurately contemplated and more forcibly communicated; because the manners of rural life germinate from those elementary feelings; and from the necessary character of rural occupations are more easily comprehended; and are more durable; and lastly, because in that situation the passions of men are incorporated with the beautiful and permanent forms of nature.

> William Wordsworth,
> 'Preface' to *Lyrical Ballads* (1800)[2]

Cadwallader Colden was a primary source of one of the central ideals of Romanticism. Born in Britain, he lived in America for over fifty-five years, negotiating with Mohawk Indians in his capacity as surveyor-general for the colonial government. His 1727 *History* showed the Indians as eloquent orators, men of dignity, honour and tradition. It gave the ideal of the noble savage a basis in factual observation. It became a standard work on native Americans, cited by later writers on the Indians and quoted by poets including Southey and Campbell. And it helped to establish an admiration for primitive rural tribes which was reflected in the emergence of a new and fashionable genre – the Indian death-song. Wordsworth and Coleridge were influenced by this genre and *Lyrical Ballads*, published to fund their trip to Germany, sought to take advantage of its popularity. Their poems of rural life were calculated to catch the vogue – and not just because they resembled the Scottish ballads which Percy and Ossian had made fashionable. Poems about, and by, Indians met a public fascination for exotic images of primitive people who seemed to retain what European civilization had lost – a bodily and spiritual harmony with nature.[3] It is such a harmony that Wordsworth attributes to unsophisticated rural folk in the 'Preface' to *Lyrical Ballads*.

(i) Braves and bards: images of Indian warriors

Indians figured in the popular imagination as warlike 'savages' given to cruelty, as ignorant barbarians mired in superstition, but also as innocent victims, as patriots, as heroes unsurpassed in courage, as people who respected courtesy and tradition, as folk full of the wisdom of nature. Interest focused on their bodies: on their capacity to endure torture without complaint, on their colour, on their ability to survive with little food, on their tattoos.[4] It also focused on their customs: in particular on the song that they were supposed to sing as they prepared for death. It was fed by travel narratives and by the accounts of traders and settlers from Peru to the Canadian Arctic. And it was renewed by visits of Indian chiefs to London,[5] and by the involvement of the Northern tribes in Britain's war against the American colonists[6] and the Southern ones in rebellion against the Spanish.[7]

The fashion for the primitive had by the mid-century assimilated the Indian into the figure of the ancient bardic poet. Drawing on Colden, Hugh Blair's *A Critical Dissertation on the Poems of Ossian* stated that 'an American chief, at this day, harangues at the head of his tribe, in a more bold metaphorical style, than a modern European would adventure to use in an Epic poem'. In primitive life, he argued, figurative speech arose from the lack of names for things: the chief's harangue showed 'that enthusiasm, that vehemence and fire, which are the soul of poetry'.[8] In 1783 Joseph Ritson took a similar view: 'We are, therefor, to look for the simplicity of the remotest periods among the savage tribes of America, at present'. And he suggested that this simplicity was legible in Indians' heroic bodies and audible in the impassioned songs they sang while suffering tortures:

> These it is the height of heroism for the victim to bear with apparent insensibility. During a series of excruciating tortures, of which a European can scarcely form the idea, he sings aloud a song[.]

To prove his point, Ritson quoted a Cherokee death-song, in which the warrior uses verbal images of weapons to fight his torturers. Arrow-shots and hatchet-blows bespeak his defiance as his words seek to (re)turn themselves to deeds of violence:

> Remember the arrows he shot from his bow;
> Remember your chiefs by his hatchet laid low:
> Why so slow? – Do you think I will shrink from the pain?
> No: – the son of Alknomook will never complain. ...
>
> I go to the land where my father is gone;
> His ghost shall rejoice in the fame of his son.
> Death comes like a friend, he relieves me from pain:
> And thy son, o Alknomook, has scorn'd to complain.[9]

J. Carver's *Travels Through the Interior Parts of North-America In The Years 1766, 1767, and 1768* made the death-song symbolic of Indians' extraordinary defiance and extreme physical cruelty. According to Carver, the warrior sang whilst under torture in order to provoke his enemies by showing his indifference to his plight. And in this rhetoric of extremity, when the tongue withered and words failed, his body became a language: 'Even in the last struggles of life, when he was no longer able to vent in words the indignant provocation his tongue would have uttered, a smile of mingled scorn and triumph sat on his countenance'. If this bodily rhetoric made the warrior savage in Carver's eyes, it also made him admirably courageous: 'it is, however, certain that these savages are possessed with many heroic qualities'.[10]

The death-song became an abiding motif in representations of Indians precisely because it constituted a heroic triumph of meaning over violence, a language whose authenticity as primitive poetry seemed vouchsafed by its emergence from bodily suffering. Immediate and oral, it existed at the opposite pole to the poetry of European civilization which was written at a remove from bodily experience and increasingly aimed at a commercial market. Torturing or tortured, the warrior-Indian and his 'savage' culture were imagined as the opposites of gentlemanly British writers and of the culture of comfort and domesticity to which their writing contributed. Cowper's *The Task,* in which civilization is symbolized by the sofa, defined gentlemanliness in terms of tamed and cosseted bodies, and for that very reason remained both fascinated and horrified by peasant bodies which suffered at others' hands or were subject to the forces of nature. The sado-masochistic imagery attached by English gentlemen to the Indian suggests that their self-repression drove their desire to extremes: their desire for powerful sensual experience could be acknowledged when confined to safely remote and ungentlemanly foreigners. Taking aesthetic pleasure in Indians' pain, readers could vicariously satisfy a wish for a knowledge of the flesh that gentlemen could not be seen to enjoy in their own persons. Yet if bodily experience was incorporated within the literary imagination of the gentleman in the form of the Indian's extreme physicality, then his extreme spirituality was equally fascinating. In enduring torture and continuing to sing, the Indian triumphed over the body by an act of mind which gentlemen could only admire even as they accepted its foreignness. Thus the Indian death-song embodied a mental heroism which enlightened Britain had left behind but for which it longed.

Britons often enlisted the heroism of the death-song in a campaign of resistance to Spanish and Catholic colonialism. This campaign was shaped by economic and political rivalry: Britain was excluded by Spain from its colonies but eager to increase its own trade and influence in South America.[11] Joseph Warton's 'Dying Indian' speaks the language of British desire to see Spanish conquest opposed by the heroism of noble savages. The Indian declares a wish for revenge that identifies him as savage, but with which civilized readers might have some sympathy.

>   – I shall soon arrive
> At the blest island, where no tigers spring
> On heedless hunters; where anana's bloom
> Thrice in each moon; where rivers smoothly glide,
> Nor thundering torrents whirl the light canoe
> Down to the sea; where my forefathers feast
> Daily on hearts of Spaniards! – O my son,
> I feel the venom busy in my breast,

Approach, and bring my crown, deck'd with the teeth
Of that bold christian who first dar'd deflour
The virgins of the sun; and, dire to tell!
Robb'd Vitzipultzi's statue of its gems!
I mark'd the spot where they interr'd this traitor,
And once at midnight stole I to his tomb,
And tore his carcass from the earth, and left it
A prey to poisonous flies. Preserve this crown
With sacred secrecy: if e'er returns
Thy much-lov'd mother from the desart woods
Where, as I hunted late, I hapless lost her,
Cherish her age. Tell her that I ne'er have worship'd
With those that eat their God. And when disease
Preys on her languid limbs, then kindly stab her
With thine own hands, nor suffer her to linger,
Like christian cowards, in a life of pain.
I go! great COPAC beckons me! farewell![12]

Eating hearts, ripping teeth from the jaw, tearing corpses from the grave – Warton's Indian defines himself by his desire to dismember and mutilate the human body. This makes him horrifying and savage. But it also makes him undaunted and brave. He is to be feared but also admired: he is sublime in his terrible violence because that violence is virtuous in terms of his own culture. Warton concentrates this virtuous violence in the remarkable phrase 'kindly stab her' – forcing readers to witness the knifing by which Indian compassion cuts into a mother and, at the same time, into Christian values. And yet Christian values are themselves imagined as a murderous violence: if the Indian feasts on men, the Spanish 'eat their God'. Violence feeds on violence, but it is the Indian's morality that is endorsed, because he has a natural belief that the cannibalistic Spanish do not. He imagines the afterlife as a 'blest island' where 'rivers smoothly glide'. He articulates, in other words, Warton's enlightenment fantasy of the religion of 'natural' man as a faith of peace, healing and reconciliation with ancestors.[13] The Indian's afterlife is an extension of his bodily oneness with nature, free from the masochistic dogma of Catholicism.

Fantasies about Indian bodies were a fundamental part of the Romantic imagination because they seemed to close the gap between civilization and savagery, present and past, language and bodily self. Ossian had been invented to close the same gap – but Indians seemed to be descendants of a still more ancient rural culture than

Macpherson's Scotland. For Rousseau, Diderot and Chateaubriand, Indian life was free of corrupt hierarchy. It was an enlightenment Christian's – or deist's – idyll, in which religion was a natural expression of a life lived in nature, free from the perversion of the Church. James Adair claimed that the Indians' life was a realization of the patriarchal community of which the Bible spoke.[14] Rather than being racially inferior to Europeans, Indians were images of the culture on which Christian Europe claimed to base itself. Adair 'observed with much inward satisfaction, the community of goods that prevailed among them, after the patriarchal manner, and that of the primitive Christians'.[15] Adair was even echoed by Benjamin Franklin in his argument that Indian society displayed more of the virtues recommended by Christianity than did the professed Christians of the New World. Franklin contrasted Indians' hospitality, courtesy, and respect for authority with the hypocrisy and meanness of the settlers, who used church meetings as opportunities to arrange ways to cheat Indian traders.[16] Adair's and Franklin's work was read by Southey while preparing *Madoc*, and had already influenced his and Coleridge's plan to establish a colony in Pennsylvania in which goods would be held in common – Pantisocracy. This radical colony was planned in the form of a patriarchal community – one free from private property and from the hierarchical institutions of Church and monarchy as were the ancient Jews and contemporary Indians.[17] Like Adair, the Pantisocrats shaped the Indians in the image of their desire to re-create in the present the uncorrupted society which the Bible showed to have existed in the past. They positioned Indians as both inferior to the Europeans (because more primitive) and superior (because less corrupted), and resembling them to the extent that their culture was also related to that of the Hebrews.

If Indians lived in harmony with each other, they also, according to European opinion, lived at one with nature.[18] Their knowledge of place was preserved by an oral memory so strong that it appeared uncanny to observers. Isaac Weld described a party of Indians who

> were observed, all on a sudden, to quit the straight road by which they were proceeding, and without asking any questions, to strike through the woods, in a direct line, to one of these graves, which lay at the distance of some miles from the road. Now very near a century must have passed over since the part of Virginia, in which this grave was situated, had been inhabited by Indians, and those Indian travellers, who were to visit it by themselves, had

unquestionably never been in that part of the country before: they must have found their way to it simply from the description of its situation, that had been handed down to them by tradition.[19]

The Indians' ability to navigate on the basis of remembered traditions was evidence of a wisdom of nature lost to Europeans. Weld argued 'the North American Indians are extremely sagacious and observant, and by dint of minute attention, acquire many qualifications to which we are wholly strangers. They will traverse a trackless forest'.[20] Such abilities allowed writers to create idealized portraits of Indian men as unalienated possessors of nature's secrets.

Lyrical Ballads was shaped by Coleridge's and Wordsworth's reading of factual accounts about the American Indians. And the volume includes an idealized portrait made in the image of those accounts, in particular that of William Bartram.[21] Coleridge's 'The Foster-mother's Tale' reflects the former Pantisocrat's desire to find a community living in harmony with nature in America. Originally composed for Coleridge's tragedy *Osorio*, this poem was included in the 1798 volume as 'a Tale in itself' (*CL*, i.412). It is a peasant's story which suggests that the freedom of nature is no longer available in Europe and must be sought among the indigenous inhabitants of other continents. In Spain the exercise of free speech has made the boy–hero a victim of religious superstition and secular tyranny:

> My Lord was sorely frightened;
> A fever seized him, and he made confession
> Of all the heretical and lawless talk
> Which brought this judgment: so the youth was seized
> And cast into that hole.
>
> (ll.54–8)

Imprisoned unjustly, the boy sustains himself with a song which identifies liberty with savage life. And this song so wins the love and pity of Leoni, the woodman who overhears it, that he helps the youth escape:

> He heard a voice distinctly; 'twas the youth's,
> Who sang a doleful song about green fields,[22]
> How sweet it were on lake or wild savannah,
> To hunt for food, and be a naked man,

And wander up and down at liberty.
He always doted on the youth, and now
His love grew desperate; and defying death,
He made that cunning entrance I described:
And the young man escaped.

(ll.61–9)

It is the power of song, felt by peasants and savages, that allows liberty to be gained. For the savage life of which the boy sings is the life to which his escape actually leads. He sails 'With those bold voyagers, who made discovery / Of golden lands' (ll.75–6), and

Soon after they arrived in that new world,
In spite of his dissuasion, seized a boat,
And all alone, set sail by silent moonlight
Up a great river, great as any sea,
And ne'er was heard of more: but 'tis supposed,
He lived and died among the savage men.

(ll.79–84)

Political freedom, a more and more distant hope in Britain by the late 1790s, takes the form of an ideal of Indian liberty, a liberty founded on a nature which magically blesses the oppressed wanderer – just as (in Coleridge's note from Bartram) it did the Seminole Indian, 'playful from infancy to Death' (*CN*, i.228).[23] '[A]ll alone', like the Ancient Mariner, the youth should logically be overwhelmed by a river 'great as any sea'. But in the logic created by the imagery this greatness opens the way for him, whilst it simultaneously closes it to those who have not cast themselves upon the elements. This logic depends on the phrase 'silent moonlight'. Moonlight lights his way without disclosing his escape to others – as the apparently redundant adjective 'silent' indicates. Nature shows him the path, but hides him from others, lighting his way when darkness is to be expected. It leads him to recesses of nature so deep that they are beyond the hearing of the Spanish. There, beyond the structures of the colonialists' knowledge, the idyll of assimilation to savage life and landscape finds its imagined place.

A few months after the publication of *Lyrical Ballads* Wordsworth located a similar recess in the Lake District life of his own boyhood, a life symbolized by the rain beating on the skin of an Indian:

Oh, many a time have I, a five years' child,
A naked boy, in one delightful rill,
A little mill-race severed from his stream,
Made one long bathing of a summer's day,
Basked in the sun, and plunged, and basked again,
Alternate, all a summer's day, or coursed
Over the sandy fields, leaping through groves
Of yellow grunsel; or, when crag and hill,
The woods, and distant Skiddaw's lofty height,
Were bronzed with a deep radiance, stood alone
Beneath the sky, as if I had been born
On Indian plains, and from my mother's hut
Had run abroad in wantonness to sport,
A naked savage, in the thunder-shower.

(*Prelude*, I, ll.291–304; cf. *Prelude* (1799), I, ll.17–26)

For Wordsworth in 1798, as well as for Coleridge, to live at one with nature was to want to feel it mark the flesh. It was to acquire the unfettered body and liberated soul of a savage, and that savage was depicted as an American Indian, his nakedness revealing his unafraid communion with his own – and nature's – physical power. And in return the landscape becomes Indian in its colouring, 'bronzed' like the naked savage who is at one with it.

It is significant that Wordsworth's 'savage', like Coleridge's 'youth', is still a boy. Adult Indians were more difficult to idealize as embodiments of natural innocence. The fantasy of Indian life as the rural paradise lost to European Christianity was always in conflict with the fixation upon the figure of the Indian warrior. Carver had argued that the courage of the warrior 'has not been outdone by any of the ancient heroes of either Greece or Rome'.[24] Comparisons with classical heroes became commonplace, and were evidence of the European desire to find living evidence of the personal heroism of which classical literature spoke. The Indian warrior satisfied this desire because, lacking both horses and guns, he fought hand-to-hand, testing his body directly against his enemies. He was depicted through the discourse of the sublime as a menacing and merciless figure, terrible in his bodily power. He was awe-inspiring (so long as he was only met second-hand in books and pictures) because he fought by exposing his body to immediate danger. He thus provided a foreign realization of an ideal of heroism in which Europeans wished to believe but which they no longer practised in their own wars – least of all colonial wars, in which muskets and artillery made the slaughter of indigenous peoples a more remote and mechanized (and safe) affair.

Crucial to this idealization was the apparent unity between the warrior's body and the signs that signified its being. The warrior's deeds were not only immediately celebrated in his own speech (as in the death-song) but, Carver noted, cut into his flesh with fish-teeth and sharpened stones:

> Their success in war is readily known by the blue marks upon their breasts and arms, which are as legible to the Indians as letters are to the Europeans.
>
> The manner in which these hieroglyphicks are made, is by breaking the skin with the teeth of fish, or sharpened flints, dipped in a kind of ink made of the soot of pitch pine. Like those of the ancient Picts of Britain these are esteemed ornamental; and at the same time they serve as registers of the heroic actions of the warrior, who thus bears about him indelible marks of his valour.[25]

In the warrior writing and self are reconciled: to Carver his being and its meaning are one, as was once the case with Britons, when bodily deeds were written on the body. Nature and the self are reconciled too, since the skin is carved with the teeth of fish dipped in pitch-pine soot.[26] The Indian is here a fantasy of unity and authenticity, having no split between soul, body and the letters which represent him – the flesh made word. He is the polar opposite of the deracinated blind beggar in Wordsworth's *Prelude*, whose inner identity is emptied out onto the demeaning paper that is merely pinned to his body to represent his alienation from himself and his dependence on others:

> a blind Beggar, who, with upright face,
> Stood propped against a wall, upon his chest
> Wearing a written paper, to explain
> The story of the man, and who he was.
> My mind did at this spectacle turn round
> As with the might of waters, and it seemed
> To me that in this label was a type
> Or emblem of the utmost that we know
> Both of ourselves and of the universe[.]

> (*Prelude*, VII, ll.612–20)

However, the alienation which London-life imposes on the beggar is also registered on the body of the Indian. The 'hunter Indian' 'from remote / America' is viewed by Wordsworth as merely one of many 'specimens of man' visible in the London streets (VII, ll.240–1, 236). He is reduced to one of the spectacles of a city which makes trivial exhibitions out of the most autochthonous cultures. Like the 'English ballad-singer' and 'Ossian ... / Summoned from streamy Morven' (VII, ll.196, 561–2), he is uprooted, at best a face in the London crowd, at worst a 'raree show' demeaning the authenticity which he embodies in his rural home.

In making the 'hunter Indian' an example of the authenticity that he thought was prostituted in London, Wordsworth was commenting on contemporary trends. In 1805 a Mohawk warrior visited London, as the poet Thomas Campbell reported:

> There is a Mohawk Indian in town, who whoops the war-whoop to ladies in drawing-rooms, and is the reigning rage of the town this season. He is an arch dog, and palms a number of old Scotch tunes (he was educated in the woods by a Scotchwoman), for Indian opera airs, on his discerning audience. Rogers the poet, somebody told me, being one of the spectators of this wonder, at hearing of proposals for the whoop, was seen to shrink with a look of inexpressible horror, and hide himself behind a sofa.[27]

Here the bodily sublimity of the fierce brave is turned into a trivial amusement. In the London drawing room the war-cry curdles the blood only of the most timid of poets, and its force is absorbed by that most domestic of eighteenth-century inventions – the comfortably and reassuringly padded sofa. And the fantasy of the primitive authenticity of Indian song is undermined by the Mohawk's colonial education (ironically enough the Scottish songs which he palmed off as Indian airs were themselves examples for Wordsworth of authentic rural poetry).

Wordsworth wanted his Indians, like his Scots and Lakelanders, to stay in their rural places. If London uprooted them and their culture, the travel narratives which he read in the 1790s allowed him to imagine them as embodiments of their native lands. At Alfoxden he read Samuel Hearne's *A Journey From Prince of Wales's Fort in Hudson's Bay to the Northern Ocean In The Years 1769, 1770, 1771, and 1772.*[28] Hearne focused to a greater degree than the other popular accounts of Indians on the warrior's bodily fierceness and on his cruelty to women. He interpreted these traits as proceeding from a culture which had no pity for the vulnerable because it was determined to overcome the vulnerability of the body. This Indians sought to do, according to Hearne, by voluntarily subjecting the body to feats which exceeded its limits.

> When a friend for whom they have a particular regard is, as they suppose, dangerously ill, beside the above methods, they have recourse to another very extraordinary piece of superstition; which is no less than that of pretending to swallow hatchets, ice-chissels, broad bayonets, knives, and the like; out of a superstitious notion that undertaking such desperate feats will have some influence in appeasing death, and procure a respite for their patient.[29]

Throats as deep as these were disturbing as well as fascinating because they subverted the boundary of the internal and external, thus cutting through assumptions about the body's relationship to the world outside itself. Hearne found it all hard to swallow, despite the fact that he could detect no imposture when he witnessed an Indian eat a knife. Likewise the missionary David Brainerd found the actions of Indian 'conjurers' (shamans) too excessive to be human:

> As he came forward, he beat his tune with the *rattle*, and danced with all his might, but did not suffer any part of his body, not so much as his fingers, to be seen: and no man would have guessed by his appearance and actions that he could have been a human creature, if they had not had some intimation of it otherwise. When he came near me, I could not but shrink away from him, although it was then noon-day, and I knew who it was, his appearance and gestures were so prodigiously frightful.[30]

These bodies bespoke the effects of belief upon the flesh. Beyond the norms of European rationality, they appeared to readers as a form of grotesque sublime.[31] And they were immediately subject to the Indians' beliefs in a way that was also inexplicable to Europeans trained to believe in the distinctness of the soul and body. (The influence of belief on the body was explored by Coleridge in 'The Ancient Mariner' and by Wordsworth in 'Goody Blake and Harry Gill', poems written when their authors were reading about Indian superstitions in Hearne and Bartram.) It was in death that the Indian was most powerfully fascinating to Europeans, since it was there that his spirit–body unity was ultimately proved. Indians, in the imagination of whites, could literally think themselves to death.

> When these jugglers take a dislike to, and threaten a secret revenge on any person, it often proves fatal to that person; as, from a firm belief that the conjurer has power over his life, he permits the very thoughts of it to prey on his spirits, till by degrees it brings on a disorder which puts an end to his existence: and sometimes a threat of this kind causes the death of a whole family; and that without any blood being shed, or the least apparent molestation being offered to any of the parties.[32]

Fascinated by the causative connection between mind and body, writers focused upon the male Indian body as an extreme (and self-contradictory) Other of 'civilized' society – heroic, savage, courageous, cruel, excessive, perverse, and superstitious, but immediately present-to-itself. This ambivalent attitude is evident in Wordsworth's 'Ruth' (*Lyrical Ballads*, 1800), where Indian life is first pictured as idyllic:

> The Youth of green Savannahs spake,
> And many an endless endless lake
> With all its fairy crowds
> Of islands that together lie
> As quietly as spots of sky
> Among the evening clouds:
>
> And then he said 'How sweet it were
> A fisher or a hunter there,
> A gardener in the shade,
> Still wandering with an easy mind
> To build a household fire and find
> A home in every glade
>
> (ll.61–72)

But this idyll (derived from Bartram's *Travels*[33]) turns out to be dangerous; American nature's wildness exacerbates the youth's irregularity and he abandons Ruth for a life of 'lawless' liberty. He is corrupted by the bodily excesses of savage men:

But ill he liv'd, much evil saw
With men to whom no better law
Nor better life was known;
Deliberately and undeceived
Those wild men's vices he receiv'd,
And gave them back his own.

(ll.139–44)

Here Wordsworth betrays doubts about nature and liberty that reflect
his growing distance from revolutionary politics. But he ponders these
doubts by setting them on a foreign stage: his Indian men pervert
themselves in an American landscape whose free growth then symbol-
izes their wildness. The idyll becomes a dystopia, the noble savage an
ignoble 'slave of low desires'. Ruth is left alone, to find solace in her
love of a tamer English nature which does not, as did America, betray
her.

(ii) Death and the Indian maiden

In 'Ruth' Wordsworth pictures Indian women in happy companion-
ship, dancing, singing, gathering strawberries all day long. But he also
shows them as victims of Indian men. And in this his poem is typical
of many European depictions. The received image of Indian women
was less complex than that of men because it highlighted their depen-
dency and chastity, both traits which were familiar ideals for women
in Europe. And it was agreed that Indian women were ill-used, an
agreement which placed readers in the comfortable position of being
able to pity them and to congratulate themselves for so doing. A
reader who extended compassion to an Indian woman (albeit at
second hand) was likely to feel that he was more chivalrous and pater-
nalistic than were her own menfolk. Images of Indian women were
calculated to make male readers feel themselves to be more noble, as
well as more civilized, than the supposedly noble savages.

Indian women's bodies were used for sex, childrearing, and work –
the latter giving them a hardihood which amazed writers who were
accustomed to regard European women as delicate. Their resumption
of work immediately after childbirth was particularly remarked upon
– and led to comparisons of Indian life with that of beasts. According
to Hearne, the point of comparison was that bodily strength was the
decisive factor in gender relations and marriage customs.

It has ever been the custom among those people for the men to wrestle for any women to whom they are attached; and, of course, the strongest party always carries off the prize. A weak man, unless he be a good hunter and well-beloved, is seldom permitted to keep a wife that a stronger man thinks worth his notice: for at any time when the wives of those strong wrestlers are heavy-laden either with furrs or provisions, they make no scruple of tearing any other man's wife from his bosom, and making her bear a part of his luggage.[34]

But the picture painted by other commentators challenged Hearne's. Carver saw Indian polygamy to be governed by custom and social rank rather than brute strength. He showed it to be compatible with chastity and idealized the numerous instances he found of monogamy: 'there are many of the Indians who have but one wife, and enjoy with her a state of connubial happiness not to be exceeded in more refined societies'.[35] Indian women were regarded on the whole as chaste, modest, and virtuous in their sexual conduct because they were governed by their husbands and the customs of their tribe. Here white men found themselves in sympathy with what they perceived to be a patriarchal society. Meek, chaste, submissive, Indian women did not, as did warriors, threaten the image of Indian life as an idyll with fierce and cruel – albeit heroic – physicality. They suited the paternalism implicit in European men's fantasy of uniting themselves to a gentle and harmonious nature, as is evident in the death-song Wordsworth composed for *Lyrical Ballads*, 'The Complaint of a forsaken Indian Woman'.

Wordsworth's Indian song stood firmly in what was by 1798 a popular genre. It was also a response to reading Hearne's *Journey*. Hearne had focused on Indian men's callousness towards women, on their lack of the values of chivalry expected from a European man. He witnessed the slaughter of a camp of Eskimos and related how two Indians of his expedition transfixed a girl to the ground and, whilst she was 'twining round their spears like an eel', ridiculed him for soliciting for her life.[36] And he recorded the abandonment of one of the Indian women who, having fallen ill, could no longer keep up with the party:

it is the common, and indeed the constant practice of those Indians; for when a grown person is so ill, especially in the Summer, as not to be able to walk, and too heavy to be carried, they say it is better to leave one who is past recovery, than for the whole family to sit down by them and starve to death; well knowing that they cannot be of any service to the afflicted. On those occasions, therefore, the friends or relations of the sick generally leave them some victuals and water; and, if the situation of the place will afford it, a little firing.[37]

The abandoned woman recovered sufficiently to rejoin the party, but could not keep pace and was finally left behind. Hearne concludes:

A custom apparently so unnatural is perhaps not to be found among any other of the human race: if properly considered, however, it may with justice be ascribed to necessity and self-preservation, rather than to the want of humanity and social feeling, which ought to be the characteristic of men, as the noblest part of the creation. Necessity, added to custom, contributes principally to make scenes of this kind less shocking to those people, than they must appear to the more civilized part of mankind.[38]

Hearne seeks to overcome his desire to condemn by explaining the practice in terms of Indian customs, which he understands as a rational response to the harsh climate. Here his ambivalence about his Indian companions is especially strong as he inclines towards blame then exculpation. And his ambivalence is reflected in Wordsworth's poem. In the voice of the woman left behind Wordsworth alternates between despair and hope. She both regrets and stoically accepts death:

> Too soon despair o'er me prevailed;
> Too soon my heartless spirit failed;
> When you were gone my limbs were stronger,
> And Oh how grievously I rue,
> That, afterwards, a little longer,
> My friends, I did not follow you!
> For strong and without pain I lay,
> My friends, when you were gone away ...
>
> My journey will be shortly run,
> I shall not see another sun,
> I cannot lift my limbs to know
> If they have any life or no.

> My poor forsaken child! if I
> For once could have thee close to me,
> With happy heart I then would die,
> And my last thoughts would happy be.
> I feel my body die away,
> I shall not see another day.

(ll.23–30; 61–70)

Wordsworth's poem gives psychological complexity to the genre of the death-song he inherited from Warton and Ritson. And crucially, it feminizes it. Wordsworth substitutes a helpless woman's entreaties for the defiant boasting of the tortured warrior. And the woman's pathetic story appeals to the European reader to provide the compassion which the Indian men failed to show her (the very title seems to allude to the piteous cry made by Jesus on the cross when he suspected God, like man, had abandoned him – 'why hast thou forsaken me?'). Wordsworth's Indian woman excites compassion more easily than did the cruel warrior men. Nevertheless, she features in *Lyrical Ballads* for the same reasons Indian men appear in Warton, Ritson, and Blair: she is the epitome of the idea that the most expressive and forceful poetry is the oral response of primitive and rural folk to the extremes of nature – in this case isolation as well as oncoming death. Her words emanate directly from her body, itself in direct contact with unmediated nature. She is thus not the exception but the defining case amongst all the rural speakers in Wordsworth's collection: his mad mothers, female vagrants are all forsaken Indian women – or at least aspire to her indigenous state. Like the Indian, all Wordsworth's women gain a certain power as they sing out their own interpretation of their bodily distress. By voicing their state orally and immediately, they come to define their being by it, and even to embrace it. What seems 'madness' may, Wordsworth suggests, be the 'Indian' voice of a woman who has come to accept and even to will the isolation and decay of her body. Freedom in nature finds its apogee in a savage remoteness from civilization experienced as an escape into insanity and death:

> Then do not fear, my boy! for thee
> Bold as a lion I will be;
> And I will always be thy guide,
> Through hollow snows and rivers wide.

I'll build an Indian bower; I know
The leaves that make the softest bed:
And if from me thou wilt not go,
But still be true 'till I am dead,
My pretty thing! then thou shalt sing,
As merry as the birds in spring.

('The Mad Mother', ll.51–60)

The language of rural life, it seems, is at its most authentic when spoken by a woman who is embracing death (physical or social). The ballad is raised up to become lyrical when it acquires the autochthonous self-identity of the Indian woman's song of death or madness. In these poetic circumstances compassion becomes vampiric as the male narrator searches for victims to feed his pity – hence Wordsworth's need to dissociate himself from the sentimental but uncomprehending spectator of female distress in 'The Thorn'.

Wordsworth's forsaken woman died in the northerly region of America. But she resembled the portraits Britons made of the women of the south. There were two reasons for this resemblance and they together reveal the uneasy combination of historical empiricism and stereotyping fantasy by which white men formed their picture of native peoples. First, many writers suggested that northern and southern tribes were similar as a result of migration southwards over the centuries. The evidence collected of such migrations fuelled a stereotype which tended to make all indigenous Americans conform to currently fashionable literary topoi and ethical scenarios. Wordsworth's first published poem had been the 1787 sonnet 'On seeing Miss Helen Maria Williams weep at a tale of distress',[39] and his Indian woman is shaped by the ethics of sensibility with which Williams had delineated native Americans in her long poem of 1784 – *Peru*. Williams introduced a subject which was to recur with great frequency in the poetry of the period – the Spanish conquest of South America.[40] Her poem attacks Pizarro and his soldiers for cruelty, bigotry, rapacity, and deceit and idealizes the Inca warriors who resist them as heroic fighters for liberty. Yet Williams does not depict these warriors in detail. Instead she claims women's domestic suffering as her subject, ostensibly because she is too 'timid' to depict slaughter. But depicting slaughter would have demanded descriptions of Indian warriors' 'cruel' deeds and 'fierce' bodies. Such descriptions might have seemed improper for a woman writer and they would certainly have undermined the gendered moral scheme by which Williams imagined the conquest. Williams concentrates on Indian women's suffering because she wishes to pity the Indians as helpless and innocent victims of Spanish aggression. Her Indians – men and women – are defined by their defeat and despair, by their need for compassion. And this compassion can be vicariously extended to them by poet and reader because their bodily defiance – and therefore their menace – is effaced from the text. Williams feminizes the Indian song, making it a woman's lament rather than a warrior's cry of defiance. Her heroine Aciloe sees her father Zamor taken captive by the Spanish:

> 'He bleeds (she cries) I hear his moan of pain,
> My father will not bear the galling chain;
> My tender father will his child forsake,
> His mourning child, but soon her heart will break.
> Cruel Alphonso, let not helpless age
> Feel thy hard yoke, and meet thy barb'rous rage;
> Or, oh, if ever mercy mov'd thy soul,
> If ever thou hast felt her blest controul,
> Grant my sad heart's desire, and let me share
> The load, that feeble frame but ill can bear.'
>
> (V, ll.99–108) [41]

No longer protected by her father and unable to protect him, Aciloe depends upon Spanish compassion. But Alphonso, the Spanish commander, has Zamor tortured in front of her so as to blackmail her into giving him sexual favours. Aciloe wishes for death for them both and the reader wishes to offer her the protection that her father cannot and the Spaniard will not.

Using female narrators who told of women's suffering rather than of the martial bodies of warriors, Williams feminized the Indian through the discourse of sensibility. She created portraits which conformed to a European view of femininity which Wollstonecraft, for one, condemned for pandering to men's desire to keep women weak and dependent. In the American context these portraits served to justify a paternalist colonialism, one supposedly opposed to military or commercial kinds. The British readers' desire to offer compassion and protection to dependent Indians distinguishes them (as paternalists) from the Spanish soldiers, whose refusal to pity and protect shows their colonialism to be rapacious rather than benevolent.

Wordsworth's Indian woman, weak of body, abandoned by men, needing compassion, is also not unmarked by his desire to offer her strength and protection. Wordsworth had inherited from Williams and the discourse of sensibility beliefs about how men should behave towards weak and dependent women – beliefs translated by images of Indian women into advocacy of paternalist colonialism.

(iii) The Lake Tribe

Lyrical Ballads was influenced by the eighteenth-century fashion for 'Indian' tales and the paternalist colonialism justified by those tales. In their turn, Wordsworth's and Coleridge's Indians influenced the 'Indian' poetry of other writers, who adopted the style and values that rapidly became associated with 'the Lake poets'. One such was P.M. James, a Birmingham banker and poet whose 'American Song'[42] resembles Coleridge's 'Foster-mother's Tale':

> Come to the green Savannah!
> To the Indian wild-wood bower!
> Where the tyrant's frown cannot daunt thee,
> Nor the oppressor's arm hath power.
> Where thy course like the winds of heaven,
> Shall be free o'er the boundless plains;
> And the realm of thy joy shall be
> Where Nature majestic reigns!

> (st. 1)

Enclosed bowers and boundless plains: James's Indian landscape, like Coleridge's, offers maternal security from oppression and freedom to roam.

A still more remote Indian descendant of *Lyrical Ballads* was James's 'The Otaheitan Mourner'.[43] This poem is the 'song' of the Tahitian maid Peggy, who had become the partner of George Stewart, one of the mutineers on the *Bounty*.[44] Stewart was living in Tahiti with Peggy and their child when he was arrested, clapped in irons, and taken back to Britain to face court martial. Eyewitness accounts found his parting from Peggy heartrending.

James was a fan of Wordsworth (another of his poems rhapsodizes about the beauty of Grasmere). His versification of Peggy's lament recalls Wordsworth's *Lyrical Ballads*, using colloquial diction and simple rhyme to make the figure of the lonely mother seem artless and pathetic in her simplicity, whilst the form is comparable to that of 'Goody Blake and Harry Gill'.[45]

> All by the sounding ocean
> > I sit me down and mourn,
> In hopes his chiefs may pardon him,
> > And speed my Love's return.
> Can he forget his Peggy,
> > That soothed his cares to rest?
> Can he forget the baby,
> > That smiles upon her breast?
>
> > > > (st. 10)

James heightens the pathos by imbuing Tahitian nature with love: the island woman speaks of love shared without the need for language.

> Before I knew his language,
> > Or he could talk in mine,
> We vow'd to love each other,
> > And never to resign.
> O then 'twas lovely watching
> > The sparkling of his eyes;
> And learn the white man's greeting,
> > And answer all his sighs.
>
> > > > (st. 2)

James shapes the native woman in accordance with his desire to find a location in which oneness with nature can be rediscovered through the love of a faithful, compliant, and artless maiden. This oneness is sensual: in a series of erotic images Peggy shows the lovers 'like dolphins' sporting with each other's bodies as they play upon and below the lithe body of the sea:

> I taught my constant white Love
> > To play upon the wave,
> To turn the storm to pleasure,
> > And the curling surge to brave,
> How pleasant was our sporting,
> > Like dolphins on the tide;

> To drive beneath the billow,
> > Or the rolling surf to ride.

(st.3)

Freedom is a pleasuring of all the senses: tasted fruits intensify rather than destroy this Eden of the flesh, heightening perception until even the ocean deep seems a sunlit grove welcoming the lovers:

> To summer groves I led him,
> > Where fruit hangs in the sun;
> We linger'd by the fountains,
> > That murmur as they run.
> By the verdant islands sailing,
> > Where the crested sea-birds go;
> We heard the dash of the distant spray,
> And saw through the deeps the sunbeams play,
> > In the coral bow'rs below.

(st.4)

All the elements of Wordsworthian primitivism are here: heartfelt love and idyllic nature are vouchsafed to the reader in a song whose apparent spontaneity makes it seem authentic. The reader is invited both to admire the maid's capacity for feeling and to pity her in her abandonment. And the poem's celebration of cross-cultural love implicitly criticizes the British for preferring the letter of military discipline to the claims of the heart. Paternal and romantic love are destroyed when Stewart, husband and father of natives, is arrested by Captain Edwards and the troops sent by the Admiralty to capture the mutineers.[46] They have not shown the paternalism or compassion which the Tahitian maid, like Wordsworth's Indian woman, invites the civilized reader to give her.

James was not the only poet to adapt Wordsworth's *Lyrical Ballads*. Thomas Campbell's *Gertrude of Wyoming* was thought by Southey to have been influenced by 'Ruth' and 'The Brothers'. It depicted a paternal Indian chief who sang a death-song as he prepared to die in battle avenging the killing of the American girl. But it was William Lisle Bowles who drew closest to the poets of the Lake District. Bowles's sentimental verse had inspired Coleridge in the mid-1790s. Indeed, Bowles had led Coleridge towards his enthusiasm for the songs and tales of native peoples. In 1784 Captain Wilson had been forced by damage to his ship the *Antelope* to spend months on the Pelew (Palos) islands. He had been welcomed by chief Abba Thule. Having repaired his ship Wilson brought Abba Thule's son Lee Boo to Britain. But Lee Boo caught smallpox shortly after arrival in Greenwich and died. Bowles responded to the sad event with a poem in which Abba Thule waits anxiously for his son's return:[47]

> Is he cast bleeding on some desert plain!
> Upon his father did he call in vain!
> Have pitiless and bloody tribes defiled
> The cold limbs of my brave, my beauteous child!
>   Oh! I shall never, never hear his voice;
> The spring-time shall return, the isles rejoice,
> But faint and weary I shall meet the morn,
> And 'mid the cheering sunshine droop forlorn!

> (ll. 57–64)

Coleridge took up Lee Boo's death in 1794, treating it sentimentally as an opportunity for lament over the death of an innocent: 'My soul amid the pensive twilight gloom / Mourn'd with the breeze, O Lee Boo! o'er thy tomb' ('To A Young Lady with a Poem on the French Revolution', ll.9–10; *CPW*, i.64).[48]

When Bowles turned again to 'Indian' poems, he adopted the voice of a primitive South American forest dweller. Bodily at one with nature, the singer is guided by tribal tradition. He is governed by an oral memory of the speech of the fathers. The poem mirrors this orality since it appears to be a transcription of an oral form – a song. And the song the Indian sings makes him an ancestor of those in Coleridge's 'Foster-mother's Tale' – a careless and free inhabitant of the verdant and idyllic forest:

> Home returning from our toils,
> Thou shalt bear the tiger's spoils;
> And we will sing our loudest strain
> O'er the forest-tyrant slain! ...
>   By the river's craggy banks,
> O'erhung with stately cypress-ranks,
> Where the bush-bee hums his song,
> Thy trim canoe shall glance along.
>   To-night at least, in this retreat,

> Stranger! rest thy wandering feet;
> To-morrow, with unerring bow,
> To the deep thickets fearless we will go.

('Song of the American Indian', ll.15–18, 25–32)[49]

Bowles's poem takes the song-form as does Wordsworth's 'forsaken Indian Woman', but his Indian is to be envied and followed rather than pitied or regarded with awe. He is fearless and the only tyrant he faces is the tiger. He welcomes the stranger to a paradise. Clearly, in Bowles's South America the landscape and its Indians are fantasies, exotic locations in which the liberal's dream of political freedom is unstained by apprehensions of cultural and colonial violence.

If poems such as 'Song of the American Indian' set the mood for Pantisocracy, by the new century it was the Pantisocratic poets and their friend Wordsworth who were influencing Bowles. It was in his long poem of 1811–13 that Bowles came closest to Wordsworth's presentation of Indians. *The Missionary* was Bowles's major work. Written with the encouragement of Samuel Rogers, it was repeatedly praised by Byron, whom it influenced. But it was Robert Southey, Wordsworth's Lakeland neighbour and himself an authority on South America, whom Bowles asked for advice concerning the Indian maid whose story *The Missionary* narrates. This maid, Olola, falls in love with Zarinel, a Spanish minstrel and a member of the army attempting to conquer Chile. They share a brief idyll in her native Andean valley before he abandons her to return to the army. She travels from the mountains to the coast in search of him, but, failing to find him, drowns herself in despair. Before she casts herself into the waters, however, she sings a death-song which is strongly reminiscent of 'The Mad Mother':[50]

> I heard the song of gladness:
>   It seemed but yesterday,
> But it turned my thoughts to madness,
>   So soon it died away:
> I sound my sea-shell; but in vain I try
> To bring back that enchanting harmony!
>   Hark! heard ye not the surges say,
> Oh! heartless maid, what canst thou do?
>   O'er the moon-gleaming ocean, I'll wander away,
> And paddle to Spain in my light canoe!

(VI, ll.75–84)[51]

Like Warton's 'Dying Indian' her song is an indictment of Spanish conquest. But like Wordsworth's 'The Complaint of a forsaken Indian Woman' it feminizes the genre, positioning Indians as victims who deserve the compassion and protection they have been denied. In this case it is the Spanish who have denied it, not the Indian warriors, and this gives the poem a political relevance. Readers are called upon to give their pity as a recompense for the betrayal of the Indian woman by their fellow 'civilized' Europeans. As a political gesture at a time when Britain was tacitly supporting Bolivar's South American independence-war[52] this is mild: feeling compassion for fictional feminized Indians merely entails a general regret at their colonized position. It demands no action and positions the reader as a benevolent paternalist, a would-be chivalrous knight who would save Indian damsels if he could. It is over the Indian maid's dead body that paternalism triumphs: Olola has to die, and has to sing of her death, to let readers feel good by feeling sad. Southey advised Bowles as much:

I could have wished your Indian maid had been spared, – because I am arrived at that age when men like to be spared from as many painful feelings as possible; – in our youth we love to shed tears over fictitious sorrows, – as we grow older we have none to spare for them, and find too much cause for melancholy thoughts ever to have them willingly excited. But you could not have disposed of her otherwise, and when happiness has been rendered impossible, death becomes the desirable termination.[53]

Death was the desirable termination because it excited compassion, and compassion, as Southey acknowledged, aligned the reader with the 'compassionate' colonialism which the poem sought to vindicate. The Christian missionary after whom it is named laments Olola and protects her brother. His compassion and paternalism redeems colonialism from the deeds of the Spanish soldiers. He is peaceful, fatherly, Christianizing; they are warlike, enslaving, cruel. Both Bowles and Southey justified British imperialism as a civilizing and Christianizing mission, in contrast to a Spanish colonialism they portrayed as a rapacious exploitation of people and materials. They needed the death-song of an Indian maid to do so. And if they politicized the aesthetic which Wordsworth had established in his 'Complaint of a forsaken Indian Woman', then perhaps their politics were present in embryonic form in his poem. Certainly Wordsworth himself later revisited the themes of Indian suffering and superstition he had explored in 1798. In *The Excursion* the Solitary searches for his ideal Indian: 'Primeval Nature's child' who is 'stronger in himself; / Whether to act, judge, suffer, or enjoy', but finds only 'A creature, squalid, vengeful, and impure; / Remorseless, and submissive to no law / But superstitious fear, and abject sloth' (*Excursion*, III, ll.919, 923–4, 953–5). Lawless, lazy and superstitious, Indians needed paternalist rule and the Protestant work-ethic. Colonization was a civilizing mission:

> 'O for the coming of that glorious time
> When, prizing knowledge as her noblest wealth
> And best protection, this imperial Realm,
> While she exacts allegiance, shall admit
> An obligation, on her part, to *teach*
> Them who are born to serve her and obey; ...
> Earth's universal frame shall feel the effect;
> Even till the smallest habitable rock,
> Beaten by lonely billows, hear the songs
> Of humanised society; ...
> Your Country must complete
> Her glorious destiny. Begin even now ... [']
>
> (*Excursion*, IX, ll.293–8, 386–9, 407–8)

Coleridge concurred when in 1810 he justified 'Coercion of those Savages, or even compelling them into a form of civilisation' through a colonization which made 'the moral good & personal Happiness of the Savages ... a part of the End' (*CN*, iii.3921). In 1833 he commented that '[c]olonization is not only a manifest expedient – but an imperative duty on Great Britain. God seems to hold out his finger to us over the sea'.[54] The Lyrical Balladeers and the 'Lake tribe' they led had developed from the aesthetics of 1798 a paternalist vision which demanded that their idealized natives gave deference to 'civilized' men in return for compassion, care and respect. What readers offered to fictional natives in the comfort of their homes, the builders of empire would give their real cousins under the hot sun of Africa, America, and India. Thus Romantic aesthetics shaped the ideology of British colonialism.

Notes

1   Cadwallader Colden, *The History of the Five Indian Nations of Canada* (London: Osborne, 1747), Dedication, p. v. (The first edition was published in New York in 1727.)

2   *WPrW*, i.124.

3   Critical preoccupation with *Lyrical Ballads'* formal innovations and radical politics has led to the neglect of the volume's exploitation of fashionable genres. Exceptions to this neglect include Robert Mayo, 'The Contemporaneity of the *Lyrical Ballads'*, *PMLA* 69 (1954), pp. 486–522; and Mary Jacobus, *Tradition and Experiment in Wordsworth's* Lyrical Ballads *(1798)* (Oxford: Clarendon Press, 1976). I am indebted to Jacobus's discussion, pp. 192–4.

4   On white people's images of Indians see Louise K. Barnett, *The Ignoble Savage: American Literary Racism 1780–1890* (Westport, Conn.: Greenwood Press, 1975); Robert F. Berkhofer, Jr., *The White Man's Indian* (NY: Vintage Books, 1978); Richard Drinnon, *Facing West: The Metaphysics of Indian-Hating and Empire Building* (Minneapolis: University of Minnesota Press, 1980).

5   In 1785, for example, the Mohawk chief Brant visited London where he was introduced to the King and Queen, and met Bishops, Lords, and James Boswell.

6   Burke and the elder Pitt both painted lurid pictures of the atrocities committed by Indians, in speeches opposing the British army's use of them. For Burke, see *The Parliamentary History of England, from the Earliest Period to the Year 1803* … (36 vols; London: Longman, *etc.*, 1806–20), xix.708, 971; and for Pitt, Basil Williams, *The Life of William Pitt, Earl of Chatham*, (2 vols; London: Longmans, Green, 1913), ii.322. In 1795 Coleridge wrote of 'human Tygers' as he described the Indians who in 1778 were used by the British to pillage Wyoming in Pennsylvania: *Lectures 1795 On Politics and Religion*, ed. Lewis Patton and Peter Mann (London/Princeton, NJ: Routledge and Kegan Paul/Princeton University Press, 1971), p. 57.

7   For sympathetic accounts of Indians fighting against the Spanish see, for example, Joel Barlow, *The Vision of Columbus* (1788); William Lisle Bowles, *The Missionary* (1811–13); and Byron, *The Island* (1823), II, ll.65–78.

8   Hugh Blair, *A Critical Dissertation on the Poems of Ossian, the Son of Fingal* (London: Beckett and De Hondt, 1763), p. 2. Blair was applying to the American Indians a point made by Robert Lowth about the language of the ancient Hebrew tribes. On Lowth, Blair, and the influence of their primitivist aesthetics on Coleridge and Wordsworth, see Nigel Leask, 'Pantisocracy and the Politics of the "Preface" to *Lyrical Ballads'*, in Alison Yarrington and Kelvin Everest (eds), *Reflections of Revolution: Images of Romanticism* (London/NY: Routledge, 1993), pp. 39–58; Stephen Prickett, *Words and* The Word: *Language, Poetics and Biblical Interpretation* (Cambridge: Cambridge University Press, 1986), pp. 114–18; and Tim Fulford, *Coleridge's Figurative Language* (London/Basingstoke: Macmillan, 1991), pp. 83–6.

9   'A Historical Essay on the Origin and Progress of National Song'; in *A Select*

Collection of English Songs (3 vols; London: Johnson, 1783), i.ii, and n. (The 'Essay' is independently paginated.)

10 Jonathan Carver, *Travels Through the Interior Parts of North-America In The Years 1766, 1767, and 1768* (London: Carver, 1778), pp. 340, 341. Southey used Carver extensively in writing *Madoc* (1805).

11 On this rivalry see Margaret Steven, *Trade, Tactics and Territory. Britain in the Pacific 1783–1823* (Melbourne: Melbourne University Press, 1983), pp. 1–63.

12 Warton's 'The Dying Indian' was published in *A Collection of Poems In Four Volumes By Several Hands*, ed. Robert Dodsley (London: Dodsley, 1755), iv.209–10.

13 The Indian's dying invocation of Manco Capac reminds the reader of the heroic Inca leader in whose name resistance against the Spanish continued. Capac became a Romantic hero in the work of Helen Maria Williams, Southey, and Barlow – an idealized resistance leader of the kind later found in Byron's Eastern Tales.

14 James Adair, *The History of the American Indians* (London, 1775); Adair echoed the argument of the early colonist Roger Williams as expressed in *A Key Into The Language of America* (1643), ed. John J. Teunissen and Evelyn J. Hinz (Detroit: Wayne State University Press, 1973), pp. 86–7.

15 Adair, *History of the American Indians*, p. 17.

16 Benjamin Franklin, *Remarks Concerning the Savages of North America*; in *Two Tracts: Information to Those Who Would Remove to America*, 3rd edn (London: Stockdale, 1784), pp. 36–9.

17 On Pantisocracy as a patriarchal community, see Leask, 'Pantisocracy and the Politics of the "Preface"'. On Pantisocracy and Indians, see James C. McKusick, '"Wisely Forgetful": Coleridge and the Politics of Pantisocracy'; in Tim Fulford and Peter J. Kitson (eds), *Romanticism and Colonialism* (Cambridge: Cambridge University Press, 1998), pp. 107–28.

18 Wordsworth and Coleridge were, of course, influenced by Rousseau's idealization of 'savage' life. See the *Discourse on the Origin of Inequality (Second Discourse), Polemics, and Political Economy*; in *The Collected Writings of Rousseau*, ed. Roger D. Masters and Christopher Kelly (8 vols to date; Hanover/London: University Press of New England, 1990–), vol. 3.

19 Isaac Weld, *Travels Through the States of North America and the Provinces of Upper and Lower Canada During the Years 1795, 1796, and 1797* (London: Stockdale, 1799), pp. 391–3. See also Thomas Jefferson's 1784 account of Indian resourcefulness: *Notes on the State of Virginia* (NY/London: Harper and Row, 1964), pp. 56–95.

20 Weld, *Travels*, p. 391.

21 William Bartram, *Travels through North and South Carolina, Georgia, East and West Florida, The Cherokee Country ... together with Observations on the Manners of the Indians* (Philadelphia: James and Johnson, 1791) was a source for the landscape-description in several of Coleridge's poems. See John Livingston Lowes, *The Road to Xanadu: A Study in the Ways of the Imagination* (London: Constable, n.d.), pp. 453–5. See also *CN*, i.218, 220, 221, 222.

22 Coleridge exports the pathetic pastoralism of the dying Falstaff to an uncolonized America.

23   Bartram described the Seminoles as 'free from want or desires ... nothing to give them disquietude, but the gradual encroachments of the white people ... as blithe and free as the birds of the air': *Travels through North and South Carolina*, p. 210.

24   Carver, *Travels*, p. 342.

25   Carver, *Travels*, p. 337.

26   I am indebted to D. Lee for showing me the meaning of inscriptions of this kind.

27   Letter of 25 April, 1805; *Life and Letters of Thomas Campbell*, ed. William Beattie (3 vols; London: Moxon, 1849), ii.51. Campbell went on to write his poem about Indian warriors, *Gertrude of Wyoming* (1809), in which a Mohawk chief is called a 'Monster' (III, st. 16).

28   Samuel Hearne, *A Journey From Prince of Wales's Fort in Hudson's Bay to the Northern Ocean In The Years 1769, 1770, 1771, and 1772* (London: Strahan and Cadell, 1795). Hearne had travelled at the behest of the Hudson Bay Company in search of a copper lode. Guided by Indians, he walked across the Arctic interior that was hitherto unexplored by whites.

29   Hearne, *A Journey*, p. 210.

30   From Brainerd's journal (1745), incorporated in Jonathan Edwards, *An Account of the Life of the Late Reverend Mr David Brainerd* ... (Edinburgh: Gray, 1765), p. 356.

31   On the emergence of a grotesque sublime see Morton D. Paley, 'Coleridge and the Apocalyptic Grotesque'; in Tim Fulford and Morton D. Paley (eds), *Coleridge's Visionary Languages: Essays in Honour of John Beer* (Cambridge: Brewer, 1993), pp. 15–25.

32   Hearne, *A Journey*, p. 233.

33   On the debts to Bartram throughout the poem see Lowes, *The Road to Xanadu*, pp. 453.

34   Hearne, *A Journey*, p. 141.

35   Carver, *Travels*, p. 372.

36   Hearne, *A Journey*, p. 179.

37   Hearne, *A Journey*, p. 219.

38   Hearne, *A Journey*, p. 219.

39   Wordsworth's poem to Williams was published in the *European Magazine* for March, 1787. In August and September, 1786, the *European* had reviewed Williams's *Poems* favourably.

40   Not least in Southey's *Madoc* (1805) and *A Tale of Paraguay* (1825).

41   Helen Maria Williams, *Poems* (1786; facs. rpt, 2 vols in one; Oxford/NY: Woodstock (*Romanticism and Revolution* series), 1994), ii.132.

42   P.M. James, *Poems* (London: Arch, 1821), pp. 97–101.

43   Southey encouraged James after reading the poem in the *Monthly Magazine* for December, 1808. He quoted it in a review article in the *Quarterly Review* 2 (1809), p. 50.

44   Stewart, a 'young gentleman' rather than common seaman, claimed not to have been willingly involved in the mutiny.

45   'P.M.J', 'The Otaheitan Mourner', *Monthly Magazine* 26 (1808–9), pp. 457–8. James published a version amended to remove some of the Wordsworthian colloquialisms in his *Poems*, pp. 76–83.

46   Testimony at the court martial made Captain Edwards notorious for an

insistence on the letter of military discipline which amounted to cruelty. He confined the arrested mutineers in a prison-house constructed on the *Pandora's* deck ('Pandora's Box') and left them ironed and locked in when the ship was wrecked. A crew member unlocked the door as the ship foundered, but not all the prisoners were able to escape in time. Stewart drowned. See Neil Rennie, *Far Fetched Facts: The Literature of Travel and the Idea of the South Seas* (Oxford: Clarendon Press, 1995).

47   See 'Abba Thule's Lament for his Son Prince Lee Boo', in *The Poetical Works of William Lisle Bowles*, ed. George Gilfillan (2 vols; Edinburgh: Nichol, 1855), i.49–50.

48   Both Bowles and Coleridge had read George Keate's narrative of Wilson's voyage, *An Account of the Pelew Islands* ... (London: Nicol, 1788). For a discussion of the affair see James C. McKusick, '"That Silent Sea": Coleridge, Lee Boo, and the Exploration of the South Pacific', *TWC* 24 (1993), pp. 102–6.

49   Bowles, *Poetical Works*, i.61.

50   Not only is Olola's 'madness' caused by a man's desertion but she, like the mad mother, is contemplating throwing herself into the sea.

51   Bowles, *Poetical Works*, i.346.

52   Salvador de Madariaga, *Bolivar* (London: Hollis and Carter, 1952), pp. 309–19, shows that, despite Castlereagh's public policy of non-interference, auxiliaries for Bolivar's armies were recruited and equipped in Britain with the connivance of ministers.

53   Southey to Bowles, January, 1816; quoted in *A Wiltshire Parson and His Friends. The Correspondence of William Lisle Bowles*, ed. Garland Greever (London: Constable, 1926), p. 152.

54   S.T. Coleridge, *Table Talk*, ed. Carl Woodring (2 vols; London/Princeton, NJ: Routledge/Princeton University Press, 1990), i.369.

4
Wordsworth and the Six Arts of Childhood

Marilyn Gaull

> Who . . . shall point as with a wand, and say
> 'This portion of the river of my mind
> Came from yon fountain?'
>
> *The Prelude* (1799), II, ll.247–49

By the art of childhood in Wordsworth's poetry I mean, first, his representation of childhood; secondly, his misrepresentation, art as artful, as dissimulation; thirdly, his depicting the artfulness of children, their dissembling; and, fourth, the tradition of childhood as recorded in art, as an artful construction. In many ways, they are all the same. When, at age thirty, the fantasies that had sustained his childhood, the experiences that inspired him, the arts of his own childhood, appear 'dead in [his] eyes as is a theatre / Fresh emptied of spectators' (*Prelude*, V, ll.574–5), Wordsworth depicts them and enacts their loss in the *Lyrical Ballads*, 1800. A place, or a time, illusory, alluring, this memory of childhood haunts Wordsworth's imagination, tempts him to repeated encounters with the disenchantment Keats was to describe in 'Ode to a Nightingale' where 'Charm'd magic casements, opening on the foam / Of perilous seas, in faery lands forlorn' (ll.69–70). Neither a world of innocence nor of joy, the childhood Wordsworth depicts in the *Lyrical Ballads* of 1800 is 'perilous' and takes place in the 'lands forlorn.'

According to historians of childhood as well as literary historians, Wordsworth and Blake introduced the theme of childhood to literature, invented literary children, shaped both the fictional representation and the perception of childhood, consequently shaping adult expectations of real children, and the self-evaluations of children themselves.[1] Although, as Richardson pointed out, four 'versions' of childhood appear in Wordsworth's poetry – the 'natural', the 'wise', the 'foolish', and the 'sinful' – the primary one with which he and Blake are identified is the innocent and therefore virtuous child, both vulnerable and harmless, a 'divine child,' as Ross Woodman calls him, redemptive and wise, enjoying visionary powers, that, Wordsworth said, 'we are toiling all our life to find.'[2] The most frequently cited sources for this reading or misreading of childhood are Wordsworth's 'Intimations Ode' and Blake's *Songs of Innocence*, both of which ultimately acquired moral, even political functions, and came to serve purposes that were the very opposite of what both Blake and Wordsworth represented: whole educational systems, to which they would have objected, forced the realities of childhood into the illusions of the poets, followed by psychological theories to free adults from the same poetic illusions and the pernicious effects of educations based on them. 'That childhood has attained a special status in our own century,' Spiegelman writes, unaware of the crushing ironies and contradictions, 'owes as much to the imaginings of Wordsworth as those of Freud.'[3]

The idealized child, of course, preceded Wordsworth's *Intimations Ode*, originating in Locke, elaborated by Rousseau, permeating the literature of sensibility, part of a primitivistic bag of tricks, equating children with a golden age of mankind, innocence with virtue, goodness with poverty, instinct with art, philosophically and artistically favouring the poor, the deranged, the savage, the disinherited, and the young, the very young, especially if they were also deprived, illiterate, mentally disabled, and orphaned. This interest in childhood coincided with a curious turn in the history of Christianity in Europe when the cult of the Son, the Infant Jesus, and the domestic ideal it promoted displaced the cult of the Virgin and the ritual of courtly love, essentially fertility rituals, she had inspired in the twelfth century.

In this context – religious, political, economic, artistic, cultural in the broadest sense – appeared another art of childhood, my fifth, what we call children's literature, the only literature written specifically for an audience that might not be able to read it, that did not write it, and seldom chose it. Along with the moral and didactic tales of Mary Wollstonecraft, Mrs. Trimmer, Mrs. Sherwood, Mrs. Barbauld, and Maria Edgeworth, Sir Walter Scott wrote a history of France for children, Charles and Mary Lamb adapted Shakespeare, Southey wrote 'The Three Bears', and Godwin published profitable adaptations of

Greek myths and of Homer. With the exception of 'The Three Bears', and 'Twinkle Twinkle Little Star', this art of childhood did not survive the generation that produced it, although it shaped the moralistic taste of those who grew up to be the Victorian generation, and became the authority against which the great children's writers of that generation rebelled.[4]

While this art of childhood, children's literature, flourished during Wordsworth's youth and provided a source of income to his contemporaries, he, like Coleridge, found it ponderous, unimaginative, heavy-handed. He preferred another art – the sixth – an art which during his lifetime, in part because of him, entered the world of childhood, and is still almost exclusively identified as children's literature. The original audience, however, was not only adult but also, because of the emphasis on fertility and courtship, an audience that would have excluded children. The tales – the *Arabian Nights*, the French and German cottage and fairy or salon tales associated with Perrault and the Brothers Grimm along with the few native ·British adventure stories – influenced both Wordsworth's childhood and, up until the *Lyrical Ballads* of 1800, his representations of children as well. As much as Milton and Shakespeare, these tales from the folk tradition, along with the Cumbrian border songs to which he often alludes, shaped his adult taste and literary mannerisms connecting him to an older and more universal text than either the classical or British traditions in which he was educated.[5]

Although the terms folklore and folktales were not coined until 1846 by a British antiquarian, the concept began evolving early in the eighteenth century, driven by the energies and curiosity of antiquarians, philologists, and philosophers, all caught up in the growing nationalism of Western Europe and a preoccupation with history. While war, trade, colonial expansion, and tourism increased encounters with alien and exotic cultures, challenged the familiar and unexamined assumptions about native identity, scholars searched for cultural origins among what the Germans, especially Herder, considered the Folk. Folk studies concentrated on historically validated native language, rituals, beliefs, manners, and experiences, a unique spirit, all reflected supposedly in a purified state among the rural poor engaged in traditional activities and their vernacular literature, either oral or written, anonymous or at least collective, valued or authenticated by historical associations, repetition, custom, familiarity, offering insights into the community that produced and preserved it.[6]

Derived mostly from Herder, shaped in the twentieth century by

Stith Thompson, this description of folklore could have been adapted from Wordsworth's 'Preface' of 1800. One can only speculate, as I shall, on how and why such narrative becomes the art of childhood, but its association with language, pure native language (accurate or not) the customary rituals and traditional beliefs, would certainly recommend it. I am not claiming that Wordsworth was a folklorist but, first, his inclinations as a poet were compatible with what will become folklore, certainly as compatible as with the popular magazine verse that Mayo identified, or with the German and English literary ballads that Parrish discovered;[7] secondly, he presents original poetry as if it were folklore (especially in poems that feature a narrative voice such as *Peter Bell* or 'The Ruined Cottage'); third, he turns folklore into original poetry (such as 'Hart-Leap Well'); fourth, folktales, in their artful artlessness, their ritualistic spontaneity, provided the techniques and forms he used to fictionalize his personal experiences, the art of his childhood.

This lore, primarily tales but also songs, embodies and preserves the language, the dialect, and the traditional knowledge, the characters and events that everyone needs to know to participate in the community. Familiar examples include the Old Testament, as well as many of the myths, *märchen, sagen*, and commonplaces that formed such familiar collections as those by Basile, Perrault, Grimm, Andersen, Bishop Percy, and even Macpherson's Ossianic poems, which, however inauthentic, stimulated scholarly activity in Europe. Like Homer, the Old Testament, Don Quixote, and Robinson Crusoe, the tales were endlessly recycled through oral and written versions, retaining the implied intimacy of oral performance although the actual authorship had become obscure and irrelevant. However remote from their origins – translated, adapted, abbreviated, moralized, customized to new settings, geographies, languages, even neighbourhoods, tribes, families – the forms of the tales, the motifs, survive. Performed on holidays, at festivals, in coffee houses, or to relieve the boredom of work or long nights in strange places, they created a sense of identity, initiated the young and alien into the common knowledge that binds the society and reminds the rest who they are and to whom they are related.

However puzzling, it is true that folk tales demonstrate a pervasive brutality, especially toward children, especially by women, and a simple relentless code of retributive justice. The Brothers Grimm, who adapted as well as collected them, believed that the brutality reflected their origins among primitive people, historical not contemporary primitives, in the childhood of the race as they conceived it. To anthropologists such as Frazer, philosophers such as Eliade, folklorists such as Propp, Dorson, Zipes, and Tartar, the brutality, which can never be totally hidden, is a vestige of the initiation, fertility, and creation rituals which are since lost.[8] *The Juniper Tree*, for example, with its murder, dismemberment, cannibalism, matricide, transformations, the evil step-mother who lures everyone into a bestial and destructive drama, depicts both the destructive power of nature and the dangers of domesticity, the rage and vindictiveness of the ancient female goddesses who have been displaced by patriarch religion. The gods in folktales, as Wordsworth described the primitive religions of nature in *The Excursion*, are 'Gods delighting in remorseless deeds'. They depict the way children, helpless, ignorant, surrounded by giants they do not understand, driven by forces they cannot control, actually experience the world. The tales then, even if they do not depict ancient initiation rituals, become initiation rituals, which, as we shall see, Wordsworth – who understood 'moving about in worlds not realized' – knew so very well.

Finding the origins of these tales is complicated by their amazing mobility, how they travel, how, like currency, they convert and acquire new values, adapt to new communities, acquire features from the settings in which they were read or performed. So, for example, because their primary informant was a descendant of French Hugenots, many tales in the collections of the Brothers Grimm, which were supposed to represent a Germanic tradition, actually derive from the French court tales of Perrault, in turn derived from local folk tales and the *Arabian Nights*.[9] Wordsworth's travels, to France, Switzerland, France again, then Germany, in some ways reflect the history of this lore in Europe during his life-time, to which he contributed. From his native tradition, he would have known, carried, and shared the cyclical Jack-tales, the British tradition of mischievous or stupid but lucky heroes, outsiders, eccentrics, iconoclasts, even the Lords of Misrule, the Jack Falstaffs, the Robin Hoods, Jack the Giant-Killer. In part, however, because of this limited native narrative tradition (about which there is much to be written) England was a great repository for the Indo-European, thus connecting Wordsworth to those Continental cultures in which he travelled even though, as in Germany, he did not know the language:

> From Homer the great thunderer, from the voice
> Which roars along the bed of Jewish song,
> And that, more varied and elaborate,

> Those trumpet-tones of harmony that shake
> Our shores in England, from those loftiest notes
> Down to the low and wren-like warblings, made
> For cottagers and spinners at the wheel
> And weary travellers when they rest themselves
> By the highways and hedges: ballad tunes,
> Food for the hungry ears of little ones,
> And of old men who have survived their joy –
>
> (*Prelude*, V, ll.203–13)

They are, he says, the 'Powers', less than Nature, but 'For ever to be hallowed... / For what we may become, and what we need', the powers to which he attributes, next to nature, his vocation as a poet. Moreover, in that brief passage, Wordsworth intuits what becomes the subject of folklore as a discipline, its range, audience, the scenes and occasions of transmission, and its transitional function in human development, helping to shape one's expectations of life:

> Oh, where had been the man, the poet where –
> Where had we been we two, beloved friend,
> If we, in lieu of wandering as we did
> Through heights and hollows and bye-spots of tales
> Rich with indigenous produce, open ground
> Of fancy, happy pastures ranged at will ...
>
> (*Prelude*, V, ll.232–7)

For the illiterate, the isolated, the uneducated, folklore provides a history – a surrogate history, the 'old unhappy far-off things', as he calls them in 'The Solitary Reaper', and 'battles long ago'. In the eighteenth century, when so much energy was invested in recovering origins, collecting, validating, organizing information about the past, when the search for origins awakened the study of myth, language, archaeology, all the historical disciplines, folklore was simply one more of the many historical illusions extending and sometimes substituting for reality. As Loren Eiseley explains, in the century before Darwin, 'Man was a creature without history': his

> oldest written records told him nothing of himself. They showed
> him a picture limited, at best, to a few millennia in which he had
> warred and suffered, changed kings and customs, marked the face

of the landscape with towns and chimneys, but, for all that, he had remained to himself unknown.

Summarizing the entire historical turn of the eighteenth century, Eiseley concludes:

> for a thinking being to be without history is to make him a fabricator of illusions. His restless and inquiring intellect will create its own universe and describe its forces, even if these are no more than the malignant personifications which loom behind the face of nature in the mythologies of the simple folk.[10]

When I cited this passage in *English Romanticism: The Human Context* (1988) to explain the invention of history in eighteenth-century England, such artificial versions of the past as the Gothic, the Hellenic, and even an invented Biblical past, I did not realize how relevant it was to the orphan writers, the poets without personal history: Byron, Keats, and, of course, Wordsworth, mostly Wordsworth, who, above all, found a surrogate in 'the mythologies of the simple folk'. Oedipus, Tom Jones, Huck Finn, even Superman – orphans are the ideal heroes because, like Adam, they are originals. Of divine, royal, or obscure origins, free of historical ties and in search of them, anything, good or bad, supernatural or magical powers can be attributed to them. In this respect, like so many others, Wordsworth is representative of his age as Eiseley defined it, and his experience symbolic of his generation: 'without history ... he had remained to himself unknown', a 'fabricator of illusions'. Because in the folk tradition, the emphasis falls on the narrator, the story teller, Wordsworth by extension is not only an author of folk heroes but a folk hero himself as he describes himself at the end of 'Home at Grasmere', when he introduces the 'lowly matter', that is himself, 'when and where and how he lived', 'All his little realities of life', and what he represents: 'May my life / Express the image of a better time, / More wise desires and simple manners.' From his own experience and his reading of folk tales he finds what Jameson calls the 'master narrative' of his age,[11] the poor boy who succeeds, the orphan who becomes Poet Laureate; or, to adapt the phrase with which Dickens begins *David Copperfield*, he becomes the hero of his own life.

Orphaned in childhood, separated from the sister with whom he was to spend most of his adult life, raised by caretakers to whom he was one among many children, by his own admission a difficult and demanding boy, 'of a stiff, moody, and violent temper', as he describes himself in his *Autobiographical Memoranda* (*WPrW*, iii: 372), there were no records, family anecdotes, historians of his infancy, none more reliable than the butterfly, the fugitive memories of his mother pinning a flower on his coat or reprimanding him, and the traumatic memories he calls 'spots of time'. However fascinated by the power of memory, he is just as often overcome by 'forgetting', as he calls it in the 'Intimations Ode', or the 'vanishings' he cannot overcome: 'I cannot paint / what then I was', he says in 'Tintern Abbey', or in *The Prelude* recover 'days / Disowned by memory'(I, 1.643), 'raptures now forever flown' (V, 1.557). And the memories he does recover are part created, part recalled, an artful recreation, such as the 'spots of time' that both renew and elude him: 'the hiding places of my power / Seem open, I approach, and then they close' (XI, ll.335–6). The loss, the limitation, became his strength, and he did indeed create an illusion, a literary childhood – not the one, however, that historians of childhood attribute to him.

It is ironic that the poet who cannot recall his own childhood or whose recollections start with being 'savage', mischievous, and confused is held responsible for that artificial and ultimately pernicious vision of infancy as pure, innocent, and ideal, a vision that haunts nineteenth century literature and life as well. By the time Wordsworth starts writing the 'Intimations Ode' in 1802, he is not so much lamenting the loss of childhood, the loss of memories of blessedness and visionary powers, but rather he laments losing his belief in the illusion that such powers are a part of childhood, when 'The earth and every common sight, / To me did seem / Appareled in celestial light,' the operative words 'seem' and 'Appareled' emphasizing the illusion. Forgetting starts at birth, and what is not forgotten is dispelled in the strange irony of development, the child 'blindly' 'at strife', with its own 'blessedness' (l. 125). Whatever childhood held for him, without historians of his infancy, it became clear in that cold and isolated winter in Goslar, 1798–99, when he was starting *The Prelude*, 'The Ruined Cottage', and new poems for the 1800 edition of the *Lyrical Ballads*, when he was most obsessed with childhood experiences, that they were as irrecoverable as Blake's state of innocence, where merely to reflect on childhood, to share and repeat it, changes it and stains the water.

In spite of his sense that childhood is irrecoverable, out of fugitive and distorted memories, out of his readings in the narrative tradition, the 'Powers' only second to nature, Wordsworth artfully constructed in *The Prelude*, starting in 1799, a childhood that is closer to reality than the *Intimations Ode* and the idealizations with which he became associated. Following Ken Johnston in *The Hidden Wordsworth*, I believe Wordsworth was his own best creation, that he imaginatively constructed a childhood out of the recollected glimpses of his past shaped and highlighted by the narratives, the ones he heard, the ones he found in his father's study, the tales in the little yellow canvas book that 'charm away the wakeful night / In Araby' (V, ll.520–1). Wordsworth's childhood was shaped by a diverse and powerful range of tales: Sinbad the Sailor, Ali Baba, and Aladdin, the native ones, the 'bye-spots of tales / Rich with indigenous produce' (ll.235–7), 'Fortunatus, and the invisible coat /... Jack the Giant-killer, Robin Hood / And Sabra in the forest with St. George' (ll.365–9), the 'tales / Traditionary' that 'round the mountains hung / And many a legend, peopling the dark woods' (*The Excursion*, I, ll.163–5), the ones he read lying on the hot stones by the River Derwent 'Defrauding the day's glory' (*Prelude*, V, ll.511–13), the local tales he heard from the packmen and peddlers, the wandering labourers, the ironmonger, the discharged soldier, weavers, shepherds, the old men who sat on the benches in Hawkshead and exchanged their stories.[12] Many of the tales have that timeless contemporaneity characteristic of the best folktales, the 'Familiar matter of today' as he calls it in 'The Solitary Reaper', 'Some natural sorrow, loss, or pain / That has been and may be again.'

A Wordsworthian child is not exemplary, charming, or cuddly. Rather, as he recalls in 1800, at age thirty, in 'Home at Grasmere':

> I breathed ...
> Among wild appetites and blind desires,
> Motions of savage instinct, my delight
> And exaltation. Nothing at that time
> So welcome, no temptation half so dear
> As that which urged me to a daring feat
> Deep pools, tall trees, black chasms, and dizzy crags,
> I loved to look at them, to stand and read
> Their looks forbidding, read and disobey
>
> (ll.912–20)

Without responsible, observant, caring, and disciplining adults, he lived as only one in a pack of boys, a

> ... race of real children, not too wise,
> Too learned, or too good, ... wanton, fresh,
> And bandied up and down by love and hate,
> Fierce, moody, [im]patient, venturous, modest, shy,
> Mad at their sports like withered leaves in winds;
> ... doing wrong and suffering, and full oft
> Bending, beneath our life's mysterious weight
> Of pain and fear
>
> (V, ll.436–44).

More than social skills, practical knowledge, moral values, this boy, this orphan-boy, tempted by danger and conflict, responsible to no one, acquired survival skills, courage, but mostly fear, the 'ministry,' the 'discipline' of fear, fostering fear, varieties of fear to prepare him for the real dangers of the real world. 'No vulgar fear', he says, 'Possessed me' when he witnessed the recovery of the drowned man from Esthwaite: 'Young as I was, a child not nine years old, / ... my inner eye had seen / Such sights before among the shining streams / Of fairyland, the forests of romance' (V, ll.473–7). Although he had always found fear in Nature, it is in the language of folk tale, the 'ghostly language of the ancient earth'(II, l.328), that he learns to live with it, with its 'mysterious weight', which is what folk tales do best.

For Wordsworth, fear, whatever its source, had a second even more primitive function; for, more than love, of which there seems to be very little in his boyhood, fear helped him overcome his isolation, connected him to his fellow adventurers. While some scholars claimed that his preoccupation with the role of fear in childhood prepared him to experience the sublime or religion, it was equally important as a socializing force,[13] which suggests another reason why the folk tales and the fairy tales based on them, the carnage, injustice, abandonment, betrayal, and danger they depicted, became children's literature, why tales contrived to keep an Emperor awake were told, however surreptitiously, to put children to sleep. According to Carl Sagan, on the frontier and in primitive communities such bedtime rituals kept children, while the adults slept, from straying into the woods where they could be abducted by demons, eaten by animals or by other people's parents.[14] However, as Charles Lamb pointed out in 'Witches and other Night-fears' (1821), whether they are told such stories or not, children will generate their own terrors: the Gorgons, and Hydras, and Chimaera, 'They are the transcripts . . . the archetypes are in us and eternal.'[15]

Wordsworth's preoccupation with fear in *The Prelude*, the pursuit and mastery of the fearful, recalls the *Arabian Nights* rather than the native trickster tales which are characterized by equally hapless heroes who have no fear or who proudly deny it. Specifically, the tales from the Sinbad cycle with their recurrent voyages for adventure, entanglements in foreign communities, imprisonments, dangerous and fretful returns (satirized in *Gulliver's Travels*) illuminate the dilemma and the powerfully evoked fear in *The Prelude*, where, having abandoned his mistress and unborn child in what on many levels was a 'country of romance', Wordsworth becomes the isolated adventurer, secluded in a 'high and lonely room' in a demonized Paris, held literally in a reign of terror, 'at the best . . . a place of fear', keeping watch by candlelight, 'Defenseless as a wood where tigers roam '(X, ll.57–82). In Paris, reality exceeded the fictions that helped him deal with the ghastly sight of the drowned man of Esthwaite: the tigers, the wood, more images from *The Arabian Nights*, become measures of his terror. By 1800, he has exchanged the literary tales, the romances of his childhood, for the realities of 'The Ruined Cottage', exchanging an exotic courtly European folk tradition for a native oral one: the 'Elysian, fortunate islands, fields like those of old / In the deep ocean' ('Home at Grasmere', ll.997–9) for 'the very world which is the world / Of all of us, the place in which, in the end, / We find our happiness, or not at all' (*Prelude*, X, ll.723–8).

Wordsworth's interest in *The Arabian Nights*, up until 1793, its lingering verbal, substantive, and formal appeal, arise in part from its unique history and the moment when Wordsworth encountered it (which I have examined in detail in 'Awake in Araby').[16] Originally part of a vast body of oral entertainment that circulated throughout the world of trade in Persia, Egypt, Italy, Spain, France, Germany, and Holland, from the ninth century on, they periodically entered the written tradition, surviving still in the oral, always as adult entertainment, vulgar, lurid, performed in coffee houses, for bachelor entertainments or at weddings. Published first in France by Galland as *Les Mille et Une Nuits* (1704–17) in five volumes, joining though probably stimulating the deluge of fantasy and fairy tale that amused and occupied the literate aristocracy, possibly, again, as oral entertainment, they were soon nationalized, published, and assimilated. Like Perrault's 'Puss in Boots', 'Cinderella', 'Blue Beard', 'Sleeping Beauty', 'Little Red Riding Hood', and the many versions of Beauty and the

Beast that circulated in the salons among the literate middle classes and aristocracy, *The Arabian Nights* served as conduct manuals, as sources of *civilité*, while encoding traditional and archetypal fertility and courtship rituals.[17] In Germany, they appeared in versions by Mozart, Goethe, Tieck, Novalis, Brentano, and ultimately the Brothers Grimm, who adapted them for the middle and lower classes, possibly children, with the emphasis shifting from a civilizing to a moralizing function.

Similarly, in England they circulated in partial, unauthorized, and some moralized translations such as *The Oriental Moralist* (1790),[18] which were not the 'lawless tales' Wordsworth read in his father's library. Nurses, tutors, tourists helped diffuse them not only through different countries but also different social classes, turning ancient primitive initiation rites into contemporary and cultural initiation rituals. At one extreme, *The Arabian Nights* influenced the gothic horror and eroticism of novels such as *Vathek* while at the opposite, by 1800, they acquired new life in stage adaptations, especially comic, often Chinese, a favourite theme for the seasonal pantomimes.[19]

Considered as folktales, more traditional than original, collective and anonymous rather than authored, *The Arabian Nights*, like Wordsworth and his contemporaries, without a history, an orphaned form, nonetheless provided a common language, experience, even a source of community wherever Wordsworth lived and travelled, in England, Switzerland, France, and Germany. Anticipating the folklorists who would study them in the future, Wordsworth recognized their nature and function: 'romances, legends penned / For solace by the light of monkish lamps; / Fictions, for ladies of their love, devised / By youthful squires; adventures endless, spun / By the dismantled warrior in old age ... / These spread like day, and something in the shape / Of these will live till man shall be no more' (*Prelude*, V, ll.522–9). War, trade, colonial expansion, travel, publishing, all accelerated the spread of this central body of writing during the last decade of the eighteenth century when Wordsworth, himself a traveller, became an intermediary, transmitting the tales he knew and the ones he learned along the way.

In France, *The Arabian Nights* connected him to the popular culture, with other travellers and revellers as well, the young men and women he met in the pleasure spots of Paris and the families with whom he lived in Orleans and Blois.[20] And while he was learning French from Annette Vallon, the tales, the body of shared knowledge, provided a theme, an admonition, illustrative sentiments for their passionate and forbidden love affair – which may explain his allusion to them in his fictionalized account of the romance in the Vaudracour and Julia episode in *The Prelude* in which Vaudracour describes Julia: 'A vision, and he loved the thing he saw. / Arabian fiction never filled the world / With half the wonders that were wrought for him' (IX, ll.584–5). He alludes to the same tales when he sees the castles in the Loire valley, the huge forests, or describing his friend Beaupuy, who 'wandered in perfect faith, / As through a book, an old romance or tale / Of Fairy' (IX, ll.306–8).

Such verbal resemblances, however, changing with each performance and in each context, are the least important and least influential aspect of folktale. It is 'something in the shape', as Wordsworth calls it, that 'will live till man shall be no more', the formal qualities that matter, the morphology, one of the most controversial and unresolved issues in the history of folklore. Most eighteenth-century scholars of myth, philology, or the native vernacular literatures, such as Sir William Jones or Richard Payne Knight in England, or Herder and later the Brothers Grimm in Germany, believed in monogenesis, in a single tale originating probably in India, evolving through Europe, from which all others descended; an idea which had something of a rebirth in the nineteenth century, when so many areas of human history were interpreted according to evolutionary theory. But most students of folklore and anthropologists in the nineteenth century such as Andrew Lang and E.B. Tyler in England or Vladimir Propp in Russia, advocated polygenesis, attributing the similarity among culturally, linguistically, and geographically unrelated tales to archetypes, that appear in similar narratives independently in each society at particular stages of development.[21] Anticipating the folklorists in describing the ease with which they spread ('like day') and the formal qualities through which they survive ('something in the shape') between 1799 and 1805, Wordsworth, drawing on his own experience, observation, and instinct, came to recognize that their power derived from their diffusion as well as their archetypal qualities. Alluding to the archetypes, in the *Two-Part Prelude*, written in Goslar, Wordsworth explains his response to the drowned man of Esthwaite:

> numerous accidents in flood or field
> Quarry or moor, or 'mid the winter snows,
> Distresses and disasters, tragic facts
> Of rural history, that impressed my mind

> With images to which in following years
> Far other feelings were attached – with forms
> That yet exist with independent life,
> And like their archetypes, know no decay.

(I, ll.279–87)

Later in the 1805 version, he imbeds the archetypes in the tales, 'among the shining streams / Of fairyland, the forests of romance' (V, ll.476–7).

I believe that the frame story either had the most decisive influence on Wordsworth or it was the characteristic with which he felt the most affinity. The frame story, common in these cyclical popular narratives, places the emphasis on the performance, on the narrator whose tales, often tales within tales, are designed to distract the audience from some discomfort or threat to their safety, to redeem a listener from madness or some terrible error in judgment, or to save the narrator's life, guarantee his safety, allow him to escape. Common examples include Homer's reciting at court, Chaucer on his pilgrimage, Boccaccio's escaping a plague, or Basile's offering tales to a woman in the last five days of her pregnancy, and the most common example, perhaps the common antecedent, Scheherazade, a male invention, whose nocturnal tales supposedly cure King Shahryar of his madness, to save her life and her sister's. 'The Ancient Mariner', 'The Thorn', 'Peter Bell', 'The Brothers', 'The Ruined Cottage', consummately in *The Excursion* where the Wanderer tells tales to redeem the Solitary, subtly in *The Prelude* when Wordsworth addresses Coleridge on the recovery of his creative life, consistently enough in the *Lyrical Ballads* of 1800 with various narrators to consider them one long cycle of tales within tales, with a whole array of narrative voices: all projections of Wordsworth whose habit of oral composition lends them an authenticity that other poets lose in adapting this technique to writing.[22]

The frame tale with the fictional narrator, usually in danger or under immense pressure to relate something pertinent and absorbing, encourages the odd morality or amorality of these works, one that makes little sense outside the folk tradition. Scheherazade is, after all, not a reliable narrator, nor a role model, exemplary or even inspiring: however beautiful, clever, and seductive, she was raised by a father who earned his living by murdering other people's daughters and uses her narrative skills to entertain a serial killer with whom she sleeps every night for three years; a heartless ogre who will, if she fails to amuse him, have her strangled by her own father leaving motherless the three children born of this revolting match. A version of the same fertility cult as Beauty and the Beast with its implied virgin sacrifice, *The Arabian Nights*, among many other things, demonstrates the role of narrative in creating civilization, in redeeming humankind from the lawless brutality or arbitrary power. Unfortunately, its fascination as a collection of tales lies in the brutality, not the redemption.

All the tales involve the same irreconcilable loyalties, irrational commitments, and savage alternatives as the frame story, all illustrating how life is both endangered and preserved in arbitrary and mysterious ways, in accidental encounters and clever stories. The first tale, one that impressed Coleridge so much that he used it to explain the morality of 'The Rime of the Ancient Mariner',[23] concerns a merchant who, mindlessly discarding the pit of a date he was eating into a well, accidentally blinds the son of a genii who in turn requires his life as punishment. Three passing sheiks save him by each telling tales to the genii in exchange for a third of his blood. Morality is as irrelevant in these tales as it was to be in the Lucy poems, 'Ruth', 'The Last of the Flock', 'The Thorn', 'Michael', the Matthew poems, 'Andrew Jones' whose sons the narrative voice curses because he stole a penny from a beggar, and 'The Ruined Cottage'. The 'Forgers of lawless tales', as Wordsworth calls them, the narrators are merely spectators, often two or three times removed from the tale, telling tales about tales, at best transitional figures between the civilized world of the implied audience, who can read, and the austere world of nature, where the stories take place. A narrator like the Pedlar in 'The Ruined Cottage' is not responsible for the justice of events, just the ordering of them, their fictional value, the awakened expectation, suspense, and resolution. The 'lawless tales', Wordsworth said, 'make our wish our power, our thought a deed' (*Prelude*, V, ll.548, 552); depicting deeds, not abstractions, principles or morality. Such tales in Perrault, *The Arabian Nights*, or the Brothers Grimm, were published for adults, literate adults, while teaching and representing the art of childhood: deeds in narrative sequences, the inevitabilities of fiction, to serve the 'dumb yearnings, hidden appetites', to overcome 'life's mysterious weight of pain and fear', to domesticate the 'unknown modes of being' with which children contend.

Wordsworth developed many of his ideas about narrative, language, and his own childhood while he was in Germany in 1798–99. But, as many scholars have noted, there is little sign of his

German experience in his writing; in fact, the poetry could have been written anywhere. Isolated, cold, unhappy, William and Dorothy, like tourists, indeed like adventurers in *The Arabian Nights*, or, as we shall see, characters in a folk tale, discovered themselves in a foreign country, came to terms with themselves among strangers, became more of what they were among people who did not know them, became more English in Germany; and, as a writer, Johnston observes, the 'poet of Englishness, ... [was] born in Germany.'[24] While Wordsworth may not have been able to read the elevated philosophical or literary works in German or engage in intellectual conversation in German, he was well equipped to learn German as he had French, travelling among the common people, living with families, sharing the common knowledge, especially the tales that were their common heritage, the French tales from which the German oral tradition was derived.[25] Moreover, they lived and travelled in the provincial towns and country villages – Goslar, Göttingen, the foot of the Harz mountains, near or possibly to Kassel, where the Brothers Grimm found their informants nearly a decade later – places where, if it existed at all, native culture and language survived, a culture in many ways reminiscent of the British Celtic and Druid past, real or legendary, which Wordsworth envisioned on Salisbury Plain in 1793, and again in *The Prelude* XII.

But William and Dorothy left a meagre record of encounters, exchanges, or even recognitions of this common tradition, and the record they did leave expressed their profound disappointment. First, they met the seventy-four-year-old Klopstock, by accident, through his brother, and Wordsworth recorded their conversations, in French, noting his swollen ankles, his bad teeth:

> Yet he expresses himself with the liveliness of a girl of seventeen – this is striking to an Englishman, and rendered him an interesting object; and such I found him, notwithstanding his enormous powdered and frizzled periwig. By the bye, old men ought never to wear powder – the contrast between a large snow white wig and the colour of an old man's skin is disgusting.
>
> (*WPrW*, i:91–2)

By his own report, in their literary exchanges, Wordsworth was equally trivial, disagreeable, and patronizing. An impoverished and obscure twenty-eight-year-old poet, Wordsworth contradicted nearly everything this patriarch of German poetry said, whether they were discussing English or German literature. Wordsworth recommended he read Dryden whose strength, he said, came from not borrowing from other languages, a trait which Klopstock admired, while Klopstock, appropriately, recommended that this young Englishman who claimed to have come to Germany to learn the language and the culture read his historical trilogy based on the life of Arminius and the ancient tribes he had dispelled in the first century Roman invasion.

If Wordsworth could read German, the plays – which by the 1790s had a cult following among the students at Göttingen – would have explained not only what Germans believed to be their history but also the many analogies between England and Germany, between Klopstock and MacPherson, with whose Ossianic poems the plays were contemporary. Although the ancient heroes were depicted as savages dressed in animal skins, living in impenetrable forests and deadly bogs, engaging in human sacrifice and worshipping the forests where they believed the gods who protected them resided, to contemporary Germans they were the source of the unique spirit, a virility they needed to survive as a nation. Invaded in the eighteenth century first by the French Enlightenment and then by the French armies, Germans such as Herder, Klopstock, Brentano, even the Brothers Grimm (in 1808, Jacob actually served as private librarian to the French King of Hanover, Jerome Bonaparte) found in these ancient stories the same historical illusions Eiseley described that the English found in their sentimental medievalism. They located it in the villages, the forests, among the Volk, as Herder called it, the simple, virtuous, hard-working, spiritual peasants, craftsmen, and tradespeople with whom the Wordsworths were to live, the familiar population of Grimm's tales – living out the plots from the French and Italian tales in the ubiquitous German forests where all terror and all redress take place.[26]

To the Wordsworths, the mountains were not high enough, the trees disappointing, and the population revolting: 'a wretched race,' they wrote, 'the flesh, blood, and bone of their minds being nothing but knavery and low falsehood', 'dirty, impudent, and vulgar', 'rude and barbarous', 'petty ... low and selfish', money 'the god of universal worship' (*EY*, pp.230–52). And the ancient altar for human sacrifice that remained in the Goslar Church was dismissed as 'the only assured antiquity of German Heathenism'.[27] But, in 1793, similar images on Salisbury Plain had turned his life around; the vision of 'a single Briton in his wolf-skin vest, / With shield and stone-ax', 'the sacrificial altar, fed / With living men', awakened him to the 'grandeur upon the very humblest face', 'if we have eyes to see' (XII, ll.323ff., 283). Could the failure of language, the frigid weather, the austere and lonely life have so alienated him from this history and these people with whom he shared so much? In his isolation, did he become like a child again, unloving and unloved, the Wordsworthian child without conscience or care, not wise, learned, or good, a creature who 'breathed / Among wild appetites and blind desires', more savage than innocent? And did he then write the poems of a child, the art of childhood, that in their moral confusion anticipate the tales the Bothers Grimm were soon to collect in the same region? And was this art of childhood a true analogy to the brutal narratives told in the childhood of the race? Was it more authentic than the sentimental ethnography that grew up around the golden age? Do children have the same savage instincts and destructive nature as primitive man, and does that explain their attraction to the brutal tales that end up in the nursery?

If Wordsworth could not connect with the people he met and the local traditions because he did not share and could not learn their language, his life with Dorothy took on the qualities of a folk tale: a self-centred orphan brother and sister, offending the local gods, disregarding the omens, are banished to a room in a remote village in the coldest recorded winter, where they are deprived of the powers of speech, communicating with no one but each other, a deaf apprentice, the widowed linen-draper who is their landlady, the fly to whom Wordsworth writes a poem, and a bird, a kingfisher, he encounters on walks he takes dressed in animal skins, as Dorothy notes, a 'helmet of black dog's fur'. His task, like spinning straw into gold, is to rediscover his feeling for his fellow man by writing poetry that depicts their terrible suffering, the unaccountable death of anonymous children, the nobility of age, loyalty and helplessness – poems that will dignify the people he has denigrated.

In Goslar, Wordsworth had tried to recover and then to invent his own history: the deaths, betrayals, mysteries, the dreams that die or, worse, fail to die, the realization that nature with its 'silent overgrowings', as he claimed in 'The Ruined Cottage', was at best indifferent to human needs or suffering. This is the Nature personified in the folktales as witches, step-mothers, evil queens, the Nature that Wordsworth invokes in the 'Intimations Ode', the 'homely Nurse' making 'her Inmate Man, / Forget the glories he hath known' (ll.81–3). Delayed until 1804, but implied in the poetry of 1800, here are the 'malignant personifications' that, Eiseley claimed, 'loom behind the face of nature in the mythologies of simple folk', the ones that men will invoke if they have, as Wordsworth had at Goslar, no other history. And in those poems, in the *Two-part Prelude* which he began, Wordsworth analysed childhood as an initiation ritual, a 'long probation':

> The time of trial ere we learn to live
> In reconcilement with our stinted powers,
> To endure this state of meagre vassalage,
> Unwilling to forego, confess, submit,
> Uneasy and unsettled, yoke-fellows
> To custom, mettlesome and not yet tamed
> And humbled down – oh, then we feel, we feel,
> We know, when we have friends.
>
> (V, ll.540–7)

The 'friends', the 'Forgers of lawless tales', the art of childhood that they create, reconcile the child's sense of omnipotence with the adult's realization of mortality, again consummately expressed in the last poem of the *Lyrical Ballads* of 1800, 'Michael' – a poem, largely because of its Biblical referents, as clearly an initiation rite as any of the folk tales.

After 1800, Wordsworth creates the art of childhood for which he is remembered in sonnets to Caroline, to Hartley, to his children, and in the 'Intimations Ode'. And because it is so artificial, so formulaic, like a folktale, it becomes anonymous, collective, diffused through the popular sentimental literature of the Victorian period. Similarly, the brutal realities of the German folk tradition, the murders, incest, mutilations, infanticide, greed, cannibalism, betrayals, and abandonments epitomized in *The Juniper Tree*, for example, or in any of the early versions of even such common tales as *Little Red Riding Hood* or *Cinderella*, were gradually moralized, indeed civilized by the Brothers Grimm themselves, translated and adapted to British taste by Edward Taylor in 1823, taking on the attributes of the most artful of the arts of childhood and the audience that Wordsworth created.

Notes

1   Philippe Ariès, *Centuries of Childhood: A Social History of Family Life*, tr. Robert Baldick (New York: Knopf, 1962); A. Charles Babenroth, *English Childhood: Wordsworth's Treatment of Childhood in Light of English Poetry from Prior to Crabbe* (New York: Columbia University Press, 1922);

Humphrey Carpenter, *Secret Gardens: The Golden Age of Children's Literature* (Boston: Houghton Mifflin, 1985); Peter Coveney, *The Image of Childhood: The Individual and Society* (New York: Penguin, 1967); U.C. Knoepflmacher, 'Mutations of the Wordsworthian Child of Nature', *Nature and the Victorian Imagination*, ed. Knoepflmacher and B.G. Tennyson (Berkeley: University of California Press, 1977), pp. 391–425; Alison Lurie, *Don't Tell the Grown-ups: The Subversive Power of Children's Literature* (Boston: Little, Brown, 1990).

2   Alan Richardson, *Literature, Education, and Romanticism: Reading as Social Practice 1780–1832* (Cambridge: Cambridge University Press, 1994), pp. 8–25; Ross Woodman, 'The Idiot Boy as Healer', *Romanticism and Children's Literature in Nineteenth-Century England*, ed. James McGavran (Athens, Ga.: University of Georgia Press, 1991), pp. 72–95.

3   Willard Spiegelman, *Wordsworth's Heroes* (Berkeley, Ca.: University of California Press, 1985), p. 50.

4   Marilyn Gaull, *English Romanticism: The Human Context*, Chapter III (New York: Norton, 1988), pp. 50–80; Geoffrey Summerfield, *Fantasy and Reason: Children's Literature in the Eighteenth Century* (London: Methuen, 1984).

5   Peter Caracciolo, ed. *The Arabian Nights in English Literature: Studies in the Reception of the Thousand and One Nights into British Culture* (New York: St. Martin's Press, 1988); Robert Darnton, *The Great Cat Massacre and Other Episodes in French Cultural History* (New York: Basic Books, 1984); Robert Irwin, *The Arabian Nights: A Companion* (New York: Penguin, 1994); James McGlathery, *Grimms' Fairy Tales: A History of Criticism on a Popular Classic* (Columbia, South Carolina: Camden House, 1993), pp. 5–58.

6   Antti Aarne and Stith Thompson, *The Types of the Folk-Tale: A Classification and Bibliography* (Helsinki: Suomalainen Tiedeakatemia, 1928); Richard Dorson, *Folklore and Folklife* (Chicago: University of Chicago Press, 1972); Stith Thompson, *The Folktale* (Berkeley, Ca.; University of California Press, rpt 1977); Barre Toelken, *The Dynamics of Folklore* (Boston: Houghton Mifflin, 1979).

7   Robert Mayo, 'The Contemporaneity of the Lyrical Ballads', *PMLA* 69 (1954), pp. 486–522; John E. Jordan, *Why the 'Lyrical Ballads'?: The Background, Writing and Character of Wordsworth's 1798 'Lyrical Ballads'* (Berkeley: University of California Press, 1976); Stephen Parrish, *The Art of the Lyrical Ballads* (Cambridge, Mass.: Harvard University Press, 1973).

8   Mircea Eliade, *Myth and Reality*, tr. Willard Trask (New York: Harper and Row, 1963) and *Rites and Symbols of Initiation: The Mysteries of Birth and Rebirth*, tr. Willard Trask (New York: Harper and Row, 1958); Vladimir Propp, *Morphology of the Folktale*, tr. Laurence Scott, 2nd, rev. edn (Austin, Texas; University of Texas Press, 1968), and *Theory and History of Folklore*, tr. Ariadna Y. and Richard P. Martin, ed. Anatoly Liberman (Minneapolis: University of Minnesota Press, 1984); Bruce A. Rosenberg, *Folklore and Literature: Rival Siblings* (Knoxville, Tn.: University of Tennesee Press, 1991); Maria Tartar, *The Hard Facts of the Grimm's Fairy Tales* (Princeton, N. J.: Princeton University Press, 1987) and *Off With Their Heads: Fairy Tales and the Culture of Childhood* (Princeton, N. J.: Princeton University Press, 1992); Jack Zipes, *Fairy Tales and the Art of Subversion* (New York: Routledge, 1991), *Breaking the Magic Spell: Radical Theories of Folk and Fairy Tales* (New York, Routledge, 1992), *Fairy Tale as Myth: Myth as Fairy Tale* (Lexington, Ky:

University of Kentucky Press, 1994), *Happily Ever After: Fairy Tales, Children, and the Culture Industry* (New York: Routledge, 1997), and *When Dreams Came True: Classical Fairy Tales and Their Tradition* (New York: Routledge, 1999).

9 Gonthier-Louis Fink, *Naissance et apogée du conte merveilleux en Allemagne, 1740–1800* (Paris: Les Belles Lettres, 1966); Manfred Gratz, *Das Märchen in der deutschen Aufklärung: Vom Feenmärchen zum Volksmärchen* (Stuttgart: Metzler, 1988).

10 Loren Eiseley, *Darwin's Century: Evolution and the Men who Discovered It* (New York: Doubleday Anchor, 1961), pp. 27–8.

11 Frederic Jameson, *The Political Unconscious: Narrative as Socially Symbolic Act* (Cornell: Cornell University Press, 1981).

12 Kenneth R. Johnston, *The Hidden Wordsworth: Poet, Lover, Rebel, Spy* (New York: Norton, 1988), pp. 55ff.

13 Alan Bewell, *Wordsworth and the Enlightenment* (New Haven, Ct.: Yale University Press 1989), pp. 109–23; Tartar (1992), pp. 22–50.

14 Carl Sagan, *The Demon-Haunted World: Science as a Candle in the Dark* (New York: Ballantine, 1996), pp. 115–30.

15 Charles Lamb, *Essays of Elia*, intro. Geoffrey Tollotson (New York: Everyman's Library, 1974), pp. 79–81.

16 Marilyn Gaull, 'Awake in Araby: The Mary Moorman Memorial Lecture', *Romanticism*, forthcoming.

17 Jack Zipes, tr. and ed., *Arabian Nights: The Marvels and Wonders of The Thousand and One Nights* (New York: Signet Classics, 1991); Irwin, *The Arabian Nights: A Companion*, Chapter II.

18 Richardson, p. 117.

19 Primarily interested in Aladdin's influence on De Quincey, Plotz offers a large collection of adaptations and astute interpretive comments on how De Quincey used the tales to express his complex relationship with Wordsworth who plays the Magician to his Aladdin. Judith Plotz, 'In the Footsteps of Aladdin: De Quincey's Arabian Nights' *TWC*, 29 (1998), pp. 120–6.

20 Johnston, *The Hidden Wordsworth*, p. 286.

21 Richard Dorson, *Folklore and Folklife* (Chicago: University of Chicago Press, 1972); Alan Dundes, *Interpreting Folklore* (Bloomington Indiana: Indiana University Press, 1980), Chapters I and II, 'Who are the Folk', and 'Texture, Text, and Context'.

22 Gregory Bateson, *A Theory of Play and Fantasy: Steps to an Ecology of Mind* (New York, Ballantine, 1954), pp. 177–93; Erving Goffman, *Frame Analysis: An Essay on the Organization of Experience* (Cambridge, Mass., Harvard University Press, 1974); Deborah Tannen, ed., *Framing in Discourse* (New York: Oxford University Press, 1993), pp. 14–56.

23 John Beer, *Coleridge the Visionary* (London: Chatto and Windus, 1959), pp. 145–6, 148, 325n.

24 Johnston, *The Hidden Wordsworth*, p. 631.

25 Gratz, *Das Märchen*.

26 Simon Schama, *Landscape and Memory* (London: Harper Collins, 1995), p. 107.

27 Johnston, *The Hidden Wordsworth*, p. 631.

5
Wordsworth's Self-Creation and the 1800 *Lyrical Ballads*

Kenneth R. Johnston

(i) The wrong book?

A bicentenary observance of the second edition of *Lyrical Ballads* (1800) is in an important sense a celebration of the 'wrong' book.[*] In the chequered history of a publication containing so many other contradictions and paradoxes, this one may not be the most important. But we can improve our understanding of the new poems which appeared in the second volume of this edition – and their long, vexed critical tradition – if we recognize that the volume, *as* a volume, was not the one Wordsworth originally intended. Many of the problems posed by the new poems of 1800 have as much to do with Wordsworth's on-going process of self-creation as with the more narrowly literary issues raised in the famous 'Preface': the language of common people, the distinction between poetry and prose, the relation of emotion and tranquillity to poetic composition, the social responsibility of poets, and so on.

Wordsworth had been composing at a great rate since arriving in Grasmere in December 1799; his production in 1800 outstrips even the *annus mirabilis* of 1798. By midsummer he had written roughly the first half of 'Home at Grasmere' and the 'Prospectus' to *The Recluse,* as well as most of the poems that would make up the second volume in the new edition of *Lyrical Ballads.* The first report of a new volume came from Coleridge to Southey on 10 April. 'Wordsworth publishes a second Volume of Lyrical Ballads, & Pastorals. He meditates a novel – & so do I – but first I shall re-write my Tragedy' (*CL,*

---

[*]This essay draws on material from *The Hidden Wordsworth: Poet, Lover, Rebel, Spy,* by Kenneth R. Johnston. Copyright © 1998 by Kenneth Richard Johnston. Reprinted by permission of W.W. Norton & Company, Inc.

i.585). This decision signalled the end of work on *The Recluse,* in the same way that it had been interrupted by the first volume of *Lyrical Ballads* in 1798. It also broke Wordsworth's solemn promise 'not to publish on his own account' (*CL,* i.543): he had vowed to Coleridge during their November walking tour of 1799 that only 'pecuniary necessity' could lead him to publish again soon (*EY,* p. 267). Judging from Coleridge's report, the first title proposed for the new volume seems to have been *Lyrical Ballads and Pastorals.* This squares with Wordsworth's note to 'The Brothers', recalling his intention to produce 'a series of pastorals, the scene of which was laid among the mountains of Cumberland and Westmoreland' (*LBB,* p. 135n.). Many of the new poems fit that description, and five have the word 'pastoral' in their sub-titles or notes, suggesting that a still more accurate title for the new book could have been *Lake District Pastorals.* Nobody planned for the entire edition to be entitled *Lyrical Ballads*; it became so only by default, when, despite seven months of Wordsworth's insistence to the contrary, his new publisher, Longman, finally refused his request to call the work by the title he really preferred: 'Poems in two Volumes[.] By W. Wordsworth' (*EY,* p. 303). This, and not *Lyrical Ballads,* was Wordsworth's repeatedly specified name for the book that finally appeared in January 1801. (This preferred title became exactly that of the *next* new collection he published: '*Poems, in Two Volumes,* by W. Wordsworth', in 1807.) Coleridge reported the preferred title as a fact to Southey, Godwin, and others throughout the summer and autumn, further specifying that the *Lyrical Ballads* element was to be 'dropt' entirely, 'and his "Poems" substituted' (*CL,* i.620–1).

The title of the 1798 volume was to be 'dropt' (or retained only for the first volume of the new edition) because most of Wordsworth's new poems did not fit the pattern established by his ten 'lyrical ballads' of 1798. They were the majority of his nineteen poems in the earlier volume; but only twelve of his forty-one new poems were ballads at all. The 'Matthew' poems can be called 'lyrical ballads'; but though the 'Lucy' poems are mysteriously lyrical, they are not ballads, except for 'Strange fits of passion'. His other new ballads were sentimental variations on the genre: 'The Waterfall and the Eglantine', 'The Oak and the Broom', 'The Idle Shepherd-Boys', 'The Two Thieves', and 'Andrew Jones'. Another reason for changing the title was, as Dorothy explained, that 'Mrs. Robinson has claimed the title and is about publishing a volume of *Lyrical Tales.* This is a great objection to the former title, particularly as they are both printed at the same press and Longman is the publisher of both the works' (*EY*, p.297). But though Wordsworth kept urging the change, Longman would not budge. At his splendid emporium in London, Thomas Longman calculated that any confusion with either the *Lyrical Ballads* of 1798 or with Robinson's *Lyrical Tales* would help sales, while the author's name, 'W. Wordsworth', would not. As late as October, Wordsworth was keeping up a clear distinction between the old volume and the new one: 'The first Volume of these Poems, under the title of Lyrical Ballads, has already been presented &c.' (*EY*, p. 304). But the published 'Preface' drops the reference to a former title, with the result that *both* volumes were presumed to be *Lyrical Ballads* – as they have been from that day forward. Neither Coleridge nor Wordsworth planned it that way, and much of the controversy caused them no end of annoyance; but at the same time it helped immeasurably to make them notorious and, eventually, famous.

If Wordsworth had secured the title he wanted, several things would be clearer. First, that he did not consider the forty-one poems now published to be 'lyrical ballads' in any meaningful sense, even though a few of them can be linked with the experimental poems of 1798. Second, that the 'Preface', composed in September, was not designed to explicate a concept that he labelled 'lyrical ballad' or 'lyrical pastoral'. The 'Preface' is not at all concerned with defending hybrid genres, except to attack arbitrary distinctions between poetry and prose; rather, it argues the need for a thorough renovation of polite definitions of poetry as a whole. Third, that, thanks to Longman's insistence on retaining the old title, discussion of 'lyrical ballads' has often, inappropriately, encompassed all forty-one of the new poems, sometimes with brilliantly ingenious results, but often with glaring inconsistencies – which are hardly surprising, since Wordsworth held no brief for them as 'lyrical ballads'.

The only part of Wordsworth's request which Longman *did* accept was the designation of a single author: 'W. Wordsworth'. This was agreed to by all parties, including Coleridge (so the loose presumption that Wordsworth forced his friend out of the picture is not true). Wordsworth wanted nothing to do with the old title which, nevertheless, remained attached to his new volume; but anyway, for him, the key word on the title page would not have been 'Poems', but 'Wordsworth'.

(ii) The new poems of 1800

The poems which finally appeared in January 1801 were notably different to Wordsworth's nineteen poems of 1798. None of the new poems approached the artistic achievement of 'Lines written ... above Tintern Abbey', but it could be argued that the overall level of literary excellence in the 1800 *Ballads* is higher than that in 1798, when we consider the 'Lucy' and 'Matthew' poems, and 'The Brothers' and 'Michael'. Dorothy hoped that 'the second [volume] is much more likely to please the generality of readers' (*EY*, p. 298): only three of the poems in 1798 had a light or humorous tone, whereas fully a quarter of the 1800 poems are amusing. There were far fewer poems containing the kind of social critique that Dr. Burney had noticed in his review of the 1798 volume (reprinted in *LBB*, pp. 324–7); only 'Poor Susan', 'Ruth', and 'The Old Cumberland Beggar' are at all comparable in this respect, and they were composed in Germany or Alfoxden or even earlier. There is also much less concern with abnormal states of mind, and with the single clearest cause of this derangement in 1798: people being cast out of their homes or communities.

Instead, Wordsworth's new emphasis falls on how communities – or more specifically *pairs or couples* as the smallest units of community – can be preserved. This theme was the motor driving 'Home at Grasmere', and it continued into 'The Waterfall and the Eglantine', 'The Oak and the Broom', 'The Idle Shepherd-Boys', 'The Pet-Lamb', 'The Two Thieves', and several others poems. The typical situation of the 1798 poems had been a narrator's conversation with a solitary outcast; in 1800, the basic situation is a threatened loss of *partnership*, or a delayed, tragic recognition of its value, heretofore naively taken for granted. Not that the poems of 1800 are all happy ones; far from it. But their unhappiness arises from a suddenly perceived loss of love, in a relationship, a family, or a community, whereas in 1798 the great danger was mental breakdown, caused by apparent rejection from English society itself. The solitaries of 1798 have long since lost their mates or partners, and are struggling to stay in touch with – as the Female Vagrant says – their 'inner self' (l.259). By contrast, the 1800 poems can be called more 'universal', since they depend less on specific social causes from the late 1790s. But the losses they express, though still real and painful, are much less extreme.

Almost all the poems Wordsworth composed for the second edition of *Lyrical Ballads* are concerned in one sense or another with the proper way to live among simple people in the country, which is usually explicitly identified as the Lake District. Setting aside the larger issues that Wordsworth addressed in his 'Preface', most of the poems actually composed in 1800 deal with the *content*-question of country living – that is to say, with his and Dorothy's everyday experience: intellectual 'culture workers' setting up business in a region far removed from the cultural capital where such business was normally conducted. The new poems concern: first, how the Wordsworths' new surroundings should be named or identified (five are gathered as 'Poems on the Naming of Places'); second, whether (and how) one should build there (four fall under the rubric of 'Rural Architecture'); and, third, how one should judge the customs of village folk (five poems like 'The Idle Shepherd-Boys'). Besides these categories, there is a 'control' group of five poems dealing with the crisis-question (similar to the theme of 'Home at Grasmere') of how *prior love relationships* can be maintained in this new setting – or cannot be. 'The Brothers' is the first of these poems in the 1800 volume, and it is the first poem Wordsworth began composing after he and Dorothy had settled into Dove Cottage. The last of this group, 'Michael', is last in every way: last-composed, and also the thematic conclusion to the book. 'Hart-Leap Well' forms a sort of travelling prologue to this theme (as well as to the second volume as a whole); while 'The Waterfall and the Eglantine', 'The Oak and the Broom', and the Scottish ballad of 'Ellen Irwin' are lighter variations on the same love theme. Finally, the remaining poems, not composed in the nervous euphoria of 1800, have significant tangential relations to these groupings: the 'Lucy' poems to the broken-pair theme, and the 'Matthew' poems both to that, and to the theme of local customs.

In 'The Brothers', a happily-anticipated homecoming reunion is spoiled by the death of one of the brothers. This is an unlikely topic for the joyous mood that Wordsworth's return home has assumed in popular cultural mythology; but it is an altogether likely one, for Wordsworth was a dialectically contrary poet who often expressed the depths of his joy by exploring its opposite. In this respect, 'The Brothers' is a direct continuation of the vexed 'Home at Grasmere', a poem whose glaring sub-text everywhere subverts the reassuring message (or desperate hope) of its title. Leonard the mariner has come home after twenty years at sea 'to resume / The life which he liv'd there' (ll.67–8). Wordsworth, too, had effectively returned 'home' after twenty years, having left his family home in 1779 following his mother's death. A related biographical signature is contained in Leonard's age, given as twelve in 1800, but changed to fifteen when

Wordsworth republished the poem in 1815 (*WPW*, ii.2, l.39 and *app. crit.*): that is to say, the same age at which John Wordsworth was sent to sea. The brothers of the poem were orphans whose grandparents outlived their parents, as also happened to the Wordsworth children. The grandfather of the poem lost the lands which had been in the family for five generations, 'buffeted with bond, / Interest and mortgages' (ll.217–18), a parallel to John Wordsworth Senior's losing his estate to the unpaid debts of Lord Lonsdale – and also to the precise number of generations ('five': l.207) through which the Wordsworths traced their family's emigration from Yorkshire to Cumberland to rebuild their gentry fortunes.

But all these parallels are given a reverse twist by Wordsworth. Leonard does not reveal his identity to the parish priest who tells him what happened to his brother James, because 'now, / This vale, where he had been so happy, seem'd / A place in which he could not bear to live' (ll.438–40). Here we see ten small words in one strong line, revealing Wordsworth's empathy with a self-created situation that holds up a tragic mirror to his own Ode to Joy. Leonard returns to sea, where he is now 'a grey headed Mariner' (l.449). This glances at Coleridge's 'Old Navigator' (see the Fenwick note to 'We are Seven': *LBM*, p. 368); but Leonard combines the roles of Ancient Mariner and Wedding Guest, becoming a sadder and a wiser man not from hearing fantastic tales of otherworldly deeds and spirits, but from a homely account of a common accident on the fells – which was very much the brief of 'Home at Grasmere', and by extension of the epic poem, *The Recluse*, of which it formed 'Part First' of 'Book First': 'is there not / An art, a music, and a stream of words / That shall be life, the acknowledged voice of life, / Shall speak of what is done among the fields, / Done truly there, or felt, of solid good / And real evil, yet be sweet withal[?]' (ll.620–6; Gill, p. 189).

The five poems on 'The Naming of Places' are less about names than about the moral propriety of bestowing them on places not one's own. Like the broken-pair poems, these Wordsworthian 'Just-So' stories are less explanations of how certain places got their names than cautionary lessons about the risk involved in presuming to *name* anything; and, as such, they reflect the lessons he had learned from the difficulties of composing the still incomplete 'Home at Grasmere'. His textual note on the poems is common-sensical:

By Persons resident in the country and attached to rural objects, many places will be found unnamed or of unknown names, where little Incidents will have occurred, or feelings been experienced, which will have given to such places a private and peculiar interest.

(*LBB*, p. 217; *WPW*, ii.111, *var.*)

But this should be balanced against Coleridge's observation, on their November walking tour, that a large number of landscape features in the North *do* have names ('In the North every Brook, every Crag, almost every Field has a name': *CN*, i.579), because many of the places named by the Wordsworth circle were *already* named, notably the lonely 'eminence' called Stone-Arthur, which they now re-named, implicitly, 'Stone-William'.

William's identification with nearby Stone-Arthur is the most straightforward in this group. He and Dorothy passed beneath it almost daily on their walks between Town-End and Town-Head. Because it was 'The loneliest place we have among the clouds', Dorothy gave it 'my Name' (III, ll.13, 17). But a heavenly portent is also registered here, whose significance is not revealed in the poem: 'The star of Jove, so beautiful and large / In the mid heav'ns, is never half so fair / As when he shines above it' (ll.10–12). In the astrology of his imagination, Jupiter was always Wordsworth's planet, which he linked to the Star of Bethlehem in the 'Prospectus' to *The Recluse* to symbolize his hopes for his poetry (ll.88–93; *WPW*, v.6). Nobody knew this but Dorothy, which gave her a title of authority to bestow the implied name, William's Eminence or Summit. This, and their love: 'She who dwells with me, whom I have lov'd / With such communion, that no place on earth / Can ever be a solitude to me' (ll.14–16). Dorothy's love removes the appearance of his solitude, and this, with the peak's association with Jupiter, makes *it* worthy to bear *his* name, not vice versa.

'Emma's Dell' is really Dorothy's, since 'Emma' was their private code for naming her in public. In fact, it is more Emma's waterfall than her dell, hinting that the waterfall in 'The Waterfall and the Eglantine' is also female: Dorothy's wild passion running roughshod over the mild compromises offered by William's eglantine. (The full text of 'Nutting' sets out, in coded country allegory, William's side of the story.) Her waterfall-wildness is stressed repeatedly: 'wild nook', 'wild place', and so on (ll.38, 46). The waterfall hits the traveller with a shock of surprise as he labours up the Easedale path to where Blindtarn Gill intersects with Sour Milk Gill: just when everything seems 'soften'd down into a vernal tone' and a 'deep contentment', one turns a corner and confronts a waterfall so 'ardent' that all calm is fled (ll.5, 13, 22). This apparently simple poem is a precursor of a kind to the visionary climbs in the already-experienced but yet-to-be-composed Simplon and Snowdon episodes of *The Prelude*. The shock woke Wordsworth up, as it did in those mountaintop revelations, to the realization that there is something *else,* beyond or different from nature's 'contentment', that is uncontrollably wild, and it is this quality he associates with Dorothy. After the sudden revelation of such wild ardency, the speaker plods onward, still 'in the confusion of my heart', reflecting obscurely, '"Our thoughts at least are ours["]' (ll.18, 38). Apparently this means that our thoughts can *resist* taking these outward evidences of identity too literally.

At the other end of the sequence, Mary's Nook is as peaceful as Dorothy's dell is wild. The pool described is in Rydal Upper Park: 'we have named [it] from You' (l.24; emphasis added). The name is assigned as the joint-title of William and Dorothy, honouring Mary-the-Peaceful. As always in these Grasmere moments of discovery, the title of authenticity is signed by death: the man who 'should plant his cottage near / … would so love it that in his death-hour / Its image would survive among his thoughts' (ll.18–22).

'To Joanna' and 'Point Rash-Judgement' correct the attempts of the other naming-poems to make one-to-one applications of their names to Grasmere's places. Coleridge makes his only appearance in 'Point Rash-Judgement', walking with Dorothy and William; all three are faulted for thinking that the peasant they see fishing should be out helping with the harvest. They have a typical middle-class reaction to the troubles of the working class: 'We all cried out, that he must be indeed / An idle man, who thus could lose a day / Of the mid harvest, when the labourer's hire / Is ample' (ll.56–9). But when they come closer, they see that he is 'Too weak to labour in the harvest field' (l.69). Unlike similar poems in the 1798 volume, such as 'Simon Lee' and 'Goody Blake', the thrust here is not against the social or human conditions that have worn the poor fisherman down, but rather against the Wordsworth circle's own status as outsiders and observing moralists, who should know better than to leap to such rash judgments.

Like the morals tacked on to 'The Ruined Cottage' and 'The Ancient Mariner', this one does not speak very adequately to the man's condition. But the poem's more important meaning comes at its beginning, in the hammer-blows it directs at the dreamy scene it establishes, which many readers would unhesitatingly label 'Wordsworthian':

> It was our occupation to observe
> Such objects as the waves had toss'd ashore,
> Feather, or leaf, or weed, or wither'd bough ...
>   ... And in our vacant mood,
> Not seldom did we stop to watch some tuft
> Of dandelion seed or thistle's beard,
> Which, seeming lifeless half, and half impell'd
> By some internal feeling, skimm'd along ...

> (ll.12–14, 16–20)

This recalls the mode of perception we find in 'Lines written ... above Tintern Abbey' ('both what they half-create / And what perceive': ll.107–8), and Wordsworth indulges himself for twenty lines of it: fairy-tale identifications with Grecian naiads, Queen Osmunda, and the 'Lady of the Mere / Sole-sitting by the shores of old Romance' (ll.39–40). But this easy reading of Nature's morality is harshly corrected by human evidence to the contrary, when they see the man 'using his best skill to gain / A pittance from *the dead unfeeling lake* / That knew not of his wants' (ll.70–2; emphasis added). The harsh corrective is commensurate with the charm of the fantasy: only a man who wished nature were humanly beautiful would need to remind us (and himself) that it is not. The 'Lady of the Mere' is not nearly as generous to beggars as is the lady (Dorothy) at Town End cottage. The 'moving soul' of natural phenomena, when entertained in 'vacant mood' and 'Feeding unthinking fancies' (ll.27, 16, 46), does not seem to amount to much.

Wordsworth linked 'Joanna's Rock' to 'Nutting' by saying that these two 'show the greatest genius of any poems in the second volume'.[1] This judgment is a bit rash for 'To Joanna'. The real point of contact between the poems is not their quality but their theme: two young women's initiation into the mysteries of a religion celebrating an independent life in nature. Nineteen-year-old Joanna Hutchinson at first laughed at William's 'ravishment' when he stood before the 'intermixture of delicious hues' on the side of a tall rock beside the River Rotha between Grasmere and Rydal. But when her laughter echoed, hyperbolically, throughout the entire Lake District, from Skiddaw in the north to Kirkstone in the south, 'the fair Joanna' drew nervously 'to my side ... as if she wish'd / To shelter from some object of her fear' (ll.53, 47, 75, 74–6). For this involuntary recognition of something akin to the laughter of the (nature) gods, Wordsworth carved Joanna's name on the rock. This amounts to enrolling her into an illicit religion, professed by we 'Who look upon the hills with tenderness' and 'are transgressors in this kind, / Dwelling retired in our simplicity' (ll.7, 9–10). His honouring of Joanna's spontaneous fear is set against the disapproval of the old religion, represented by the 'gloomy' Grasmere vicar who chides Wordsworth for apparently 'reviving obsolete Idolatry, / ... like a Runic Priest' (27–8). Though not a Druid, Wordsworth *was* becoming, in effect, the priest of a new dispensation, one that finds and worships spirit in different places and in different ways to those of Christianity: 'To Joanna' is the only poem, besides the re-christening of Stone-Arthur, in which his view of place-names is presented unqualifiedly as the correct one.

The four poems on 'rural architecture' present the negative corollary to the positive lessons of the 'Poems on the Naming of Places'; Wordsworth's handling of the dialectics of nature and the mind of man is so flexible that there can be no simple *for* and *against* on the matter. Though he was self-indulgent toward his group's naming of places, he was very hard on any improper building in paradise. His main complaint was against newcomers white- washing their houses, making them stand out too starkly from the surrounding landscape. A close second was their cutting down stands of native trees to replace them with more 'picturesque' varieties or, worse, plantations of fast-growing, profitable larches for the lumber industry.

The tonic-note of the 'architecture' group is struck by the 'Lines written with a Slate-pencil upon a Stone, the largest of a heap lying near a deserted Quarry, upon one of the Islands at Rydale'. It explains how Sir William Fleming, ancestor of Michael le Fleming of Rydal Hall, finally did *not* build his 'pleasure-house' on the tiny island just off the shore of Rydal Water: he desisted when he discovered that 'a full-grown man might wade' from the shore to the island, 'and make himself a freeman of this spot' (ll.9, 10). The place itself prevented him from committing an outrage upon it, and the remaining heap of building stones is thus a monument to his educability. The poem refuses to blame him, calling him 'a gentle Knight' (l.21). Instead, it cautions those who, like William and Dorothy, are 'On fire with ... impatience to become / An Inmate of these mountains ... disturb'd / By beautiful conceptions' (ll.26–8). But the stones of Sir William's *un*built 'trim mansion' provide a symbolic context for the right kind of local builders: 'the linnet and the thrush, / And other little builders who dwell here' (ll.30, 18–19).

Against this negative example, Wordsworth sets three other examples of architecture that are appropriate to the region – that is, to his unique recasting of it. The 'outhouse' or small barn on Grasmere island makes the obvious connections for modern, post-Romantic readers, though they were novel in 1800. Though it is 'Rude', and though other buildings 'have maintain'd / Proportions more harmonious', still 'the poor / Vitruvius of our village' has here created 'a homely pile', whose form follows its function of sheltering lambs and heifers ('Inscription for the House ... on the Island at Grasmere', ll.1, 2–3, 6–7, 13). But it also has another, more special, function, which combines the ordinary and the fantastic in a new measure: it provides a place where 'one Poet' can make 'his summer couch' and look out through its door to see 'Creations lovely as the work of sleep, / Fair sights, and visions of romantic joy' (ll.16, 21, 28–9). This 'poor Vitruvius' 'had no help / From the great city', and, in the poem actually entitled 'Rural Architecture', Wordsworth explicitly distances himself from the kinds of work he had seen going forward in cities in the 1790s. He joins some well-to-do neighbour boys, 'George Fisher, Charles Fleming, and Reginald Shore', in building a stone man on top of Great How at the north end of Wythburn (now Thirlmere); they name him 'Ralph Jones', 'the Magog of Legberthwaite dale' (ll.1, 10, 12). This stone construction is perfectly attuned to the celebration of both man and nature: when the winds blow it down, 'the very next day / They went and they built up another' (ll.17–18). In 1800 (but cancelled thereafter until 1820), Wordsworth included a final stanza that made the application of this simple lesson considerably more pointed:

> – Some little I've seen of blind boisterous works
> In Paris and London, 'mong Christians or Turks,
> Spirits busy to do and undo:
> At remembrance whereof my blood sometimes will flag.
> – Then, light-hearted Boys, to the top of the Crag!
> And I'll build up a Giant with you.
>
> (ll.19–24; cf. *WPW*, i.244, and *app. crit.*)

In these lines, Wordsworth joins in the boys' sport as therapy for his traumatic years in Paris and London. The 'Spirits busy' there were not building houses but a 'Giant' New Man – either actively in the French Revolution, or abstractly in the perfectibilian extremes of Godwin's *Political Justice*, both of which Wordsworth had come to regard as 'blind boisterous works'. 'Christians' and 'Turks' enter the picture as code words for theists (like Robespierre) or infidels (like Godwin and Thelwall). Running light-heartedly with the neighbour-boys to the top of Great How, to 'build up a Giant' with them, Wordsworth also has his own hidden agenda, for a new architecture built not with stones but with spirit: *he* is that Giant, but in a new dispensation. A poem that looks like a moment of country comic relief was also, in the mind of the very 'busy spirit' of its author, a poem of revenge and vindication against the world's more public agenda – as though he were emulating, in his own way, that special set of epic heroes whom he was later to entertain as models for his epic of self-creation: Mithridates, Sertorius, Dominique de Gourges, Gustavus the First, and William Wallace (*Prelude*, I, ll.185–219).

The deep message of his 'Inscription' for the site of St. Herbert's Hermitage on the island in the middle of Derwent-Water is the same: that, now, there *is* a spirit in these Lake District places that recognizes, and can build upon, the spirit of the place. According to Bede's *Ecclesiastical History*, St. Herbert prayed every night that he might die at the same moment as his former helpmate, St. Cuthbert, who had moved to a similar solitary confinement on Windermere. And his prayer was answered: 'Those holy men both died in the same hour' (l.21). Wordsworth has altered Bede's account to make the two hermits separate forever (in Bede, they paid each other annual visits), making the inscription one not really for the building, but for the kinds of spirits that inhabit it, and about isolated spots where one stays true to – keeps faith with – one's beloved. It is, then, addressed to a person who is a version of Wordsworth himself, in a version of his own present love-situation, whether the reference be to Dorothy or to Coleridge, or to both:

> If thou in the dear love of some one friend
> Hast been so happy, that thou know'st what thoughts
> Will, sometimes, in the happiness of love
> Make the heart sink, then wilt thou reverence
> This quiet spot.

(ll.1–5)

Such moments are those states of mind that Wordsworth called 'Strange fits of passion', and they illustrate his dire need for 'emotion recollected in tranquillity' (*WPrW*, i.148). But though Herbert on Derwent-Water and Cuthbert on Windermere are close enough stand-ins for Coleridge in Keswick and Wordsworth in Grasmere, it was not really for his friend that Wordsworth harboured this kind of sentiment. Emotion sanctified by death was, rather, the state of feeling that had been mystically induced over and over again by William and Dorothy during the previous five years to sublimate and subdue their passion for each other.

The five poems in *Lyrical Ballads* of 1800 about local people and customs are milder versions of the tales of tragic fortitude that Wordsworth added to 'Home at Grasmere' in 1806, to give it the moral ballast he needed to be able to finish it. Among them, only 'The Childless Father' tries to be serious, and even it only wonders if – 'perhaps' – old Timothy the huntsman thought of his dead daughter (who died but six months earlier) when he took the house keys with him as he left to join the fox hunt. The spectator-narrator cannot say anything directly about the state of Timothy's moral refinement, for 'in my ears not a word did he speak'. But he is pretty sure on the basis of other evidence: 'he went to the chase with a tear on his cheek' (ll.18, 20). In an era when orphans were less common than dead children, the peculiar force of Wordsworth's deceptively simple title might have seemed less strange, but it is surprising how often modern readers treat the title of this poem as if it were the more expectable, 'Fatherless Child', rather than the other way around.

The other local-colour poems treat real or potential moral dilemmas with a much lighter touch. The idle shepherd boys don't attend to their business, daring each other to cross a deep crevice on a narrow outcropping, and very nearly lose a valuable lamb as a result. They fetch a conveniently nearby 'Poet' to rescue it, who 'gently' upbraids them: 'And bade them better mind their trade' (ll.84, 99). This is brave: a poetical newcomer instructing the locals in their moral duty. But Wordsworth actually *did* try out his views on some real Grasmere shepherds. In a fragment drafted for 'Michael', he notes that a shepherd 'would have [stared] at you' 'if you in terms direct / Had ask[']d' if he loved the place, and, more likely than not, he would have said it was 'a frightful pl[ac]e'.[2] But if you talked with him 'of common things / In an unusual way, and g[a]ve to them / Unusual aspects', then 'this untaught shepherd stood / Before the man with whom he so convers'd / And look'd at him *as with a Poet's eye*'.[3] The man who would 'so converse' with the shepherds was of course Wordsworth; but the trite moral of 'The Two Idle Shepherd-Boys' is not its point. Instead, its theme is a redaction of *Et in Arcadia ego*, but with a happy ending, thanks to a savior who is 'A Poet ... who loves the brooks / Far better than the sages' books' (ll.84–5). (There is no reason in the world that he should, except for the fact of his very particular identity: William Wordsworth.)

A 'Poet' happens to be nearby not just by a wild coincidence, but because, imaginatively, Wordsworth *is* one or both of the shepherd boys. For the immediate consequence of one of the boys' leap across the crevice is to make him appreciate what he possesses only when he seems about to lose it all. Halfway across the arch, 'he hears a piteous moan – / … his heart within him dies – / His pulse is stopp'd, his breath is lost … / And, looking down, he spies / A Lamb, that in the pool is pent / Within that black and frightful rent' (ll.60–66). In this, its moment of truth, 'The Idle Shepherd-Boys' anticipates the two crucial visionary self-recognition scenes of *The Prelude*. They also occur among mountains, but their lost sheep is William Wordsworth, and their 'frightful rent' is 'the mind's abyss' (in the Simplon Pass: *Prelude* (1850), VI, l.594) and the 'deep and gloomy breathing-place' (on Snowdon: *Prelude*, XIII, l.57).

'Andrew Jones' is about a hateful man who steals pennies from crippled beggars and teaches his children to do the same. Hence Wordsworth's opening line, 'I hate that Andrew Jones', only seems like comic hyperbole. He really does hate Jones, and wants to deport him out of paradise in what is, in contemporary terms, the worst possible way: 'I wish the press-gang, or the drum / With its tantara sound would come / And sweep him from the village!' (ll.3–5). The press-gang and the recruiting officers were villains to the victims of Wordsworth's earlier poems, like the sailor and soldier in the Salisbury Plain poems. But here they have become subsidiary demons policing paradise, wishfully summoned to rid it of unworthy spirits. 'The Two Thieves' provides a comic antidote to Andrew Jones. The 'thieves' were real people, old Daniel MacKeith and his grandson, aged ninety and three respectively, who went about Hawkshead stealing wood-chips, peat, and other small things lying about; everyone in the village knew, however, that Daniel's daughter would 'gladly repair all the damage that's done'. In just letting him be, Wordsworth treats him as he does the Old Cumberland Beggar, and a surprising last line drives this moral home harder than we expect: 'Long yet may'st thou live, for a teacher we see / That lifts up the veil of our nature in thee' (ll.43, 47–8). What's that? Wordsworth's note to the poem pretends that its moral is the recognition that we may all come to such pitiable senility (*LBB*, p. 304–5; *WPW*, iv.447); but the repeated action of the poem more strongly suggests that behind 'the veil of our nature' is a fundamental larceny in our souls – and this, rather than the sheer fact of ageing, is the problem of evil that 'Home at Grasmere' confronted, and that the *Lyrical Ballads* of 1800 tries to defuse.

Finally, little Barbara Lewthwaite, the Wordsworths' next-door neighbour, cannot understand why her 'Pet-Lamb' will not eat or drink. '"Drink, pretty Creature, drink!"' she urges. Wordsworth identifies with her to such an extent 'That I almost receiv'd her heart into my own' (ll. 11, 12), and the rest of the poem is a poetical transmigration into Barbara's mind and heart, as Wordsworth imagines what she would say if she could write a poem. The apparent subject of the poem is thus programmatic for the volume: the poetry implicit in the souls of ordinary people. But the deeper subject, unstated but strongly implied, is again the troubling one of 'Home at Grasmere', the question as to whether *either* of its characters, little girl or adult narrator, can penetrate to the sense of loss that makes the *lamb* unhappy:

> – poor Creature can it be
> That 'tis thy Mother's heart which is working so in thee?
> *Things that I know not of* belike to thee are dear,
> And dreams of things which thou can'st neither see nor hear.

> (ll.49–52; emphasis added)

The poet tries to interpret the girl trying to interpret the lamb; but it is one thing to receive a little girl's heart into one's own, quite another to inhabit the soul of another species. Although the poet pretends to wonder how much of the song is his and how much Barbara's, neither of them directly addresses the more basic point: that there are relations to the natural world that are better and more appropriate than even the best of human arrangements.

Last of all, there is one poem that fits no category in the volume, belonging neither with those written in Germany in 1799 nor with those written in Grasmere in 1800; and, like many exceptions, it has rule-proving properties. Nothing is known about the genesis of the 'Song for the Wandering Jew', aside from the fact that it may refer to the Jews William and Dorothy saw being ill-treated in Hamburg (*DWJ*, i.29). It reminds us of Wordsworth's ability to say something completely different to what he seems to be saying, or to what he usually says – his ability, marked in the 'Preface', to admit doubts and qualifications that, if taken seriously, would upset his entire train of thought (as in, 'If this / Be but a vain belief, yet oh! . . .': 'Lines written . . . above Tintern Abbey', ll.50–1). The Jew's song is an adaptation of the famous passage of *Matthew* 8:20 ('The foxes have holes, and birds of the air have nests; but the Son of man hath not where to lay his head') to the Lake District. The torrents, eagles, and ravens all have their resting places, but not the speaker:

> Day and night my toils redouble !
> Never nearer to the goal,
> Night and day, I feel the trouble,
> Of the Wanderer in my soul.

(ll.17–20)

The poem, as Mary Moorman comments, 'deserves to be better known than it is, if only for the last two lines'.[4] One reason it is not more widely remarked may be that paying honest attention to those last lines uncomfortably confirms what is implicit in almost all of Wordsworth's poems written at Grasmere in 1800: namely, that his homecoming was fraught with doubt and disappointment, which he could celebrate only with difficulty, or ratify by allying it to the final homecoming – of death.

(iii) The 'Preface' to *Lyrical Ballads*

All these poems were finished by the beginning of July, and Wordsworth began sending them off in batches to Biggs and Cottle. With this work in train, he turned in early September to composing the preface which he thought the new edition needed. But in the immediate circumstances of his life and career, the famous 'Preface' to *Lyrical Ballads* arose from issues having as much to do with *The Recluse* as with the poems in the 1800 edition. Just as the new volume's title was in a real sense inaccurate, or at least unintended, so the 'Preface' is frequently concerned with issues quite different to those animating the poems in the volumes – especially if they are considered all together as 'lyrical ballads'. Like his preferred title (which was still '*Poems*, by W. Wordsworth' at this point, so far as he knew), the 'Preface' was an introduction of himself as an ideal Poet-figure, and of his views on poetry, more than it was of the individual poems in either volume.

Coleridge promised to help compose the 'Preface', but didn't, though he later claimed that it was 'half the child of my own Brain' (*CL*, ii.830). Indeed, though its ideas arose out of 'mutual Conversations', said Coleridge, 'it was at first intended, that the Preface should be written by me' (*CL*, ii.811). This would have been a sensible arrangement: one man writing a preface to a new edition of his friend's work. Coleridge was far better qualified to write such a piece, and he would come to wish very much that he *had* written it, for he spent much time over the next fifteen years explaining which ideas in it were his and which were not, trying to extricate himself from what soon became a permanent English cultural tradition: attacking or defending the literary and linguistic claims of the 'Preface' to *Lyrical Ballads*. Defending himself against the excesses of Wordsworth's 'Preface' was Coleridge's most important motive for writing his *Biographia Literaria* (1817), which explained his entire literary life in terms of its relations, pro and con, to Wordsworth's theory and practice. For Coleridge was in a unique position to recognize what is only now becoming apparent: that much of Wordsworth's 'Preface' is itself a literary biography, displaced into another literary genre from Wordsworth's other contemporaneous efforts to write himself large, *The Recluse* and *The Prelude*.

Coleridge had had ideas similar to those expressed in the 'Preface' about the philosophical tendency of poetical expressions at least since 1796, when he told Thelwall that 'My philosophical opinions are blended with, or deduced from, my feelings' (*CL*, i.279). In the 'Preface' to his 'Sheet of Sonnets' by various authors that same year, he spoke of his poems generating 'a habit of thought' which tends to 'create a sweet and indissoluble union between the intellectual and the material world' (*CPW*, ii.1139). In a brief prefatory note attached to his 'Introduction to the Ballad of the Dark Ladié', he coyly apologized for publishing 'a simple story, wholly un[in]spired with politics or personality' in these days when, 'amid the hubbub of Revolutions', one novelty followed after another 'so rapidly' (*CPW*, ii.1053). This anticipates Wordsworth's statement in the 'Preface' about the debilitating effects of mass media in modern urban life:

> The most effective of these causes [that 'blunt the discriminating powers of the mind, and ... reduce it to a state of almost savage torpor'] are the great national events which are daily taking place, and the encreasing accumulation of men in cities, where the uniformity of their occupations produces a craving for extraordinary incident.
>
> (*WPrW*, i.128)

Both men shared the same conviction, that poetry – their kind of poetry – was more important than these great events, and that it might even provide a way toward solving the dilemmas that they create. Typically, however, Wordsworth took Coleridge's playful, tentative formulations and recast them into blunt, provocative assertions.

In Coleridge's idealist mind-set almost any topic could be immediately generalized to universal, metaphysical dimensions. While Wordsworth was composing the 'Preface', Coleridge told Davy he was meditating an essay on poetry that 'would in reality be a *disguised* System of Morals & Politics' (*CL*, i.632). This too is an aspect of Wordsworth's 'Preface', for many of the poems in the volumes were still, in the two authors' minds, part of a covert programme of cultural warfare waged against established moral systems and political powers as well as literary ones, carrying on politics by other means. This purpose was implicit – though very heavily disguised – in the motto on the title page of the new second volume: 'Quam nihil ad genium, Papiniane, tuum!' (*LBB*, p. 125), a phrase that translates, 'How utterly unsuited to your taste, Papinianus!' Papinianus was a Roman lawyer, and the allusion was a slap at James Mackintosh for his embarrassingly public recantation of his former sympathies for the ideals of the French Revolution, in his 1799 lectures on 'The Laws of Nature and of Nations'.[5]

In short, like *The Recluse,* the 'Preface' was a text of philosophical social reform that Coleridge first wanted to write himself, but then urged Wordsworth to write instead. It covers many of the same topics as *The Recluse*, obscurely transposed into issues of rhyme, metre, and diction. The motive of the 'Preface' is thus vastly incommensurate with its matter. Many of its issues are displaced versions of the questions of imaginative authority and poetic identity Wordsworth and Coleridge had been writing and talking about for three years. But they had been doing this in relation to *The Recluse,* not in relation to *either* volume of *Lyrical Ballads*. Not only is 'the ambition behind the *Lyrical Ballads* pastorals ... quite as large as that which had conceived *The Recluse'*,[6] it is in essence the *same* intention. The key terms of *The Recluse* – 'On Man, on Nature, and on Human Life' – are present in the central formulations of the 'Preface', when Wordsworth refers to 'the most valuable object of all writing whether in prose or verse, the great and universal passions of men [Man], the most general and interesting of their occupations [Society], and the entire world of nature [Nature]' (*WPrW*, i.144). But the scope of *The Recluse*'s ambition, which was nothing less than the secular redemption of society, was much too big for a preface, especially one that appears to introduce poems which, whatever their merits, are much slighter productions than we would expect for an epic of human redemption. Nonetheless, enough of the heroic impulse imbedded in the 'Preface' does shine through to help explain how it achieved its hold on English-speaking audiences everywhere. Of all the creative confusions and cross-purposes which helped to make the 'Preface' such a controversial document – guaranteeing the centrality of Wordsworth's reputation both as a target of attack and as a rock of defence – none has been more overlooked than this one: that the 'Preface' is motivated by the poet's duty to renew his entire culture, English in the first instance, but implicitly universal. A theory of the creative imagination's role in improving human society is presented mainly in terms of a theory of poetics: metrics, diction, and style. The connections between the two can be worked out, but it takes a lot of time and hard work, far beyond what readers normally expect to give to a preface, and many loose ends are still left hanging.

At some point toward the end of the summer, Coleridge shifted the burden of preface-writing onto Wordsworth, provoking him into prose: 'I trust ... that I have invoked the sleeping Bard with a spell so potent, that he will awake & deliver up that Sword of Argantyr, which is to rive the Enchanter GAUDY-VERSE from his Crown to his Fork' (*CL*, i.611–12). Wordsworth marked the spot where they made the decision: the deserted quarry on the southerly shore of Rydal Water, where Sir Walter Fleming had quarried the stones for his pleasure house.[7] This is not to suggest that the 'Preface', like the pleasure house, might better have gone unfinished, but it might imply that, once it lost its architect, Coleridge, the builder's energy and enthusiasm soon made him lose sight of the original proportions which they had in mind. Once it was clear that Coleridge was not going to help, Wordsworth completed the entire 'Preface', arguably the most influential document of literary theory in English, in the last two weeks of September (*DWJ*, i.61, 62). He was so full of energy for his self-defining project that he began and nearly finished yet another 'Preface', which would have introduced the second volume. But he decided not to print it because it grew too long from the many quotations that 'must unavoidably be spun' into it (*EY*, p. 309).[8] If we take the first 'Preface' as a measure of Wordsworth's ideas of length, this second one must have been very long indeed. From his mention of the many quotations in it, it sounds like an early version of the 'Essay, Supplementary to the Preface' that he published with his first collected edition in 1815 (*WPrW*, iii.62–84). That essay is essentially a polemical history of English literature, framed as a spiritual progression toward the works of one man, William Wordsworth.

In the 1800 'Preface', Wordsworth speaks in a voice at once aggressive and defensive. It is the voice of a man convinced of the purity of his goals and motives, but unsure of the arguments he is using to defend them, and of the audience to which he is speaking. He seems to assume his audience will disagree with his premises. Coleridge's Spenserian image of Wordsworth as wielder of 'the Sword of Argantyr', roused to slay the enchanter GAUDY-VERSE, is apt for the intention of the 'Preface'; but many readers have had the uneasy feeling that the sword was somehow directed at them, or might glance off in their direction. Repeatedly, Wordsworth goes further than he needs to in urging his claims, particularly in his long, turgid insistence on the essential identity between the language of poetry and that of prose. He was trying to say everything he most deeply believed, all at once, on the first real occasion he had had to do so. He strains to unify everything, to assert the kind of moral authority he felt he must have as the bard of *The Recluse:* high seriousness and low subjects, poetry and prose, the great literature of the past and his own poems in the present. He often starts much further 'down', at the foundations of his subjects, than he needs to, or than most readers would expect of a mere preface. But this foundational or metaphysical aspect of the 'Preface' is what forces its claims upon our permanent attention: its delving into the nature of the human mind, and the mind's relations to language and to the external world.

The vehemence of Wordsworth's tone and the extremes to which he forces his arguments betray his inexperience in critical discussions of style and diction. At the very outset, he set aside the 'full account' which his theoretical principles would require, lacking sufficient space to develop it. But even the little he says about it reveals the presence of the *Recluse* ideal: philosophical, bold, and far ahead of its time. For example, his full theoretical account would require his 'pointing out' how language and mind 'act and react' on each other (*WPrW*, i.120). This is still a lively controversy, as to whether human thought precedes language, or can only be done in terms of language – which is to say, *in terms.* But Wordsworth says he would have provided this fuller 'account' for a purpose, not as an abstract scientific project, for his concern is with the 'present state of the public taste in this country', and whether it is 'healthy or depraved'. This, in turn, would require 'retracing the revolutions not of literature alone but likewise of society itself' (*WPrW*, i.120). In short, the 'Preface' is a revolutionary document in two senses, both in what it sets forth, and in that it is *about* revolutions – and, even more, about the interaction, or interdependence, of cultural and political revolutions.

Wordsworth was implying a full-field theory of the way in which language-in-culture affects and even constitutes human nature in its social forms. The presumption that language and mind *do* interact in this way to produce culture and society is now very largely accepted, two hundreds years later, in societies worried about cultural products far more pernicious than 'frantic novels, sickly and stupid German Tragedies, and deluges of idle and extravagant stories in verse' (*WPrW*, i.128). Wordsworth's interest was partisan, not abstract, because he wished to *change* the present unhappy situation. He clearly believed that 'the present taste' of the country *was* 'depraved'. He even set up a standard of value according to which progress could be measured. In a time when talk of 'the rights of man' had begun to sound a bit hollow, if not seditious, Wordsworth proposed a theory not of human equality but a hierarchy based on the value of the healthy human mind in a 'depraved' society. '[O]ne being is *elevated above another* in proportion as he possesses this capability' of *not* requiring 'gross and violent stimulants' for the excitement or healthy exercise of his mind (*WPrW*, i.128; emphasis added). This sets up a hierarchy of sensibility, or imagination, separate from the civil rights of birth or citizenship. Stimulating this higher type of imagination is 'one of the best services' in which a writer 'can be engaged ... at the present day' (*WPrW*, i.128), because there are so many more forces working to support and extend these degrading forces than there are counteracting them. Such forces are pervasive and interconnected: the 'great national events which are daily taking place', the growth of cities (as poor country people come to find employment in the war economy), the boring, uniform tasks of the emerging industrial system (stimulated by the war), which produce a craving for 'extraordinary incident', which is in turn 'gratified' by 'hourly intelligence' (newspapers), bringing full circle the system of language-mind stimulation and degradation to which Wordsworth alluded at the outset.

The 'Preface' thus aims at a whole system of cultural production, setting up an oppositional cottage industry to counter 'great national events', just as he had recast Grasmere as a national centre in 'Home at Grasmere': 'a multitude / Human and brute, possessors undisturbed / Of this recess, their legislative Hall, / Their Temple, and their glorious dwelling-place' (ll.825–8; Gill, p. 194). Wordsworth's confidence was, however, not based on his poems alone; he is not so unguarded.

Rather, it was his faith in 'certain inherent and indestructible qualities of the human *mind*', and in 'the great and permanent objects that act upon it' (that is, natural forms) that gave him the confidence to await that '*time* ... approaching when the evil will be systematically opposed by men of greater powers and with far more distinguished success' (*WPrW*, i.130; emphases added). No one has ever suggested who these 'men' might be, but from their position at the end of a long sequence of arguments promising a vast vindication in the future, we immediately recognize the signature of Wordsworth's rhetorical strategy (or habit), from 'Lines written ... above Tintern Abbey' in 1798, to the 1799 *Prelude,* to the 1800 'Prospectus' to *The Recluse.* As at those moments, his point of reference is himself and Coleridge, and he is referring to their major projects, to which *Lyrical Ballads* was, in 1800 as in 1798, dedicated primarily as a prospectus, fund-raiser, and advertising-flyer.

(iv) 'Christabel' and 'Michael'

While Wordsworth was pushing the 'Preface' to a conclusion, riding roughshod through logical impasses, guided by the light of his emerging conception of the Poet, Coleridge, instead of helping Wordsworth's argument, was trying to finish a great work of his own. For about two months, between August and October, the plan was that 'A Poem of Mr. Coleridge's was to have concluded the Volumes' (*EY*, p. 309). This poem was 'Christabel'. Wordsworth thought that the second 'Preface' he drafted was justified by the bulk of a volume that would contain a 'new long poem' by his friend; and as late as the first week in October, 'Christabel' was still scheduled with the printers for inclusion.

On 4 October, Coleridge read to William and Dorothy at Grasmere all that he had completed of his poem – largely the poem as we know it today, ending with any further action ominously suspended between the protagonists. William and Dorothy were '[e]xceedingly delighted' with it the night they heard it, and they heard it again the next day with 'increasing pleasure' (*DWJ*, i.64). But Wordsworth soon began to have doubts about it, and three days later it was out of the project. Wordsworth's unilateral decision against 'Christabel' severely damaged Coleridge's self-confidence as a poet. He had crucially recognized Wordsworth as Milton's successor when nobody else in the world would have done so, but Wordsworth's brutal commitment to his poetic programme did not permit him a similar generosity toward Coleridge.

Wordsworth's reason for dropping it was that he thought there was too abrupt a change between Parts I and II, as the poem's setting shifted from Somerset to Grasmere.[9] More justifiable was his feeling that the poem, slightly longer in its final form than 'The Ancient Mariner', was ill-suited to the contents of the rest of the volumes. He told Longman that 'the Style of this Poem was so discordant from my own' that it was better to omit it (*EY*, p. 309). In fact, its difference in style, otherwise unexceptionable (after all, it was announced as being by another author), amounted to a contradiction in terms, once the high argument of the 'Preface' had been set forth at such length. The same could be said of 'The Ancient Mariner', of course, but its place was assured, and 'Christabel''s similarity to it was no good argument with Wordsworth for including it.

By rejecting 'Christabel', Wordsworth not only lost the justification for his long second 'Preface'; he also effectively cut off the last quarter of the second volume as it then stood, so presenting himself with the necessity of coming up with a poem or poems of similar length to replace it. This poem was 'Michael'. Publication was delayed for a full three months until Wordsworth could finish it, beginning from October 12. First he rummaged about in his stock of manuscript poems, but rejected what he found there because, 'being connected with political subjects I judged that they would be injurious to the sale of the Work', whereas 'there can be no doubt that the poem alluded to ['Michael'] will be highly serviceable to the Sale' (*EY*, p. 309). The rejected poems in question were most probably 'The Ruined Cottage' and 'Adventures on Salisbury Plain', which in their extant versions of ca. 1800 could still be characterized as political – especially when compared with Wordsworth's new productions for the second volume.[10]

'Michael' is the conclusive poem of the 1800 *Lyrical Ballads* in every sense. Wordsworth's composition of it in two months was a remarkable indication of his fully-developed powers as a professional poet. He could, virtually on demand, write a powerful poem to order, appropriate to both the contents of the volume in question and, even more impressive, fully congruent with the theoretical requirements laid down in its 'Preface'. 'Michael' is the only poem in the entire collection to have been written to the specification of a previously enunciated model, since it alone follows rather than precedes the 'Preface' in time of composition. It fulfils, particularly, Wordsworth's dictum that, in these poems, unlike most narrative poems, the feeling was to give importance to the action rather than vice versa.

The action of its story is quickly told: Michael's son Luke leaves home to earn money to save the family's lands, but falls into dissipation and flees the country. But the *feeling* of the story is almost unspeakable, either in Michael's last charge to Luke or in his thoughts after Luke's fall, which are entirely contained in the vignette of his repeated returns to the sheepfold which the two of them started on the day Luke left: he 'never lifted up a single stone' (l.475). Wordsworth confirmed the poem's theoretical importance by claiming that 'Michael' contained his most important 'views'. 'Michael' at the end of the second volume forms a natural complement to 'The Brothers' near the beginning: both are sad stories of the ultimate failure of efforts to preserve the integrity of home and family in the harsh economies of the district.

As a place-bonding story 'Michael' does have the archetypal quality of telling how someone who left a tightly-knit community suffered bad consequences, and left his family to mourn. This effect is strongly reinforced by Wordsworth's allusions to tales of the Patriarchs of *Genesis* and their sons, and (in reverse) to the story of the Prodigal Son. Since the impulse of young people in provincial places is often to escape, especially when times are hard, such a tale serves as a cautionary threat. But usually such stories put the onus for blame (or praise) on the young man, whereas in 'Michael', Luke is sent away by his father to save the family: he fails, but the responsibility falls back on the father for the course of action he chose for his son.

Wordsworth found several aspects of both Michael's and Luke's situation easy to develop because they applied to his own life in the region, allowing him to enter his material quickly by self-identification. This was a necessity for almost every poem he wrote, particularly those in a collection at once as personal and prophetic as (what it still was at the time of composing its last poem) 'Poems in two Volumes. By W. Wordsworth'. He too had been a promising local boy of suddenly reduced expectations who was sent out into the world to help recoup his family's fallen fortunes. And he, like Luke, had failed in that effort, both in the world's eyes and in the eyes of most of the members of his extended family. To them, and perhaps to himself, it might well have appeared that 'in the dissolute city [he] gave himself / To evil courses' (ll.453–4). This could as easily have been radical political activism as the fleshly pleasures we more usually supply for such a reference, though both played their part in Wordsworth's youthful experience.

But the poem's blame falls hardest on Michael. If we pay attention to the poem, rather than to the sentimental images often conjured up from it, we can see that much more goes through the old man's mind than the simple fact that Luke will never return, or even that he may lose half his land and that things will never be the same again. As a Lake District tragedy, and a common one at that, the blame in Wordsworth's poem falls squarely on the hubris of the father – as it does in its supernatural double, 'Christabel', which it replaced. It is Michael's decision that Luke should be sent to *earn* the needed bond money that sets the tragedy in motion. This decision, not Luke's weakness and errors, is what goes through Michael's mind as he contemplates the unfinished sheepfold. Michael is something like the shepherd in 'The Last of the Flock', but his possessiveness is brought out, not by poverty, but by pride of ownership – to give a higher name to the perfectly understandable desire to hang onto one's house and lands at all costs. The lands had been 'burdened' (under lien) when they came to Michael, and not till he was forty was even half of his inheritance really his. Now, by the failure of his nephew ('his Brother's Son': l.221), exactly half is put under threat of loss again. He was a workaholic, and it only occurs to him late in life that he might want an heir to receive all that he has built up: he is sixty-six when Luke is born. He starts taking the boy out to work with him at a very early age: by five, Luke was 'to his office *prematurely* call'd', and by age ten, he 'could stand / Against the mountain blasts' (ll.197, 204–5; emphasis added) – Wordsworth mentions his age because he wants us to remark it. Things in nature 'Were dearer now' to Michael than they were before because of the promise represented by his son; but Wordsworth rejects this observation impatiently, as something trite and irrelevant: 'why should I relate / That … ?' (ll.210, 208–9). All the emphasis is on the father's feelings for his son *in relation to* his land.

The pathetic scene of Michael's last conversation with Luke at the sheepfold opens into language that comes close to revealing both the selfish tendency of Michael's reasoning and its close parallels to Wordsworth's project of self-creation. Michael lays a heavy burden of paternal guilt, or psychological debt, on Luke, telling him how much he has loved him since his birth. Though 'Luke had a manly heart', he soon starts sobbing aloud, leading Michael to realize, belatedly, 'Nay … I see / That these are things of which I need not speak' (ll.367, 369–70). As an alternative, he converts the same story of family indebtedness back through his own parents, but this only turns back into another duty laid on Luke: 'I wish'd that thou should'st live the life they liv'd' (l.381). His language begins to stutter as his deepest fears start to emerge: 'I knew that thou could'st never have a wish / To leave me, Luke, thou hast been bound to me / Only by links of love' (l.410–12). But these, as Wordsworth knows, are the strongest indentures of all, and Michael here sounds almost as much like 'The Mad Mother' as he does the father of 'The Last of the Flock' – or like Wordsworth himself at the end of 'Lines written ... above Tintern Abbey', pleading with Dorothy to keep his life in her mind forever: 'save *me*', is the message.

'Michael' rounds off the defining pattern of broken pairs and broken homes that dominate all the new poems that Wordsworth wrote in 1800 at Grasmere. The pair-poems, the place-poems, and the local-people poems of the new volume all come together in it, in the up-gathering conclusion of the entire volume. The unfinished structure of the sheepfold stands for human disappointment amid nature's beauty: it thus represents the tragic disappointment of the very hopes that its central symbol was supposed to represent. The unfinished sheepfold is the broken bond of love, as it seemed to William and Dorothy from the first moment they saw it, looking like 'a heart unequally divided' (*DWJ*, i.66). The poem, completed on December 9, 1800, represented a strong corrective to what Wordsworth now recognized as the very naive hopes which he had held for Grasmere almost exactly twelve months earlier. Everything is gone: 'the ploughshare has been through the ground / On which it stood' (ll.486–7). Like the village tales he later tacked on to 'Home at Grasmere', 'Michael' shows Wordsworth's awareness that any assumption of an easily enduring link between land, man, and language could not stand the test of reality. In 'Home at Grasmere', another bonding symbol of the human significance of the natural landscape, the paired swans, was all too easily broken, throwing both poet and his poem into disarray. But 'Michael', rather than rationalizing an explanation why this ideal is not tenable, conveys instead the devastating realization that it cannot be so.

Just as the self-world concerns of *The Recluse* are buried beneath the alternatively turgid and splendid arguments of the 'Preface', so are they evident in 'Michael'. Wordsworth defended his reference to 'The earliest of those tales that spake to me / Of Shepherds' because they spoke to him 'On man; the heart of man and human life' (ll.22–3, 33), words virtually identical to those with which he announced the birth of the *Recluse*-project two-and-a-half years earlier. But where 'Home at Grasmere' finally achieved a satisfactory conclusion by Wordsworth attaching the forward-looking vision of the 'Prospectus' onto its tales of tragedy, 'Michael' finds no such satisfaction: he knows that his lands are lost and his dreams destroyed. Yet by telling Michael's story, Wordsworth hoped to achieve what was denied Michael, not in his land holdings but in his own stock-in-trade, poetry:

> *Therefore,* although it be a history
> Homely and rude, I will relate the same
> For the delight of a few natural hearts,
> And with yet fonder feeling, for the sake
> Of youthful Poets, who among these Hills
> Will be my second self when I am gone.
>
> (ll.34–9; emphasis added)

This bequeathing of himself to his successors parallels that to Dorothy in 'Lines written ... above Tintern Abbey' and to Coleridge in *The Prelude*. Wordsworth will perpetuate himself through his poetical 'heirs', precisely as Michael could not. But, like Michael's desire to propagate himself, Wordsworth's legacy is expressed in language that suggest his heirs may get more than they bargained for, or that the gift may entail the assumption of an identity not their own: *'be my second self* when I am gone'.

This is to read the poem at its deepest autobiographical level, which is concerned preeminently with the creation of 'The Poet'. Wordsworth's contemporary readers understood it as a poem about human nature; Humphry Davy said it was full of just pictures of what human life ought to be like. But at the biographical level, Wordsworth's sympathy for the composite character of Michael – great as it is – was not just for the difficulties of poor country life in 1800, nor even for the private cautionary lesson it taught Wordsworth about the dangers of a naive identification with place. It was also a symbol of Wordsworth's own disappointment at his failure to push forward on *The Recluse*. He had piled up 'stones' for it and worked on it 'many a day'. But there were also many days, as there were in the composition of 'Michael', when he went either to his study or out to Easedale and other favourite composing haunts, 'And never lifted up a single stone'. Michael's sheepfold, begun but never finished, becomes a permanent record of failure. So too did Wordsworth's *Recluse* manuscripts, as they mounted up through the years.

Notes

1   As recorded in a letter from John Wordsworth to Mary Hutchinson, 25 February, 1801; quoted in Mary Moorman, *William Wordsworth: A Biography: The Early Years 1770–1803* (Oxford: Clarendon Press, 1957), p. 506.

2   See William Wordsworth, Lyrical Ballads *and Other Poems, 1797–1800*, ed. James Butler and Karen Green (Ithaca, NY: Cornell University Press, 1992), p. 623; and cf. the transcription of fragment (b) in *WPW*, ii.482.

3   Fragment (b), ll.13–15, 18–21; *WPW*, ii.482 (emphasis added).

4   Moorman, *Wordsworth*, p. 480.

5   See Moorman, *Wordsworth*, p. 501; and *LBB*, p. 124.

6   Stephen Gill, *William Wordsworth: A Life* (Oxford: Clarendon Press, 1989), p. 189.

7   'I recollect the very spot, a deserted Quarry in the Vale of Grasmere where he pressed the thing upon me': note to Barron Field's memoir of Wordsworth; quoted in *WPrW*, i.167.

8   And see *Lyrical Ballads*, ed. Butler and Green, pp. 739–40.

9   See the remarks recorded in Moorman, *Wordsworth*, p. 490.

10   See the 'Introduction' to *Lyrical Ballads*, ed. Butler and Green, p. 30.

6
Lyrical Ballads and 'Pre-Established Codes of Decision'

Michael O'Neill

The 1798 'Advertisement' to *Lyrical Ballads* (mainly, for the purpose of this essay, Wordsworth's poems in the 1800 edition) wags an admonishing finger at 'that most dreadful enemy to our pleasures, our own pre-established codes of decision'. Wordsworth has in mind presumptions about poetic value held by readers 'accustomed to the gaudiness and inane phraseology of many modern writers'. In its poetic modes, *Lyrical Ballads* frequently contends with these and other presumptions as it wrestles to redefine 'the solitary word Poetry, a word of very disputed meaning' (*WPrW*, i.116).

Certainly, the volume is unafraid of appealing to 'solitary', individual experience as the ground of poetic 'meaning'. In 'Nutting' the poet summons up 'a day' (l.1) that is 'One of those heavenly days which cannot die' (l.3): 'One of those' makes the day typical, and yet it is intricately 'singled out' (l.2) by the poetic imagination. By the time the poem has re-entered the memory of 'one dear nook' (l.15), and the disturbing, quasi-sexual 'ravage' (l.44) that took place there, it is possessed by an experience which can be evoked, but not translated into general terms. This resistance to translation is only pointed up by the almost knowingly inadequate last three lines. Even the recollection of lying 'with my cheek on *one* of those green stones' (l.34; emphasis added) insists, through the halting monosyllables, on an irreducible factuality. As the poem mixes up childhood and sexuality, serenity and violence, it confuses 'pre-established' categories – doing so less in a spirit of conscious polemic than as a result of absorption in memory.

Again, one of the volume's most famous poems begins by confessing, with mock-embarrassment, 'Strange fits of passion I have known'. The self-perplexed yet upbeat stress on the first two words evokes a speaker determined to insist that he has 'known' what is, admittedly, 'Strange': the adjective itself works strangely, open to being inter- preted as 'odd' or, more impressively, as 'uncanny'. The poet's 'fit' demands, he tells us, a reader on his affective wavelength; he will confide his tale 'in the lover's ear alone' (l.3). But the reader, while sensing that a cue has been given, will be less than sure about being able to occupy the position of echoing second self. Wordsworth unveils his motiveless presentiment of death through a lyric structure that has a spectral, jaunty weightlessness. The poem is attuned to vagaries as well as fixations of passion, communicating this attune- ment through, for example, the increase in emphasis on 'All' in the following lines: 'Upon the moon I fix'd my eye, / All over the wide lea' (ll.9–10). The second line, there, fails solely to buttress the first, since it sends the eye and imagination scampering over the 'wide lea': a darkened space, we may suppose, removed from the luminous unique- ness of the moon.

This is a poetry of misleadingly limpid surfaces and dissonant sub- texts. Its scenic ordinariness – the plodding horse, the distant cottage – cohabits with a barely spoken awareness of the mysterious. Wordsworth appeals to common experience when, later, he describes his trance-like state of moon-gazing as 'one of those sweet dreams ... / Kind Nature's gentlest boon!' (ll.17, 18). But the poem positions itself at the limit of comprehensibility. If its concluding stanza begins with another reference to typical experience (the 'fond and wayward thoughts' that 'slide / Into a Lover's head': ll.25, 26), the final words stage a talking to the self ('"Oh mercy!" to myself I cried': l.27) that makes us into enthralled if puzzled eavesdroppers. Emotionally, the poem thrives on its departures from the 'pre-established', and owes its value, in part, to involving the reader in what he or she cannot wholly comprehend.

Lyrical Ballads takes as a central topic the issue of 'pre-established codes', sometimes contesting, always making us look hard at, agreed norms of behaviour, judgement, and feeling. 'The Ancient Mariner: A Poet's Reverie' (its 1800 title) is the most disturbingly flamboyant example: the Mariner, 'Alone on the wide wide Sea' (l.225), is, at least temporarily, unmoored from a 'pre-established' (primarily Christian) value-system. Against the traditional values of community embodied in the wedding-feast, Coleridge sets the Mariner's haunting and haunted experience of dislocation, of being catapulted, by the killing of the albatross, into a parallel universe in which the God- or angel- like sun is bloody-red, and in which the Mariner is, indeed, acted upon to the depths of his hallucination-sensitive mind.[1] But in a variety of ways opposition to the 'pre-established' is pervasive: 'It is the first mild day of March', for instance, frees 'Our living Calendar' ('Lines written at a small distance from my House ...', l.18) from the would-be regulatory effect of 'joyless forms' (l.17), while in 'Anecdote for Fathers' the speaker learns a 'lore' (l.58) from his son that exceeds his own anxious rationalism.

'Fools have laughed at, wise men scarcely understand them' (Hazlitt, xi.87): Hazlitt's comment on *Lyrical Ballads* hints at the volume's deployment of complicatedly simple tactics. If Wordsworth's effects challenge 'pre-established codes of decision', they often do so by incorporating themselves in structures that allow for surprise and reversals of the expected. 'The Last of the Flock' troubles us by setting the obsessive narrative entropy of the weeping shepherd's tale – the relentless dwindling of his flock down to one sheep – against the illogical yet corresponding waning of his love for his children. The peculiar combination of empathy and alienation here is contrived by Wordsworth's ventriloquism. For all its eruptions of pantheistic joy, the volume is full of voices that are bereft of delight and express deep hurt, as in these lines from the same poem:

> Another still! and still another!
> A little lamb, and then its mother!
> It was a vein that never stopp'd,
> Like blood-drops from my heart they dropp'd.
>
> (ll.61–4)

In its chiastic expression of endless loss (l.61), graphic imagery (l.64), and rhyming that seems to enforce the dictates of an unavoidable fate, this way of speaking overrides any supposed moral about the naturalness of attachment to property. It comes close to morbid self-preoccupation, and yet Wordsworth's listening stance has about it an unsentimental charity of acceptance.

Elsewhere, the poet foxes himself and us. The fourth poem in the sequence of 'Poems on the Naming of Places' works ironically at the expense of rashly premature judgement, as the poet and his party mistake an angler 'Attir'd in peasant's garb' (l.51) for an idler, before realizing more compassionately that he is 'a man worn down / By sickness' (ll.64–5). Yet it also captures the faintly shocking way compassion comes into being. The poem's close is given up to 'serious musing' and 'self-reproach' (l.76), but at its centre is a moment of horrified fascination as the poet confronts a figure whose physique is the subject of one of nature's cruel jokes. His legs were 'so long and lean / That for my single self I look'd at them, / Forgetful of the body they sustain'd' (ll.66–8). That split-second sense of the bizarre, the whole of the poet's attention being taken up, as in some Dickensian vignette, by the long, lean legs, validates the poem's turn. This turn might have been in the direction of a conventional self-rebuke. What makes it new is the way the poet's whole being, his 'single self', attends so concentratedly yet 'forgetfully' to a detail of the peasant's physical appearance.

The 'single self' is by no means lauded in the volume, but it is a recurring concern. In 'She dwelt among th'untrodden ways', the significance of the elegized, solitary 'she' is discovered posthumously through the loss experienced by the elegizing poet. Wordsworth relies, in this lyric, on a stripped-down bareness of utterance that makes the slightest modulation a poetic event. So, the second stanza's first image of 'Half-hidden' violet (l.6) gives way to a bolder assertion of the value of singleness: in the lines, 'Fair, as a star when only one / Is shining in the sky!' (ll.7–8), the incipient hint of disappointment in '*only* one' (emphasis added) quickly discovers its erroneousness as the next line allows for a spreadingly developed 'shining'; 'only one', it turns out, celebrates uniqueness. The poem's close suggests that Lucy's value lies in her opaqueness to others, 'She *liv'd* unknown' (l.9), and the virtually inexpressible 'difference' she made to the poet: 'But she is in her Grave, and Oh! / The difference to me' (ll.11–12). Rhyming the exclamatory 'Oh!' with the word 'know', Wordsworth implies the superiority of singular feeling to shared knowledge. At the same time, his poem recognizes how close it has come to wordlessness in its challenge to such knowledge.

This kind of challenge has always bothered critics of *Lyrical Ballads*. Emile Legouis writes of Wordsworth that 'A reproach that was often and justly made against him was that he attributed to certain expressions or incidents more emotion than other people could reasonably associate with them'.[2] An exasperated Robert Southey complained to Coleridge about Wordsworth in August 1802: 'Does he not associate more feeling with particular phrases, and you also with him, than those phrases can convey to any one else?'[3] Legouis picks up Southey's post-Hartleyan use of 'associate', and, like Southey, he suggests that potentially arbitrary processes of authorial association present Wordsworth's readers with their greatest challenge. Though in the

'Preface' Wordsworth claims for each of his poems 'a worthy *purpose*' communicable to any reader who is in 'a healthful state of association' (*WPrW*, i.124, 126), he also concedes that 'my associations must have sometimes been particular instead of general' (*WPrW*, i.152). It is a revealing admission, given the volume's efforts to tie together the particular and the general, while insisting that the general always takes account of, or arises from, the particular. Yet Wordsworth follows this admission by reminding the reader that he 'ought never to forget that he is himself exposed to the same errors as the Poet, and perhaps in a much greater degree' (*WPrW*, i.152). In keeping with this reminder, *Lyrical Ballads* frequently dramatizes the poet's and reader's exposure to possible errors of judgement and feeling. Equally, if the volume is covertly fearful of uncontrollable readerly 'association', it also allows for the creative possibilities of what Wolfgang Iser calls 'reader participation in the text'.[4]

Wordsworth's disappointment with the inadequate reactions of others can verge on the comic. However, it reflects his concern about the effectiveness of his verbal representations. Often this effectiveness is discernible only when the underlying emotion has been grasped, as is asserted and conceded by the Latin quotation, adapted from Quintilian, on the half-title page of the 1802 and 1805 editions, which translates as follows: 'For it is feeling and force of imagination that make us eloquent; it is for this reason that even the uneducated have no difficulty in finding words to express their meaning, if only they are stirred by some strong emotion' (as translated in *LBM*, p. 94). The Latin tag, when juxtaposed with the elusively mocking epigraph also in Latin (and translating, in one of its inflections, as 'worthless and insignificant according to your taste, Papinian!' (*LBM*, p. 95)), prepares us for the poet's simultaneous expectation that the reader should grasp the underlying emotion and that he or she may well not do so. When Lamb showed insufficient admiration (in the poet's view) for *Lyrical Ballads* (1800), his response brought forth 'almost instanta-neously a long letter of four sweating pages from my reluctant Letterwriter [Wordsworth] ... [w]ith a deal of stuff about a certain "Union of Tenderness & Imagination"'.[5] As Kenneth Johnston points out, 'though Lamb was as usual funny, Wordsworth was, as more often than not, right'.[6] 'Written', to adapt the poet's wording from his fragmentary 'Essay on Morals', 'with sufficient power to melt into our affections ... , to incorporate itself with the blood & vital juices of our minds' (*WPrW*, i.103), Wordsworth's contributions to *Lyrical Ballads* address, cajole, admonish, and seek to re-educate an imagined reader.

And yet the fineness of his poems often has to do with a fastidious complicating of their apparent *'purpose'*, so that each poem establishes its own aesthetic and ethical code.

When Wordsworth explains his purposes, such explanations, as in 'Simon Lee', often explain little more than the fact that we have entered into unmapped territory: 'O reader!', writes Wordsworth half-mockingly, 'had you in your mind / Such stores as silent thought can bring, / O gentle reader! you would find / A tale in every thing' (ll.73–6). The apostrophes conjure up a reader who is at once 'gentle' (from the upper echelons and not without sensibility), and the target of amused scorn. The phrasing 'had you in your mind' implies that the gentle reader is, in fact, unused to the disciplines and strange liberations made possible by 'silent thought'. At the same time, there is a suggestion in the concluding line-and-a-half that, were the reader to have 'Such stores' in mind, the poet's job would be redundant. This job could be defined as making 'you think' (l.79), which is what the calculatedly thought-provoking conclusion does. Yet Wordsworth makes us think by dramatizing the response of the narrator to Simon Lee's effusive gratitude; in other words, he makes us think by showing himself (or his surrogate) being made to think:

> – I've heard of hearts unkind, kind deeds
> With coldness still returning.
> Alas! the gratitude of men
> Has oftner left me mourning.
>
> (ll.101–4)

The poem is sometimes read as voicing opposition to Godwin's disapproval of gratitude in *An Enquiry Concerning Political Justice*. Godwin took gratitude to refer to 'a sentiment, which would lead me to prefer one man to another, from some other consideration than that of his superior usefulness or worth'. Wordsworth's challenge to Godwin in 'Simon Lee', however, does not simply involve restitution of the human value of gratitude; it involves a questioning of the emotion itself, in a spirit of troubled kinship with other human beings. Viewing the emotion as 'no part either of justice or virtue', Godwin himself provides a critique of a pre-established code, according to which gratitude is expected, natural, and virtuous. His reason for doing so is a denial of the relevance of any feelings other than 'the consideration of my neighbour's moral worth and his importance to the general weal'. Godwin does believe that it is the 'duty' of any individual to grant 'relief' to a 'person in distress' who applies for it: 'It is my duty to grant it, and I commit a breach of duty in refusing'.[7] Wordsworth's narrator, by contrast, does not wait to be asked for 'relief' by a 'person in distress', before offering help. Yet if the conclusion to 'Simon Lee' parries *Political Justice*'s elimination of difficult feelings, Wordsworth, in his own way, is no less enquiring than Godwin about the meaning of 'gratitude'. The fact of gratitude has, after all, in a self-questioning final feminine rhyme, 'oftener left me mourning'. What for the philosopher is sorry evidence of 'the present imperfection of human nature' is for the poet the catalyst of an insight into 'human nature' that is obscure, dark, and possibly permanent.[8] The narrator is less worried by evidence of 'hearts unkind' than he is distressed by the predicament of others driven to express 'gratitude'. It is possible to make a critical 'tale' out of this distress that is political in emphasis, and to stress the poem's implied attack on a system that has reduced a man to physical suffering and want because he has 'spent about half his adult life devotedly helping the local aristocracy in the pursuit of one of their recreations' (Mason: *LBM*, p. 147). But the poem is reluctant to press home any such attack; there are, for instance, equally strong if knottily parodic hints of Burkean lament over the loss of feudal ties: 'His master's dead, and no one now / Dwells in the hall of Ivor; / Men, dogs, and horses, all are dead; / He is the sole survivor' (ll.21–4). The mixture of tones here – tugging us between the grim and the oddly bouncy – is crucial to the poem's challenge to established codes of feeling. 'Simon Lee' challenges even the new code of feeling it is seeking to establish; it watches itself both sharply – as it watches its sometimes hapless reader – and helplessly, as if conscious that poetry can never avoid verbal strategies, in the face of a human predicament that makes all strategies seem like evasions.

'A Poet's Epitaph' emphasizes the work required of a reader; the poem, written in briskly rhyming octosyllabic quatrains suited to caricature and aphorism, sends packing various social types (Statesman, Lawyer, Doctor, Soldier, Physician, and Moralist), then brings forward a character like Gray's '*youth*'.[9] This figure, a double of the poet whose epitaph he is reading, induces a change of tone. The use of the interrogative in lines 37–8 ('But who is He with modest looks, / And clad in homely russet brown?') is now wondering, no longer sardonic as it is in earlier uses of questions. Again, whereas earlier the pronoun 'thou' (ll.4, 5, 9, 13, 17) served to express scorn for worldly visitors to the grave, the shift to 'you' registers a reaching-out towards the possibility and necessity of 'love' if someone is to be appropriately understood: 'And you must love him, ere to you / He will seem worthy of your love' (ll.43–4). These lines pick up and modify the scornful directive addressed to the 'Statesman' (l.1): 'First learn to love one living man; / *Then* may'st thou think upon the dead' (ll.3–4). The later lines imply that one learns to love by supposing that the object is worthy of love, and, further, that the worth of the object is discovered through love. The poem's shift of tones recapitulates much in the volume and the 'Preface': there is the dismissal of 'pre-established' ways of looking, followed by a suggestion of a more rewarding mode of feeling and living, in which the reader is enjoined to participate. The poem puts us on our mettle by asking us to make distinctions even when it implies unexpected affinities. Both the (possibly Godwinian) Moralist and the poet-figure, for example, live in a world of their own: the former is 'Himself his world, and his own God' (l.28); the latter 'broods and sleeps on his own heart' (l.52), noticeably differing, in this respect, from Gray's Youth reposing in the 'EPITAPH' of the 'Elegy' on '*The bosom of his Father and his God*' (l.128). Unlike the Moralist, however, the poet-figure is responsive to the world outside him. Its 'outward shews' are connected to the 'impulses of deeper birth' he experiences 'in solitude' (ll.45, 47, 48). The Moralist is stigmatized as 'A reasoning, self-sufficing thing, / An intellectual All in All' (ll.31–2); the poet-figure may be solitary, but he finds value 'In common things that round us lie' (l.49).

Here, and elsewhere, the sense that the solitary poet-figure illuminates the 'common' prevents this figure from seeming alienated, even though the poem departs from Burns's 'A Bard's Epitaph' by stressing the lack of sympathy between visitors and the lamented poet. The final stanza reverts to an imperative, addressing the poet-figure come to mourn his double, but its meaning is markedly less clear than the corresponding stanza in Burns's poem. Burns asks that the 'Reader attend' (l.25) in the time-honoured manner of epitaphic poems, and draws from such imagined attention the – in context, touching – moral that 'prudent, cautious, *self-controul* / Is Wisdom's root' (ll.29–30).[10] Wordsworth has already refused to aggrandize a figure who is 'Contented if he might enjoy / The things which others understand' (ll.55–6). In the final stanza, he indicates that this figure has still much to 'understand':

> – Come hither in thy hour of strength,
> Come, weak as is a breaking wave!

Here stretch thy body at full length;
Or build thy house upon this grave. –

(ll.57–60)

Typically Wordsworth fails to point up an obvious moral, letting the stanza pivot on the contrasting notions of 'strength' and 'weakness', and the value for the poet-figure of developing a sense of affinity with 'this grave', the resting-place of a particular, if hardly knowable, individual. Shelley re-employs Wordsworth's technique of doubling and intermingling in his presentation of a surrogate poet-figure in *Adonais*, 'a Power / Girt round with weakness', whose characteristic mode is compared to 'A breaking billow' (ll.281–2, 285).[11] Both poems confess possible 'weakness'; both poems create a complicated relationship between their portrait of a poet and the poet doing the portraying; both poems invite the reader to construct his or her empathetic understanding of the poet-figure, without specifying exactly what that understanding should be. In *Adonais*, the 'power' of the creating poet will, in ensuing stanzas, jettison any suggestion of 'weakness', if not of rapturous fear; in 'A Poet's Epitaph', Wordsworth concludes his poem with a redefining twist that stops his challenge to the worldly and self-important from seeming itself to be self-important or complacent.[12]

Hazlitt spoke memorably of the 'unaccountable mixture of seeming simplicity and real abstruseness in the *Lyrical Ballads*' (Hazlitt, xi.87). 'Michael' is a fine example of this 'unaccountable mixture'. As Mason has observed, 'one of the distinctive rhetorical features of the poem is the turn of phrase in which the reader's assent to particular psychological effects is assumed' (*LBM*, p. 342). Yet the poem's jockeying of the reader to see from the right perspective (as in ll.14–16) gives way at the end to something less controlling. The close sees that, for the poem to do its work fully, the poet must treat the reader with the same respect for his or her otherness as is granted to the hero. The conclusion to 'Michael' shows how Wordsworth's challenge to 'pre-established codes of decision' affects the poetry's texture, underpinning his practice of confiding in and hiding from the reader. Luke, having given way to 'evil courses', experiences 'ignominy and shame' and, in an anticipation of a phrase Wordsworth will associate in *The Prelude* with his own creativity, seeks 'a hiding-place beyond the seas' (ll.454, 456). Luke in hiding brings into view the hiding-places of the poem's power, as it conveys, without milking, the pathos of his loss. Understatement and implication combine to create simultaneous yet distinct ways of responding to Michael. If we pity Michael, we also respond to him as beyond our understanding, at once tragic and uninterpretable.

We are invited to assent to the generalization in line 457 ('There is a comfort in the strength of love'), even to take 'comfort' from it. In the ensuing lines, the poetry tests the reader and flatters in so doing. The reader is required to look below the steady surface of the blank verse and to spy depths of barely formulated pain. When the narrator tells us, ''Twill make a thing endurable, which else / Would break the heart: – Old Michael found it so' (ll.458–9), the comforting gesture hears itself, and asks to be heard, as just that: a comforting gesture. But if 'strength of love' passes into 'endurable', it brings to mind, too, the anguish associated with the experience of endurance. Wordsworth breathes into endurance's apparent alternative, 'which else / Would break the heart', a mixture of inflections: for the heart to break seems undesirable, yet, as an under-whisper, the lines murmur that it may be desirable, if by the phrase is understood a possible end to anguish (through death or the kind of loss of reason suggested by the 1820 revision, 'Would overset the brain, or break the heart': l.450; *WPW*, ii.93). Moreover, as the passage will come close to establishing, heart-break and the capacity to endure may be indistinguishable. 'May be', because any certainty, the certainty in, say, 'Old Michael found it so', is complicated by the revelation that the narrator depends on second-hand information: 'I have convers'd with more than one who well / Remember the Old Man, and what he was / Years after he had heard this heavy news' (ll.460–2). To 'Remember the Old Man' may not be, despite the next phrase, to know 'what he was': a phrase momentarily rested on, in an unsignalling way, as a result of the slowed enjamb-ment. What was Michael? He was not quite, despite the memories of 'more than one', the man who 'as before / Perform'd all kinds of labour for his Sheep' (ll.466–7), as if nothing had changed. 'As before' in this passage annuls itself, and turns out to mean that nothing is what it was before. The poetry achieves this effect of evaporated comfort through recollections of earlier actions that point up differ-ence, 'half-echoes', as Jonathan Wordsworth comments, that 'throw into relief the finality of Luke's absence'.[13] So lines 463–4 ('His bodily frame had been from youth to age / Of an unusual strength') repeat lines 43–4; only, this time, the word 'strength' has been coloured by its associations with the complex of feelings surrounding 'the strength of love' and its ability to 'make a thing endurable'. Affecting the poetry's offer of comfort is a pleasing sham, and yet its slide into a truer portrait of Michael's feelings is managed by a further appeal to communal memory:

> 'Tis not forgotten yet
> The pity which was then in every heart
> For the Old Man – and 'tis believ'd by all
> That many and many a day he thither went,
> And never lifted up a single stone.
>
> (ll.471–5)

The communal and the individual come together and fly apart. Michael's actions (and inaction) are now 'believ'd by all' rather than remembered by 'many a one'. The famous line 475 could easily be heard as the half-incredulous expression of communal pity (he never lifted up a single stone); it also detaches itself from communal belief and becomes an image of incommunicable, private emotion that carries forward into the internal rhyme a couple of lines later when Michael is said to be seen 'Sitting alone' (l.477). In lines preceding line 471 Wordsworth has insinuated the possible unreliability of communal memory; in lines 471–5, he implies that when such memory is accurate (about the fact that Michael did no work day after day), it cannot have access to the whole truth about Michael's feelings. The reader, obliquely thematized from the poem's opening as the poet's 'second self' (l.39), occupies a mid-way space between believing community and solitary hero. Even as we are provoked into speculation about Michael's feelings (was he, in Mason's words, 'paralysed by a sense of futility', or was he, in the same critic's formulation of a conceivable alternative, 'remembering the boy Luke lovingly and feeling grateful for that love, even if he does no building'?: *LBM*, p. 342), such speculation is stilled by the finality of emphasis and cadence in line 475. Matthew Arnold found in the line 'expression of the highest and most truly expressive kind'.[14] 'Truly expressive' the line may be, yet what it is truly expressive of is the screened-off unreachability of specific experience.

Throughout 'Michael', Wordsworth has played the many against the single. The opening steers us off 'the public way', until we find ourselves 'alone / With a few sheep', our attention being drawn, with moving awkwardness, to 'one object which you might pass by' (ll.1, 10–11, 15). The 'story' itself is unique, the original of others, 'the first, / The earliest of those tales that spake to me / Of Shepherds' (ll.21–3). It is a single form that makes available the experience of many: a

'Tale' that has the power to make the poet 'think', albeit 'At random and imperfectly', 'On man; the heart of man and human life' (ll.27, 31, 32, 33). Luke's precious, implicitly precarious singleness is stressed: he is 'An only Child', and an 'only son' (ll.89, 92). Even when Michael's sheep-dogs are brought into the story, Wordsworth praises one above the other as 'of an inestimable worth' (l.94); Michael's and Isabel's cottage 'Stood single' (l.140); its light has a particular name, 'The Evening Star', given to it 'by all / Who dwelt within the limits of the vale, / Both old and young' (ll.146, 144–6). That way of putting it might seem garrulous, until one recognizes the poet's emphasis on the fact that 'all' the community agree that a single light should be 'nam'd', and regarded as 'a public Symbol' (ll.146, 137). No gap opens, here, between the communal and the individual, nor is there any strain placed on the reader's capacity to interpret. Moreover, the poem goes on to suggest the multiplying of happiness made possible through shared experience: Michael experiences a doubling of existence through Luke's participation in his daily life. This doubling is the more valuable for the fact that Luke does not merely echo what Michael is experiencing; rather, 'from the Boy there came / Feelings and emanations, things which were / Light to the sun and music to the wind', so that 'the Old Man's heart seemed born again' (ll.210–12, 213). It is these 'Feelings and emanations' which will be painfully present to Michael when at the poem's close it is said that he 'still look'd up upon the sun, / And listen'd to the wind' (ll.465–6).

The full force, then, of 'And never lifted up a single stone' derives from the clash between the many and the individual: the poetry spirals down from 'all' to 'many' to 'single' (ll.473, 474, 475), achieving a shocked, though not completely mist-clearing, intensity of vision. An important part is played by the preposition 'up' in the phrase 'lifted up', which recalls the fact that Michael has just been described as looking up upon the sun. That Michael should be looking 'up upon' gives the looking a quality of yearning that bears upon the inability to lift up a single stone (and makes one wonder, for a flicker, whether 'sun' in the earlier line hints at a pun on 'son'). But the adjective that devastates is 'single', whose operations are paradoxically manifold. The word sends us back to Michael's instruction to Luke, in proposing the covenantal sheep-fold, that he should 'lay one Stone' (l.396). There is a suggestion that this 'one Stone' has a significance that means no other stone can, in view of the subsequent disaster, be added to it. Above all, 'single' transfers itself back to the hero's 'singleness'. The poetry manages both to bring out this singleness and to respect it, to allow it its own privacy.

When the contemporary poet Bernard O'Donoghue, in a recent poem 'Ter Conatus', sets up a similar scenario to Wordsworth's in 'Michael', he exercises an intertextual tact that allows us to renew our awareness of the power of the original. In O'Donoghue's tragic pastoral about a brother and sister who farm together for sixty years, but never touch, even after she finds she has cancer, the brother's response to the sister's death is the object of communal sympathy. If Wordsworth asserts, ''Tis not forgotten yet / The pity which was then in every heart / For the Old Man', O'Donoghue writes, 'The neighbours watched // In pity'. But difference is as marked as affinity. Wordsworth's depiction of silent endurance is finally enigmatic. We do not know, though we may suppose we can guess, what Michael thinks about, as day after day he 'never lifted up a single stone'. By contrast, the curiosity of the brother's neighbours about 'what he could / Be thinking of' in 'Ter Conatus' is immediately satisfied.[15]

Throughout *Lyrical Ballads*, Wordsworth plays out the paradox inherent in lines from *The Prelude*: 'Points have we all of us within our souls / Where all stand single' (*Prelude*, III, ll.186–7). This passage places individual creative strength 'far hidden from the reach of words' (l.185): a remark that reminds us how often Wordsworth associates the communication of 'impassioned feelings' with 'an accompanying consciousness of the inadequateness of our own powers or the deficiencies of language' ('Note' to 'The Thorn': *LBB*, p. 289). In *Lyrical Ballads*, he sets up poetic scenarios in which, to borrow Frederick Garber's phrase, 'the presence of singularity' is discovered.[16] The reader, too, is made to recognize his or her singularity since Wordsworth breaks the convention 'that by the act of writing in verse an Author makes a formal engagement that he will gratify certain known habits of association' (*WPrW*, i.122). Wordsworth is more likely to disappoint 'certain known habits of association', and yet he avoids solipsism, nor is the reader marooned within his or her isolation since Wordsworthian 'singleness' shades into, and is shadowed by, the encroaching 'singleness' of others, and of nature.

Garber concludes a list of the numerous times 'a single thing ... becomes and remains the center of attention in the poems' with the intriguing comment that these occasions 'indicate the overwhelming substantiality, however equivocal and qualified and uncertain, of the world Wordsworth shapes out'.[17] What springs into being, as a result, for Garber, is Wordsworth's 'poetry of encounter'. Yet Wordsworthian poetic encounters often discover singular subjectivity in the act of affirming a shared human nature. For all the didactic ambitions of *Lyrical Ballads*, these discoveries occur unpredictably and often reveal in their linguistic texture an absence of palpable design. When Yeats sets up 'stylistic arrangements of experience' in *A Vision* and elsewhere, he does so 'to hold in a single thought reality and justice'.[18] Such 'a single thought' can be felt at work amidst, sometimes cutting against, the dynamic complexities of Yeats's thought. Yeats's reader is troubled and impressed by the aesthetic ruthlessness of such 'stylistic arrangements'. Wordsworth's reader is more likely to experience a sense of being disconcerted as he or she seeks to come to terms with the poetry's offer of what, in a letter to John Wilson, the poet calls 'new compositions of feeling' (*EY*, p. 355). When Dr Burney found aspects of 'Anecdote for Fathers' 'not quite obvious' (quoted in *LBB*, p. 325), he stumbled, despite himself, on a major feature of *Lyrical Ballads*: the volume thrives on avoidances of the obvious.

Characteristically the poet meditates on a single figure, such as the Old Cumberland Beggar, who is subdued to the level of on-going being: 'He travels on, a solitary Man' (l.44). True, the poem will go on to turn him into an exemplary figure, whose uniqueness confirms another kind of singleness, the view expressed in the more hortatory second half of the poem 'That we have all of us one human heart' (l.146). Though the reader may feel, with Lamb, 'that the instructions conveyed ... are too direct and like a lecture', the poem's different sections are linked.[19] It moves from celebrating the Beggar's uniqueness (one form of singleness) to assert the existence of 'one human heart' (another form of singleness). Wordsworth's imagination may be most effectively engaged in the poem by the experiential reality of human otherness. But one can see the more hortatory section as condemning wrong ways of reading the figure described in the unsentimental opening.

Elsewhere Wordsworth is quite able to sustain avoidance of sermonizing. In 'There was a Boy' the poetry's opening formula suggests that a moral of sorts will be presented, as it is, say, in 'Lines left upon a Seat in a Yew-tree', in which the fate of the disappointed visionary provokes the poet to instruct us 'that true knowledge leads to love' (l.56). However, in 'There was a Boy' the realization dawns that the Boy is being presented for his own sake, not to support a generalization. The second word of 'There was a Boy' (l.1) takes a complexly neutral but ultimately elegiac stress. The much-glossed Boy is, among other things, a version of the ideal reader of a lyrical ballad:

attentively 'Listening', he also takes in, 'unawares', the 'solemn imagery' of his surroundings (ll.19, 22, 23). The Boy is also a portrait of the incipient artist. Yet Wordsworth's lines carry their freight of suggestions easily, even, one is tempted to say, 'unawares', the blank verse 'interwoven' (l.7), like the Boy's fingers, with discoveries of relationship and isolation; indeed, the two abstractions generate each other. The Boy's 'mimic hootings' (l.10) are responsive to a circumambient world of forces and energies that he wishes to imitate and compel into relationship. But the poetry quietly establishes his aloneness amidst the natural world, even as the syntax struggles to define connections:

> ye knew him well, ye Cliffs
> And Islands of Winander! many a time,
> At evening, when the stars had just begun
> To move along the edges of the hills,
> Rising or setting, would he stand alone,
> Beneath the trees, or by the glimmering lake ...

> (ll.1–6)

The half line 'would he stand alone' briefly stands alone, for all the situating work done by prepositions and temporal markers. Glossing the poem in his 1815 'Preface', Wordsworth would write that he had 'represented a commutation and transfer of internal feelings, co-operating with external accidents, to plant, for immortality, images of sound and sight, in the celestial soul of the Imagination' (*WPrW*, iii.35, *app. crit.*). Though this gloss is abstract, even grandiloquent, its bringing together of 'commutation and transfer' shares with the poem a shrewd refusal to pin down exactly how 'internal feelings' co-operate with the 'external': if 'commutation' allows for 'interchange', 'transfer', more pointedly, insists on the element of projection in the process. The projection works inversely, so that the Boy appears to be acted on by 'the voice / Of mountain torrents, or the visible scene' (ll.20–1), even as his shaping Imagination, prompting a 'gentle shock of mild surprize' (l.19), unconsciously interprets the 'scene' in metatextual terms, marked by 'solemn imagery'.

But the poem's conclusion gives a twist to this inconspicuously triumphant allegory of the way 'internal feelings' and 'external accident' conjoin. When the Boy, in a line-ending that might have been precipitous, but is, in fact, open to experience, 'hung / Listening (ll.18–19), he occupies a creatively provisional position between inner and outer, projection and reception. His posture is less a symptom of de Manian 'dizziness' and '*vertige*' than of an enviably deft balance.[20] Yet that balance shifts at the end where 'the Church-yard hangs / Upon a slope above the village school' (ll.27–8), mimicking the earlier hanging with the infinitely withheld irony that is a characteristic of death's intrusions in *Lyrical Ballads*. So, the energies of 'mimic hootings' and responsively shouting owls give way to the fixity of a 'Mute' narrator standing by the Boy's 'grave' (ll.10, 32, 30). 'Mute' closes itself, in unexpressed grief, against the expressively rich 'pauses of deep silence' (l.17) celebrated earlier. The give-and-take between 'uncertain heaven' and 'steady lake' (ll.24, 25), where the adjectives stabilize and de-stabilize one another, passes into the assertion that 'beauteous is the spot, / The vale where he was born' (ll.26–7). What insinuates into this assertion a note of forlornness is the unspoken knowledge that Nature has betrayed the life of one who loved her. The Boy, who was known well by the 'Cliffs / And Islands of Winander', withdraws from comprehension, while a spate of first-person pronouns (three in successive lines) announces undeclared agitation on the part of the narrator.

Singleness has subsumed interplay and variety, and the narrator's final mood is not wholly beyond the reach of Geoffrey Hartman's perception that *Lyrical Ballads* is full of 'people cleaving to one thing or idea with a tenaciousness both pathetic and frightening'.[21] It is, one would guess, for its meaning as well as for its comparative avoidance of ornate diction that Wordsworth, in his 'Preface', exempted from blame these lines in Gray's 'Sonnet on the Death of Richard West': '*A different object do these eyes require; / My lonely anguish melts no heart but mine; / And in my breast the imperfect joys expire*' (*WPrW*, i.134). Gray's expression of 'lonely anguish' has an affecting straightforwardness that works (as Wordsworth inadvertently makes clear) because of its artful positioning in the poem. Relevant, too, to the later poet's obsession with obsession is the yearning embodied in 'object'. 'The Thorn' cunningly sets object-fixation against the centrifugal energies of surmise. Its 'loquacious narrator' ('Advertisement': *WPrW*, i.117) begins with a formula – 'There is a thorn' (l.1) – similar to that with which 'There was a Boy' begins, as the poet seeks to make the thorn 'permanently an impressive object' (Fenwick note: *LBB*, p. 290). The thorn's objectness provokes, resists, and survives the interpretations of villagers and narrator alike. If the thorn remains 'permanently impressive', it does so because Wordsworth brings it into ambiguous and displaced association with the sufferings of the deserted and probably unchilded Martha Ray.

The poem works by dramatizing the step-by-step approach to a glimpse of another's sorrow and grief that can never be anything like complete knowledge. Wordsworth's narrative skills are evident in, and his method illustrated by, stanza XVIII. Here the story advances by taking a step backward, recounting the narrator's visit to the mountain 'Ere I had heard of Martha's name' (l.184). Momentarily we step outside the web of hearsay, surmise, and reported rumour, and experience the narrator's recognition that he must rely on his senses. The stanza begins with a vision of 'mist and rain, and storm and rain' (l.188), a vision of unaccommodated existence ('No screen, no fence': l.189) that seems hostile to the human. The very wind, so the encroaching narrator supposes, 'was' – placed forcefully at the end of the line – 'A wind full ten times over' (ll.190, 191). Thinking he 'saw / A jutting crag' (ll.192–3), and wishing to gain 'The shelter of the crag' (l.195), the narrator ran 'Head-foremost, through the driving rain', only to discover 'Instead of jutting crag' 'A woman seated on the ground' (ll.194, 197, 198). The movement of the stanza generates a frisson of shock, but it does much more than this, setting going a three-handed exchange between poet, reader, and narrator in an effort to break through the 'driving rain' and confront the endlessly complex singleness of another person.

In enacting the highly unsimple process of recording the 'fluxes and refluxes of the mind when agitated by the great and simple affections of our nature' (*WPrW*, i.126), *Lyrical Ballads* is an unsettling, remarkable congery of diverse impulses: deeply sane and earthbound, it is at ease with idiocy and madness; aware of, and tacitly celebrating, the recalcitrant otherness of others, it is impelled by a 'sense sublime / Of something far more deeply interfused' ('Lines written … Tintern Abbey', ll.96–7); sometimes sealing its vision within stanzaic structures that are impenetrably tomb-like, it also commits itself, often with high spirits, to laying bare the building and re-building of poetic shapes (allegorized in the rough-and-tumble joking of 'Rural Architecture'). Above all, in its disagreement with 'pre-established codes of decision', the artistic vision of *Lyrical Ballads* engages in constantly changing dialogue with its reader.

Notes

1 This sentence alludes to the comparison in ll.93–4 of the 1798 version, in which the sun is likened to 'God's own head', not (as in 1800) to 'an

Angel's head' (see *LBB*, p. 13 and *app. crit*; and *CPW*, i.190 *app. crit.*). The
sentence also alludes to Wordsworth's criticism of the Mariner, that 'he
does not act, but is continually acted upon' (*LBB*, p. 276).

2 Emile Legouis, *The Early Life of William Wordsworth 1770–1798: A Study of
  'The Prelude'* (1896), with a new introduction by Nicholas Roe (London:
  Libris, 1988), p. 315.

3 Quoted in *William Wordsworth: A Critical Anthology*, ed. Graham McMaster
  (Harmondsworth: Penguin, 1972), p. 74.

4 'Interaction between Text and Reader'; in *Readers and Reading*, Longman
  Critical Reader, ed. Andrew Bennett (London/NY: Longman, 1995) 20–31,
  p. 29.

5 *The Letters of Charles and Mary Anne Lamb*, ed. Edwin W. Marrs (3 vols to
  date; Ithaca, NY: Cornell University Press, 1975–), i.273.

6 Kenneth R. Johnston, *The Hidden Wordsworth: Poet, Lover, Rebel, Spy*
  (NY/London: Norton, 1998), p. 760.

7 *An Enquiry Concerning Political Justice*; in *Political and Philosophical Writings
  of William Godwin*, ed. Mark Philp *et al.* (7 vols; London: Pickering and
  Chatto, 1993), iii.51, 52.

8 *Political Justice*; in *Writings of Godwin*, iii.51. *The Borderers*, ll.1543–4; *WPW*,
  i.188.

9 Thomas Gray, 'Elegy Written in a Country Church Yard', l.118; in *The
  Poems of Thomas Gray, William Collins, Oliver Goldsmith*, ed. Roger Lonsdale
  (London: Longman, 1969; repr., 1976), p. 138.

10 'A Bard's Epitaph'; in Robert Burns, *Poems in Scots and English*, ed. Donald
   Low (London: Dent (Everyman), 1993), p. 126.

11 'Adonais'; in *Shelley's Poetry and Prose*, ed. Donald H. Reiman and Sharon
   B. Powers (NY/London: Norton, 1977), p. 400.

12 See Michael Baron's fine reading of this conclusion in his *Language and
   Relationship in Wordsworth's Writing* (London/NY: Longman, 1995). Baron
   stresses the significance of the final dash (present only in the 1800
   edition), suggesting that it might be read in two ways, the second of which
   ('an invitation to the reader to complete the poem himself or herself' (p.
   41)) is relevant to my essay's argument.

13 Jonathan Wordsworth, *The Music of Humanity: A Critical Study of
   Wordsworth's* Ruined Cottage ... (London: Nelson, 1969), p. 82.

14 'Introduction' to *Poems of Wordsworth*; in McMaster, *William Wordsworth:
   A Critical Anthology*, p. 233.

15 '*Ter Conatus*'; in Bernard O'Donoghue, *Here Nor There* (London: Chatto and
   Windus, 1999), p. 52.

16 Frederick Garber, *Wordsworth and the Poetry of Encounter* (Urbana, Ill.:
   University of Illinois Press, 1971), p. 28.

17 Garber, *Wordsworth and the Poetry of Encounter*, p. 39.

18 W. B. Yeats, *A Vision* (London: Macmillan, 1937), p. 25.

19 *Letters of Charles and Mary Anne Lamb*, i.265.

20 Paul de Man, 'Time and History in Wordsworth', *Diacritics* 17:4 (Winter,
   1987) 4–17, p. 7.

21 Geoffrey H. Hartman, *Wordsworth's Poetry 1787–1814* (New Haven, Conn.:
   Yale University Press, 1964; repr., 1971), p. 143.

7
Wordsworth's Loves of the Plants
Nicola Trott

(i) Sacred nature

When Wordsworth began writing *Lyrical Ballads*, he was flush with his newly conferred status as the philosophic poet of *The Recluse*. His epic 'plan' was announced, in a letter to a friend, at the very moment that his sister's Journal recorded the earliest signs of spring (6 March, 1798: *EY*, p. 212; *DWJ*, i.11); and it was 'the first mild day of March' which suggested the first lyrical ballad of the new poetic 'season' also ('Lines written at a small distance from my House': ll.1, 28). This coincidence is important: the originality of the 1798 collection has been much disputed; but in one respect, at least, it could hardly fail to be unique, since its borrowings from widely-imitated models in the magazine-poetry of the period were idiosyncratically combined with wholly private formulations deriving from *The Recluse*.

Happily, Wordsworth's manuscripts register the impact of his new philosophical role. In early 1798, another kind of poetic 'experiment' was going on side-by-side with that of the lyrical ballads: the tragic story of 'The Ruined Cottage' turned, almost overnight, into a case history for *The Recluse*; and the optimistic philosophy which inspired Wordsworth's epic intentions demanded a drastic plot-reversal. Existing material was not especially promising: the Pedlar–narrator had left off, bleakly, the previous summer, by commemorating Margaret as the 'Last human tenant of these ruined walls'. Now he had to become the spokesperson for meditative 'happiness'. Even more improbably, he had to announce this peripetaeia on no sounder a basis than his sight of a 'spear-grass' growing on a broken wall. By the Pedlar's own account, this improbable object proved a source of lasting consolation: 'So still an image of tranquillity' was fixed in

141

itself, but also the means by which a corresponding 'calm' was 'convey[ed]' from natural form to human heart ('Ruined Cottage', ll.492, 525, 514–18). Once there, the image was able to soften the prior, exclusively human, sympathy with grief and pain. And, in concluding lines that were drafted by 10 March, 1798, and later discarded, the Pedlar's memory of the 'spear-grass' led him to make the following observations:

> Not useless do I deem
> These quiet sympathies with things that hold
> An inarticulate language, for the man
> Once taught to love such objects as excite
> No morbid passions, no disquietude ... cannot choose
> But seek for objects of a kindred love
> In fellow-natures ...

> > > (ll.1–11; Gill, p. 678)

The grass has now been generalized into 'things that hold / An inarticulate language'. That plants should be objects of love is sufficiently extraordinary. But the Pedlar makes a further, and still stranger, assertion: that this species of floraphilia necessarily makes for a growth in philanthropy, or a search for 'objects of a kindred love / In fellow-natures'.

Wordsworth has already arrived at the thesis he will later state, more succinctly, as 'Love of Nature Leading to Love of Mankind' (the title of *Prelude* Book VIII). In the earliest *Recluse* materials, his phrasing has the ungainly insistence of the recent convert; but the world-view is secure enough to produce a creed – 'There is an active principle alive in all things', another manuscript draft proclaims, running over the pentameter line-ending in its enthusiasm – and a benignly circular logic: given that there is a benevolent 'Spirit' in all things, all things are as one, 'from link to link / It circulates the soul of all the worlds'; and the love of natural objects, which best reflect that benevolence, will ensure that 'we shall move / From strict necessity along the path / Of order and of good'.[1]

In the context of *The Recluse*, nature is both holy and holistic. However, Wordsworth's testing of this ideology emerges almost in the same instant as the project itself.[2] 'Lines written in early spring', written – that is, just a month after the Pedlar's lines quoted above – are as close to the spirit of *The Recluse* as a lyrical ballad can get; yet here the speaker's experience of the theology – his trusting acceptance that 'To her fair works did nature link / The human soul that through me ran' – suffers a sinister reversal from his own thought-processes: 'And much it griev'd my heart to think / What man has made of man' (ll.5–8). Human thoughts and human behaviour combine to break the chain that ties the speaker to the world. The fairness of nature is despoiled by the foulness of man. Wordsworth's refrain is adapted from Burns's 'Man was Made to Mourn, a Dirge', with its outspoken questioning of social injustice: 'Or why has Man the will and pow'r / To make his fellow mourn?' (ll.71–2).[3] When these same lines surfaced in the phrasing of the Pedlar's blank verse, about a month earlier, the necessary optimism was upheld: tellingly, natural forms were found to 'give the will / And power which by a [   ] chain of good / Shall link us to our kind'.[4] Now, though, the 'sweet air of futurity', which *The Recluse* predictably and hopefully 'breathe[s]',[5] has been poisoned by a balladic apprehension of the dark side of life.

'Credal lyrics', Richard E. Matlak's useful name for poems of the type to which the 'Lines written in early spring' belong,[6] does not quite prepare us for the effect of this ballad component; or for the schematic opposition it produces between natural pleasure and human pain. And yet the speaker's conviction remains in place: ''tis my faith that every flower / Enjoys the air it breathes' (ll.11–12). Matters of 'faith' are more than merely fanciful. They do, however, demand a leap, here, to a belief in the 'pleasure' of plants (plant-life being the poet's wishful synecdoche for nature in general). The notion that flowers 'breathe', on the other hand, is taken as a matter of fact. In this case, Wordsworth's matter-of-factness probably rests on a scientific basis: Erasmus Darwin, whom he was reading at this moment in connection with both *Lyrical Ballads* and *The Recluse*,[7] refers to leaves as the 'lungs' of plants in a lengthy note on the subject of 'Vegetable Respiration'.[8] While the 'pleasure' principle adds a distinctively Wordsworthian quality of life to the 'Lines' (ll.16, 20), it also assumes with Darwin that there is no essential difference between vegetative and animal life.[9] At the same time, it assumes more than Darwin's argument from 'analogy'[10] is willing to allow – the redemptive 'creed' of *The Recluse* requiring that the analogical theory of contemporary science be replaced by a God-given *identity* of man and nature.

Nevertheless, it is just this claim to unity that Wordsworth challenges. In the Pedlar's lines, love of plants leads to love of man. In Wordsworth's 'Lines', it leads to a 'lament' for man (l.23). To this extent, the poem is his first response to the disturbing example of 'The

Ancient Mariner', finished on 23 March (*DWJ*, i.13): even as Coleridge's Unitarian theology was being established as the basis of the philosophical *Recluse*, it was also undergoing torture and trial, in the tale of his archaic alter-ego, the Mariner. The Wordsworthian division of mind arises out of the speaker's reluctant admission of a sad and superior realism, the reality being that much suffering is inflicted rather than strictly necessary. That kind of cruelty escapes the jurisdiction of a sacred nature, but is still, apparently, part of *human* nature. Unlike *The Recluse*, then, the lyrical ballad shows the strain involved in maintaining the 'plan' of its 'creed', its speaker has 'thoughts' he 'may not prevent' ('Lines', ll.21–2). These 'thoughts' may be seen as coming from the ballad form itself: the undermining of confidence is partly, it seems, a function of genre; but they also involve Wordsworth's complicating resistance to the totalizing optimism on whose ground the 'plan' of *The Recluse* has so recently been laid.

'Nutting' inherits this resistance; and finds Wordsworth revealingly at cross-purposes in all sorts of other ways as well. For one thing, its composition, in Germany, at the end of 1798, is suggestively poised between the first and second editions of *Lyrical Ballads*. For another, it is connected at once with the thinking of *The Recluse*, and with the emergent identity of the earliest *Prelude* episodes. Finally, though, it belongs with neither of these works in progress, but with Wordsworth's first named collection, the 1800 *Lyrical Ballads*, where, however, it appears as an autobiographical 'fragment', its anomalousness underlined by a half-line opening, and a footnote uniquely identifying the situation as Wordsworth's own (*LBM*, p. 296).

Though it starts innocently enough, 'Nutting' quickly establishes an air of artifice in language and action: the boy going nutting in bramble-proof clothing becomes 'a Figure quaint, / Trick'd out in proud disguise of Beggar's weeds / Put on for the occasion'. His 'Motley accoutrement' (ll.7–11) jests in the manner of Spenser, and entertains the same kind of affectionate mock-heroizing of the boyish adventurer as is found in the early *Prelude* drafts. Here, though, the dressing-up leads to a more extended sort of roleplay. The sacred bower is discovered, or penetrated, almost at once: 'I forc'd my way / Until, at length, I came to one dear nook / Unvisited' (ll.14–16). The effort involved is a 'sign' of things to come. That the boy's ultimate intentions are not in doubt is cunningly implied by the way in which the bower is first described: the negative expression of its perfection – 'not a broken bough / Droop'd with its wither'd leaves' (ll.16–17) –

ensures that the destruction which has not yet happened already exists in thought. The reader is inevitably drawn to the catastrophe – the sudden act of 'ravage' starting at line 42 – but the great bulk of the poem is given up to delay. Between the thought and the action, surprisingly, lies a waiting game.

The delaying tactics appear in different guises and voices.[11] The adult narrator contributes in the form of digressive surmise ('Perhaps it was a bower...': l.29) and selective generalization ('A temper known to those...': l.26). The child's hanging back, meanwhile, is registered in the taut suspensiveness and hesitancy of the line-endings ('hung, / A virgin scene', 'I stood, / Breathing', 'eyed / The banquet': ll.19–24). The romance fantasy, from which both boy and poem set out, offers a means of delay, but also of escape from normal constraints. As his 'Beggar[ly]' yet 'proud disguise' seems to prompt, the child assumes two, quite contrary roles. In the first, he is a shepherd, 'nutting crook in hand' (l.6), and acting on the traditional association of hazels with shepherding. In the second, he is a sexual adept, startlingly miming the practised responses of the voluptuary. The first role is taken up in a pastoral interlude, during which 'green stones', under the watchful eye of the 'shepherd'-boy who is lying among them, are seen as 'fleec'd with moss' and 'scatter'd like a flock of sheep' (ll.34–6). The second role is more complex and disturbing, since it involves the feigning of innocence for the purpose of heightening the experience of pleasure. It comes as something of a shock to find 'joy', that keyword of the Alfoxden ballads – see the rhyme-scheme of 'The Idiot Boy' (ll.86, 388, 401, 406), and 'the deep power' of 'Lines written ... above Tintern Abbey' (l.49) – being adapted to a consciously sophisticated and deferred gratification: 'such suppression of the heart / As joy delights in' ('Nutting', ll.21–2). Faced with the overwhelming beauty of the bower, the boy assumes a 'wise restraint / Voluptuous' (ll.22–3). In this superbly judged Miltonic construction, a noun is surrounded by contrary adjectives, in order that the artfulness of language may draw attention to a parallel complexity of manner. The child's wisdom comes laden with connotations imported from the disguised figure of Satan in Paradise;[12] the reining-in represented by the enjambment allows a full, Latinate, luxuriousness to be released in 'Voluptuous'; while its oxymoronic tension with the 'wise restraint' knowingly places discipline in the service of desire.

This pent-up energy is finally released from its perplexity by an assumed carelessness. Immediately before the act of ravage, the 'heart' is observed 'luxuriat[ing] with indifferent things, / Wasting its kindliness on stocks and stones' – a combination of stock phrase[13] and transferred epithet that catches the moment at which a callousness or nonchalance towards the beauty of the surroundings emerges. In addition to the uneasy completeness of the 'ease' with which the boy plays, there is a lurking awareness of his lack of a definitive object of sympathy, comparable, perhaps, to the vision of vacant beauty in 'Lines left upon a Seat in a Yew-tree'.[14] In the context of *The Recluse*, stocks and stones had led to 'objects of a kindred love'; here, such 'kindliness' is merely 'Wast[ed]' (as the homocentrism of 'kind' deftly insinuates). Where affective excess and objective inadequacy meet, violence suddenly erupts, unleashed by laborious force in an entirely monosyllabic line: 'Then up I rose, / And dragg'd to earth both branch and bough, with crash / And merciless ravage' (ll.39–44). Yet no sooner have the hazels yielded to the destroyer than they are, painfully, humanized: 'Deform'd and sullied', they 'patiently gave up / Their quiet being' (ll.46–7), a passive action which echoes the moment in the Passion when Christ 'gave up the ghost' (Mark, 15.37). In a language that is heavy with both moral opprobrium and moral ambivalence, the desecrated bower yields a crop of moral knowledge, in which 'wealth' and 'pain' coincide (ll.50–1). This is, as it were, the experienced forerunner of Keats's *Ode on Melancholy*, where the way of restraint promises the ultimate indulgence, yet also reveals the inescapable mutuality of loss and gain.

The final lines of 'Nutting' move into the present tense and – as has often been remarked – into a most unexpected address to the 'Maiden' for whose edification the tale has apparently been told: 'Then, dearest Maiden! move along these shades / In gentleness of heart with gentle hand / Touch, – for there is a Spirit in the woods' (ll.53–5). A tentativeness of gesture – the 'hand' made to 'Touch' across a line-ending – offsets the imperative mood; but the poet's authority rests on a thesis, or theology, whose tautological circularity is familiar from the *Recluse* drafts of early 1798: 'gentleness of heart' leads to a 'gentle hand', and both are underwritten by the assertion of a 'Spirit' in nature. While the 'Spirit' returns to the echo of Christ's suffering ghost, the sexual specificity of the 'Maiden' corresponds to the 'virgin scene' discovered in line 20.

And yet this innocent nature is only half the story. If the Pedlar's floraphilia was immersed in Coleridgean theology, the presence of Erasmus Darwin, in the 'Lines written in early spring', has already suggested another, and altogether racier, love of plants.

(ii) Sexual nature

When Don Juan first falls in love, Byron casts him as a Wordsworthian nature-worshipper, wandering narcissistically among 'glassy brooks', while the narrator puts the Lake-poet and his public back on track: 'If *you* think 'twas philosophy that this did, / I can't help thinking puberty assisted'.[15] But Byron's taunting of Wordsworth for his ignorance of sex has itself to ignore the sexy case of 'Nutting'. There, the ecstatic exclamation, 'A virgin scene!', is made in response to a markedly priapic display: 'the hazels rose / Tall and erect' (ll.18–20).

As both Wordsworth and Coleridge were aware, contemporary botany was based entirely upon sexual reproduction. The 'Sexual System', as it was called, was the unlikely brainchild of a Swedish Calvinist, Carl Linnaeus, who developed existing knowledge into a comprehensive taxonomy.[16] Linnaeus's method involved 'classifying plants solely by the number of stamens and pistils', or male and female parts.[17] As a result, 'the precise description of their organs of generation, became the explicit focus of botanical research and illustration'.[18] The simplicity of the system – to say nothing of its other attractions – made it widely practised, especially among women, whose ancient decorative association with flowers was given a new, and controversial, lease of life: 'Flora' had re-emerged as a scientific classification.[19] Since botanists habitually used terminology deriving from anatomy, plant reproduction quickly cross-fertilized with the human variety. (It still does: witness the aural pun in the punk band 'Sex Pistols'.) The aptly named Hugh Rose, who translated Linnaeus in *The Elements of Botany* (1775), could hardly have been more overt:

> The calyx then is the marriage bed, the corolla the curtains, the filaments the spermatic vessels, the antherae the testicles, the dust the male sperm, the stigma the extremity of the female organ, the style the vagina, the germen the ovary, the pericarpium the ovary impregnated, the seeds the ovula or eggs.[20]

Despite being restricted to the 'marriage'-relation (the most quaint thing, perhaps, to modern ears), the Linnaean system had to stretch its governing metaphor to allow for the enormous variety thrown up by botanical specimens. To some extent, then, it was able to disguise the sexual threat while presenting diverse and amusing permutations on the marriage-tie: 'intermarriages', polyandry, polygamy, promiscuity, adultery, even, though no explicit homosexuality is available, 'feminine males', as Erasmus Darwin called them (*gynandria*, which occur where stamens are attached to the pistil).

Darwin's versification of Linnaeus, *The Loves of the Plants*,[21] made botany one of the fine arts. It also, as Tim Fulford points out, further 'elaborated upon the Swede's analogies between plant reproduction and human promiscuity'.[22] Darwin's title suggests the euphemism and the anthropomorphism of the enterprise: by translating 'stamens' and 'pistils' into men and women, rather than sexual parts as such, *The Loves of the Plants* turned the language of flowers into a codified way of discussing social as well as sexual relations. By implication, the two were nearly identical. Like the plants whose reproductive behaviour they themselves reproduced, Darwin's human beings were governed by 'Nature's laws' (*Loves of the Plants*, IV, l.406). This idea of nature was both sacred *and* sexual – or rather, the sacred was the sex-drive, the generative principle that the life-sciences were discerning throughout the vegetable and animal worlds. In Darwin, then, the modern Tree of Knowledge was to be found among the 'Paphian groves' (*The Economy of Vegetation*, IV, l.441).

Thanks largely to *The Loves of the Plants*, botany entered mainstream culture in a surprising variety of forms. In a lighthearted vein, the Revd James Plumptre's comic opera, *The Lakers* (1798), invented a loco-botanical plot. Combining scenery- with husband-hunting, Plumptre's heroine set off, Claude-glass and guide-book in hand, to take in a spot of sexual tourism along with her more conventional round of the Lake District 'stations' recommended by West, Gilpin, and Gray. To gardening types, Beccabunga Veronica was recognizable from her name alone: a genuine Linnaean classification, she is a 'succulent' variety of veronica, and a diandria monogynia, whose flowers – appropriately enough, given her predelictions – show two males to a single female.[23]

In a less genial mood, botany provided ammunition for the ongoing ideological crossfire of the 1790s. The 'Sexual System' was a useful addition to the anti-jacobin armoury.[24] That Wordsworth picked up on the pejorative connotations is clear from 'A Poet's Epitaph' (one of the 1800 *Lyrical Ballads*, and written about the same time as 'Nutting'), which caricatured the 'sensual' or materialist 'Philosopher' as 'a fingering slave, / One that would peep and botanize / Upon his mother's grave' (ll.18–21). For those with ears to hear, the second verb, consciously modish and slangy,[25] added a certain incestuous insult to the injury. In addition to Darwin, Wordsworth quite possibly had William Godwin, his former mentor and jacobin philosopher *par excellence*, in mind.[26] Botany had surfaced even more viciously in the aftermath of Godwin's *Memoirs* of his dead wife and lover, Mary Wollstonecraft. Wordsworth received a copy on 14 April, 1798 (*DWJ*, i.15); and later that same year it provided the story-line for Richard Polwhele's couplet-satire, *The Unsex'd Females*, which sought to ruin Wollstonecraft's posthumous reputation by putting her in bed, so to speak, with Erasmus Darwin. The existing association of botany with sexual experience, its fashionable role in the education of young ladies, and its advocacy as a subject of study by Wollstonecraft herself,[27] all contrived to turn 'botany' into a trope for her adventurous sexual history, as narrated by Godwin.

Polwhele, a clergyman–poet, recognized in Darwin's *Botanic Garden* the Fall of woman into knowledge, and set about returning the Dissenter's version of the myth to its biblical roots. 'With bliss botanic as their bosoms heave', his precocious girls 'Still pluck forbidden fruit, with mother Eve'. Their interest in the fruit being more than gastronomic, they 'Dissect its organ of unhallow'd lust, / And fondly gaze the titillating dust'.[28] 'Dust' or pollen is Linnaean code for sperm, and, as Polwhele's annotation implies, this is a scene of (figurative) impregnation.[29] The botanical Tree of Knowledge is expressly encrypted into bourgeois life in some lines that Coleridge (who later regretted 'the sneers against women who study Botany'; *NB*, ii.2600) is thought to have written, in 1801, during the parliamentary scandal and debate surrounding the Adultery Prevention Bill:

> Botanic science charms sweet Miss,
> She views the flow'r's enraptur'd kiss,
>   And rolls a sparkling eye;
> ANTHER, and PISTIL, she explains,
> And dear delicious knowledge gains,
> Mamma sits smiling by.[30]

Cutting out the decorous euphemism of Darwin, Coleridge has an unmarried daughter refer her unwitting mother directly to the male and female organs. The invidiousness of the scene lies in its very domesticity, just as the source of knowledge seems innocuous because it, too, is homely or indigenous: this 'Forbidden fruit on hawthorn blows'.[31] Much like a Lake District hazel, in short.

Critics have recently given up thinking of Wordsworth's hazel bower as straightforwardly female, and, with varying degrees of ingenuity, have sought to explain its sexual characteristics.[32] Botanically speaking, the trees are precisely heterosexual, in that the nuts the boy gathers are the fruit of the union of male and female parts (and the hazel, or *Corylus avellana*, is heavily sexed: an octandria digynia, its flowers boast eight males and two females). Enviably well-endowed in the poet's memory, 'the hazels rose / Tall and erect, with milk-white clusters hung'; and yet they are addressed as 'A virgin scene!' Wordsworth's bower is sexualized, from two opposite directions, and in immediately juxtaposed lines (ll.18–20).

The ambiguous ground on which both these sexualizations meet recalls Milton's Eden, 'where delicious Paradise ... crowns with her enclosure green, / As with a rural mound, the champaign head / Of a steep wilderness, whose hairy sides / With thicket overgrown, grotesque and wild, / Access denied'.[33] Milton's grafting of experience onto innocence had horticultural offshoots, as, for instance, in Samuel Collins's work, entitled *Paradise Retriev'd* (1717), and 'demonstrating the most beautiful, durable, and beneficial method of managing and improving fruit-trees'. The hazel, for its part, came of rich folkloric stock, according to Geoffrey Grigson: though its catkins prompted the innocent nick-name of Lamb's Tails, in Ireland it was called the Tree of Knowledge. Belief in its supernatural protection made hazel the proper material for all rods of power; and these magical and taboo properties may add to the air of trespass in Wordsworth's poem: in the ballad of Hind Etin, the demon or elf guards the unripe hazel-nuts from May Margret, whom he at first threatens to kill and then takes as a fertile wife.[34] But Wordsworth's sharpest awareness of the nutting-scene as a sexual encounter would have come from the highly literary landscape cultivated by the georgic tradition: in Thomson's *Seasons*, 'Autumn' calls upon its 'swains [to] hasten to the hazel-bank'. While their 'active vigour crushes down the tree', a feminine fruitfulness falls 'ripe from the resigning husk', with a maturity that is 'of an ardent brown, / As are the ringlets of Melinda's hair'. The 'secret shade', the 'virgins' whose dress is 'Fit for the thickets and the tangling shrub', the tree-crushing, and the final resignation or surrender, are all transposed onto the solitary pursuits of the Wordsworthian child.[35]

If Thomson's is the invigorating example, it is perhaps because his untroubled, adult virility allows for such compelling disturbances. That Wordsworth requires a pastoral simplicity against which his own complexities can register themselves is again apparent in 'Ruth', another poem from the Goslar period which looks back to English scenery. Slighted by her father, Ruth has from childhood 'built a bower upon the green', and, like the purest sort of nature-poet, plays entirely neutral tones, 'of winds and floods', upon an 'oaten pipe' (ll.8–10). Yet her name brings with it the shadow of sexual deflowering and sorrow, and it is her very proximity to the natural that makes her at once attractive and vulnerable to another kind of wildness. Like 'Christabel', 'Ruth' dramatizes the mysterious crossing-over of uncorrupted innocence into morally ambiguous territory. Unlike Christabel, Ruth has a conventional tempter, 'a Youth from Georgia's shore', whose tales of life among the Indians match Othello's exotic 'dangers' (ll.13, 37–42);[36] but the means of her seduction comes as something of a surprise:

> He spake of plants divine and strange
> That ev'ry day their blossoms change,
> Ten thousand lovely hues!
> With budding, fading, faded flowers
> They stand the wonder of the bowers
> From morn to evening dews.
>
> (ll.49–54)

These lines rely on a traditional sexual symbolism – and, amid all their exquisite 'change', foretell of the withering of love: the verbal triad of 'budding, fading, faded flowers' ominously reverses the perpetual blossoming of Milton's Eden, while the tropical climate briefly re-enacts the daylong fall of Mulciber, 'from morn / To noon he fell, from noon to dewy eve'.[37] A more interesting, and unexpected, development occurs when the narrator turns to record the prior effects of the American landscape on the Youth himself. What emerges is not a single but a double seduction, of the Youth as well as of Ruth, and by precisely similar means:

> Nor less to feed voluptuous thought
> The beauteous forms of Nature wrought,
> Fair trees and lovely flowers;
> The breezes their own languor lent,
> The stars had feelings which they sent
> Into those magic bowers.
>
> (ll.127–32)

Repeating the process maximizes the felt beauty of the temptation – such entwinings of erotic abandonment and energy have rarely been equalled (except, perhaps, by Tennyson: 'Now sleeps the crimson petal, now the white...'). As the repetition also makes clear, it is the *plants* that are the seducers here, their 'inarticulate language' having suddenly become all too articulate and 'dangerous' (l.117).

Among the Youth's exotica Americana, three plants are specified: 'the Magnolia, spread / High as a cloud, high over head', 'The Cypress and her spire' – a gender fusion comparable to that of 'Nutting'[38] – and the azalea with its 'scarlet gleam' (ll.55–8). Wordsworth's note in the 1800 *Ballads* refers the reader to Bartram, as the source from which his flora are taken. In doing so, it identifies, not just a book of 'Travels', but a work in which a virgin territory has been mapped and botanized.[39] If 'Ruth' exchanges a 'green shade' for magnolias 'High as a cloud' and 'flowers that ... seem / To set the hills on fire', it is because the poem represents a kind of sexual progression, from a virginal English pastoralism to the dreamy sensuousness and fiery passion of 'savage lands' (ll.41, 56–60, 112). The movement towards arousal is extremely deft; but a similar, if much more overt, botanical progression takes place in Darwin: calling on the sylphs 'who fan the Paphian groves' (that is, the pollen-bearing breezes) to awaken nature to life, his verse proceeds from 'slumbering Snow-drop' to 'pale Primrose' and 'bashful Violet', to the more 'playful Tulip' and 'blushing' Carnation; until at last the 'silken curtains' enfolding the 'virgin *Style*' are parted, and 'bursting *Anthers* trust / To the mild breezes their prolific dust' (*The Economy of Vegetation*, IV, ll.441–54). This orchestration of the rites of spring effectively simulates a sexual climax. Lest the reader be left in any doubt, a note eagerly supplies Darwin's latest instance of plant-promiscuity: 'I was this morning surprised to observe, amongst Sir Brooke Boothby's valuable collection of plants at Ashbourn, the manifest adultery of several females of the plant Collinsonia, who had bent themselves into contact with the males of other flowers of the same plant in their vicinity, neglectful of their own' (*Economy of Vegetation*, IV, l.455n.).

This very passage, together with its annotation, is used by Polwhele in recording 'the manifest adultery' of Mary Wollstonecraft with the married Fuseli and, equally scandalously, her affair with the unmarried Imlay, with whom she had a child, in revolutionary France: transferring her affections from one to the other, in Polwhele's version of 'the Paphian grove', 'the Fair-one greets the bower, / And ravishes a flame from every flower'.[40] 'Ruth', notably, urges the seductiveness of the flamy azalea; and is concerned with how the 'Irregular in sight or sound' is carried over into sexual relations: the Youth's return to the wild is complete when 'once again he wish'd to live / As lawless as before' (ll.122, 161–2); and 'lawlessness' is Wordsworth's code for infidelity or polygamy – in spring 1798, it was Peter Bell, of 'lawless' men 'the wildest far of all', who serio-comically had no fewer than 'a dozen wedded wives' (*Peter Bell*, ll.246, 249, 250). Here as elsewhere, readers may feel that, however remotely, Wordsworth's lingering qualms about his own sexual history find an echo. The larger point to be made is that his crossing of Bartram's *Travels* with Darwinian botany returns us to the divisions within his attitude to nature.

In the grand climax of *The Loves of the Plants*, 'the Loves laugh at all, but Nature's laws' (IV, 1.406). Although for variety's sake it has disrupted the Linnaean taxonomic order, the poem as a whole has observed a progression from monogamy to promiscuity, beginning with the strictly faithful *Canna* or Indian Reed (I, ll.39–44) – one male, one female (a plant, incidentally, that Bartram illustrates[41]) – and ending with the riotously active *Adonis* or Pheasant's Eye, which presents 100 sexual pairings in a single flower, and which in turn elicits Darwin's final sociological comparison, to life among the Tahitians: 'The society called the Areoi in the island of Otaheite consists of about 100 males and 100 females who form one promiscuous marriage' (IV, ll.387–406; IV, 1.388n.). Led by the goddess of Botany, the poem has arrived at a model of natural sexual organization, common to the *Adonis* and Tahitians alike.

Darwin's anthropology of plants was no doubt aided by his own passions, since at the time of writing he was also declaring his love for Elizabeth Pole, the married lady who was to become his second wife (and the third woman to bear his children). It also welcomed the wider ramifications or analogies between the observations of modern science and the allegorizing of 'heathen mythology' or the study of 'primitive' cultures.[42] 'Ruth', on the other hand, dramatizes a deep ambivalence about the primitivist impulse, and the idea of nature which promotes it. Its shorthand for that impulse is Rousseau, or rather the popular idea of the 'noble savage'; and the presence of Rousseau brings together the Youth's primitivism with both his revolutionary and his sexual experience. It also, though how consciously is hard to say, brings all three elements into contact with botanical science, since Rousseau himself wrote some well-known *Letters on Botany* which were a target of anti-jacobin jibes.[43] The 1805 edition of *Lyrical Ballads* underlines the Youth's vision of America as a moment of Rousseauist, and revolutionary, liberation: '"It was a fresh and glorious world, / ... I looked upon those hills and plains, / And seemed as if let loose from chains / To live at liberty"' (ll.73, 76–8; *LBM*, p. 278; cf. *WPW*, ii.232, and *app. crit*). In the 1800 edition, he has fought for a 'free' America; but bears with him the symbol of another kind of freedom – a military helmet with a Cherokee head-dress, whose 'feathers nodded in the breeze / And made a gallant crest' – and, in his descent from naturalism to sensualism, becomes at last 'The slave of low desires' (ll.22, 17–18, 147). Professing a Rousseauist ideal (ll.67–78), he instead illustrates the return to nature as an ignoble savagery: 'Nature's laws' cannot, as in Darwin, become man's without becoming 'lawless'.

Wordsworth's Youth is a hybrid, formed by two worlds, the 'Indian' and the 'English' (ll.19–20). Unlike Robert Bage's Hermsprong, who successfully transplants himself from America to Europe, the Youth regresses in the other direction. His American experience parodies the archetypal divine-and-human relationship in which the natural world of 'Frost at Midnight' had hoped to instruct the new-born child. In Coleridge's words, that 'Great universal Teacher ... shall mould / Thy spirit, and by giving make it ask' (ll.63–4; *CPW*, i.242). Wordsworth dares to use the terms of giving and receiving to show mutual contamination:

> Deliberately and undeceiv'd
> Those wild men's vices he receiv'd,
> And gave them back his own.
>
> (ll.142–4)

Love of plants has led to love of man, certainly, but it is love of the wrong kind. The untamed nature of the Americas produces an extraordinary version of the 'interchange' of influence that is *corrupting* rather than redemptive. And in this exception to the schema of natural beneficence, the exception becomes the rule. Unlike Peter Bell, to whom a 'yellow primrose' was 'nothing more' than a flower (*Peter Bell*, ll.219–20), the Youth began life as a lover of the natural world: 'The moon, the glory of the sun, / And streams that murmur as they run / Had been his dearest joy' (ll.28–30). Even in America, it seems, similar feelings are possible: 'For passions link'd to forms so fair / And stately, needs must have their share / Of noble sentiment' (ll.136–8). And yet neither his passions, nor the forms themselves – the 'Nature' which, in 'Lines written ... above Tintern Abbey', had promised 'never [to] betray / The heart that loved her' (ll.123–5) – are redeeming: quite the contrary.[44]

'Those wild men's vices' directly contradict the evidence given by

Bartram, whose Indians 'must ... claim our approbation, if we divest ourselves of prejudice', and 'have been able to resist ... the complicated host of vices, that have for ages over-run the nations of the old world'.[45] In Wordsworth, interestingly, imperialist expansion appears as a contamination, not of the colonized, but of the colonizer and the old country. Ruth never leaves her Somersetshire woods, the Youth deserting her as they are due to board ship; and it is on English soil that he has succumbed to the influence of his American experience. In wooing Ruth, the 'green' girl, the Youth has been drawn to the innocent or natural in himself. In deserting her, he is reverting to a 'wild' self that is also natural (though it has actually been *acquired*). There is, then, an unexpected kinship and attraction between the 'green shade' of Somerset and the 'green Savannahs' of Georgia (ll.41, 61, 106). For all his obvious 'prejudice', Wordsworth brings his wildness dangerously close to home. Why? Perhaps because, here, his testing of *The Recluse*, and a Coleridgean idea of nature, is at its most exacting. Or, putting it another way, perhaps because the Youth's self-contestation, between 'lawful' and 'lawless' natures, suggests Wordsworth's own (ll.107, 162).

As we have seen, Wordsworth is a floraphile through Darwin as well as through Coleridge. In 'Ruth' as in 'Nutting', there are two, antithetical sexualizations in play: one is the perception of nature's innocence, and its destruction and desecration by man; the other, conversely, is the experience of nature's passion, its likeness to man's, and its provocativeness as such. In the first story, nature is 'virgin', signalling man's first entrance on the scene. In the second story, she is 'voluptuous', anticipating and enacting human desire. The first story suggests that man is opposed to nature by virtue of his violent will to power (the straightforward line taken, for instance, by Byron's *Giaour*, ll.46–67). The second story both entertains and questions an anthropomorphic impulse, in ways that reflect disturbingly upon the loves of men.

For Darwin, all life, animal and vegetable, is united by a single generative principle. For Coleridge, on the contrary, all is united by the 'God in nature' ('Fears in Solitude', l.188; *CPW*, i.262). In Wordsworth, both ideas of unity are, for a time, allowed fruitfully to contradict one another: holy plants and sacred nature are disconcertingly coupled with sexy plants and a sexual nature. Together they produce what might be seen as a counter-Unitarian heterogeneity – or, a Unitarian heterodoxy. In Wordsworth's hands, the *Lyrical Ballads* take on the qualities of a hybrid form.

That there are these two 'natures' in Wordsworth is not generally recognized, because he himself marginalizes or moralizes one of them almost out of existence: in Shelley's famous tease, 'He touched the hem of Nature's shift, / Felt faint – and never dared uplift / The closest, all-concealing tunic (*Peter Bell the Third*, ll.315–17).[46] 'Nutting' is 'struck out' of the poem on the poet's own life, where it first arose, 'as not being wanted there' (Fenwick Note; *LBB*, p. 307); 'Ruth' falls for, but then rejects, the call of the wild, leaving Ruth herself, poignantly, to a damaged or deranged imitation of her 'happy' pastoral childhood (l.222). But for all that, it is the unsocialized and uncontaminated energy that Wordsworth relishes in his own primal self-image, 'A naked savage in the thunder-shower' (*Prelude* (1799), I, l.26). Traces of a *sexualized* nature also remain, in extremely potent, though mostly heavily disguised or sublimated forms. At one crucial juncture, however, Wordsworth assimilates the 'sexual system' as a governing metaphor for his own mental life: the 'fructifying virtue' of the 'spots of time', in their earliest appearance, has an inescapable, if now largely invisible, sexual drift, 'fructification' being a technical botanical term and 'the essence of the plant' in Linnaeus's system, providing the 'only characters ... properly to be used in classification above the level of species'.[47] And that distinctive power of creation carries over into the fruitfulness of another line, which is retained in later versions, where the unconscious memories of natural 'scenes' return 'To impregnate and to elevate the mind' (*Prelude* (1799), I, ll.290, 429, 426).

'Three years she grew', the most mythic of the Lucy series, rests on a sexual impulse that is at once creative and mortal. As has been pointed out, the mythic structure of the poem stems from the rape of Proserpina by the king of the underworld: in Milton's lovely synopsis of the story, 'Proserpine gathering flowers / Her self a fairer flower by gloomy Dis / Was gathered, which cost Ceres all that pain / To seek her through the world'.[48] In Wordsworth's re-telling, it is *nature* who takes possession, and of a three-year-old child:

> Three years she grew in sun and shower,
> Then Nature said, 'A lovelier flower
> On earth was never sown;
> This Child I to myself will take,
> She shall be mine, and I will make
> A Lady of my own.[']

(ll.1–6)

'Nature', here, is both nurturing and death-dealing, combining in one ambiguous figure the masculine ravisher Dis and the fertility-goddess Ceres, mother of Proserpina. The fusion is the more powerful because Wordsworth fails to specify the sex of the figure who speaks with such abrupt and capricious authority. 'Nature' envisages giving itself to the child in the mode of a lover, using the gracious devices of erotic poetry: 'The floating clouds their state shall lend / To her, for her the willow bend...' (ll.19–20). And, although this power is itself unsexed or androgynous, the force of its intention is to sexualize Lucy in ways that are already familiar from the bower in 'Nutting': her natural education 'Shall rear her form to stately height, / Her virgin bosom swell'. As in 'Nutting', however, the verge of maturity is also the moment of sacrifice: 'Thus Nature spake – The work was done – / How soon my Lucy's race was run!' (ll.32–3, 37–8). The age at which Lucy is claimed is certain; the age of her death is not; and yet the two are finally made to seem almost simultaneous, just as the poem itself is simultaneously love lyric and elegy or epitaph.

The girl's maturation has been imagined as a delicate symmetry of equal and opposite forces: moulded by 'an overseeing power / To kindle or restrain', she 'shall be sportive as the fawn', yet gifted with 'the silence and the calm / Of mute insensate things' (ll.11–13, 17–18). Significantly, Nature echoes the Pedlar's praise for 'quiet sympathies with things that hold / An inarticulate language'. Now, though, the floraphilia of *The Recluse* has become entangled with the myth of Proserpina's abduction, 'Her self a fairer flower'. Lucy's life-cycle is determined by an eerie convergence of Wordsworth's sacred and sexual natures. The Ovidian trope which turns the human form into a 'flower' effloresces in the girl's immaculate openness to natural influence: 'And beauty born of murmuring sound / Shall pass into her face' (ll.29–30). But her beautiful receptiveness is also a kind of extinction, as though she were already more than half assimilated to the earth – or, to put it another way, as though she were becoming an allegorical figure for natural process. As such she approximates the interpretation of classical myth, including as it happens 'the Rape of Proserpine', which is proposed by Darwin's *Economy of Vegetation*.[49] In Wordsworth, Nature's deathly possessiveness produces a nature that is both possessed by, and dead to, the poet: in the devastating litotes of the ending, 'She died and left to me / This heath, this calm and quiet scene' (ll.39–40). Here as elsewhere in the Lucy cycle and in 'There was a Boy', a fear of absorption gives a sinister bent to the quiet and beneficent sympathies of *The Recluse*. Equally, one might say that, as in 'Ruth', it is the sexual and seductive in nature that is finally extinguished.

(iii) Home at Grasmere

The Wordsworth who was reflecting on his creation and education by natural agencies, in the *Prelude* drafts of 1799, seems to have required these lyrical ballads as more extreme examples of his own case. Their enigmatic dramatizations of sexual disturbance and its suppression continue into the ballads of 1800; except that, there, the story is consciously taken up as a narrative of domestication.

The Youth who roamed 'through savage lands' also imagined that he and Ruth would 'find / A home in every glade' ('Ruth', ll.112, 71–2). This possibility of a domestic pastoral gathers a new impetus in Wordsworth's Grasmere poems. The paradigmatic homing poem is 'Hart-Leap Well', the first work of the fresh volume in *Lyrical Ballads* (1800). For one thing, it is occasioned as Wordsworth and his sister approach their new home at Grasmere, and written shortly after their arrival. For another, it has connections with lines composed, as part of *The Recluse*, for 'Home at Grasmere' itself (see *WPW*, ii.514–15). Most of all, it seeks to erase the traces of a sexual nature. A country-squire Kubla Khan, Sir Walter decrees 'a Pleasure-house upon [the] spot' where the hart has died and his own heartless 'chace' has come to an end (ll.57, 25). At the spring where the animal has perished, nature is constrained to offer a passable imitation of herself:

> And near the fountain, flowers of stature tall
> With trailing plants and trees were intertwin'd,
> Which soon composed a little sylvan hall,
> A leafy shelter from the sun and wind.

> And thither, when the summer days were long,
> Sir Walter journey'd with his paramour;
> And with the dancers and the minstrel's song
> Made merriment within that pleasant bower.

> (ll.85–92)

The artfulness with which the bower is 'composed', its Latinate and architectural motif, and, still more, those priapic and entwining plants, give the game away. Nature here is not only sexual, she is a

kind of courtesan, acting in concert with the 'paramour' for the pleasure of the man who has has brought them together. This sexualizing
of nature celebrates its compliance with the sensual desire which
follows on from the savage aggression of the chase. But, in the second
part of the poem, this imposed sexuality is doubly erased. Left to its
own devices after Sir Walter's death, the landscape becomes termi-
nally ill: 'It seem'd as if the spring-time came not here, / And Nature
here was willing to decay' (ll.115–16). This unnaturalness is taken by
the poet as a sign of supernatural intervention – a purging of the
ground which confirms his own, *Recluse*-inspired, belief that 'The
Being, that is in the clouds and air, / That is in the green leaves among
the groves, / Maintains a deep and reverential care / For them the
quiet creatures whom he loves' (ll.165–8). The poet's importation of
the hopeful 'creed' of *The Recluse* makes possible his prediction of
another, more effective and natural sort of erasure: the phase of
perishing or mourning will eventually give way to oblivion, and
'These monuments shall all be overgrown' (ll.162, 176).

The renewal of growth, in a restored harmony of man and nature,
and the purging from both of their disturbing sexual content, are
closely tied up with Wordsworth's move to Grasmere. 'Sir William
[Fleming]', the regenerate Sir Walter of the 'Lines written with a Slate-
pencil upon a Stone', makes the point: he leaves 'monuments of his
unfinish'd task' for a 'pleasure-house' to be commended by the
natural medium of the poet and taken over by 'the bramble and the
rose', 'the linnet and the thrush, / And other little builders who dwell
here' (ll. 8, 13, 6, 33, 18–19). These 'Lines' utter the poet's first public
strictures against the 'blaze' of 'snow-white' buildings in a Lake
District landscape, while at the same time quietly assuming the
propriety of his own imaginary inscription (ll.30–1). In building *their*
new home, the Wordsworths were prompted to a new and vivid
curiosity about the local flora: on 16 May, 1800, Dorothy, who was
busy gathering wild specimens for the garden at Dove Cottage,
exclaimed 'Oh! that we had a book of botany' (*DWJ*, i.38); by 7
August, her brother's Longman account had been charged for two
botanical microscopes and two copies of *An Arrangement of British
Plants* by William Withering.[50] Evidence of Withering's role in
Coleridge's enthusiasm for the region he had so recently come to
know is provided by the reams of common plant-names which Sara
Hutchinson was soon transcribing into the *Notebooks* (*CN*, ii.863 and
n.).

Wordsworth, meanwhile, had already found 'A home in every glade'

('Ruth', l.72), but was now attempting to take root there. The representation of his domestication or naturalization, in the 1800 *Lyrical Ballads*, takes a number of willed or conscious forms, from the family-group of the 'Poems on the Naming of Places' to the inscribing of local monuments;[51] and from indigenous species of pastoral to the hardy vernacular of the fable. As Mary Moorman has pointed out, this last category had a model in *The Fables of Flora* (1771) by John Langhorne.[52] Once again, then, poetry is being crossed with botany in surprising ways; except that, in 1800, it is the homely associations that are uppermost: like Wordsworth, Langhorne was a Cumbrian with Somerset connections (he was Rector of Blagdon); and, just as Withering's was 'An Arrangement of British Plants', so Langhorne's 'Fables' specialized in the flora of common names and native species.[53] This preference for indigenous or uncultivated varieties enters the poetic landscape that Wordsworth is beginning to define. It also seems to involve a toning down of the sexual language of flowers: in Langhorne's fable, 'The Violet and the Pansy', an inexperienced young bee mistakenly goes to the gaudy garden pansy for nectar, until a wise old drone suggests he try the 'modest flower' instead, 'and to the Violet's breast / The little vagrant faintly flew'. Such implicitly maternal succour is meant to illustrate the wisdom of the opening stanza, which counsels the shepherd whose 'artless breast' is visited by 'the god of fond desires' to 'Implore him for a gentle guest, / Implore him with unwearied prayer'.[54]

A similar prayer to Love frames the story of ''Tis said, that some have died for love', Wordsworth's revival, in a Grasmere setting and pindaric ode-form, of the 'complaints' of the 1798 collection. This dramatization of a lover's grief wonderfully adopts the voice of a man whose 'pretty Barbara' has died and left him restlessly tormented by the liveliness of nature. Last, and worst of all, the eglantine, or briar-rose, appears as a cruel tease, a love-plant that flirtatiously mimes his memory of the woman's body: 'Thou one fair shrub, oh! shed thy flowers, / And stir not in the gale. / For thus to see thee nodding in the air, / To see thy arch thus stretch and bend, / Thus rise and thus descend, / Disturbs me, till the sight is more than I can bear'. Here (if proof were needed) is evidence that a sexual nature is never altogether banished from the scene. Significantly, however, this painfully erotic disturbance is distanced from the poet by the form of the dramatic monologue, which acts as a kind of cordon sanitaire by which he superstitiously hopes to ward off the threat of a similar fate from his own state of 'happiness' with Emma (ll.45, 9, 39–44, 52).

Wordsworth's domestication is associated with a kind of purification. And this, too, has a specific botanical context. Although Withering was necessarily a follower of Linnaeus, he also tried to de-sexualize his terms so as to make his own work more suitable for lady readers – much to Darwin's humorous impatience: '["]Pedunculis axillaxilus" "Flower-Stems in the angles" ... surely in the angles will be as intelligible as armpit, or Groin, or any other delicate Idea'.[55] Withering's purified botany has a discernible influence upon the new *Lyrical Ballads*. Remarkably, Wordsworth twice identifies his Lakeland home with one class of plants in particular. Describing a state of pastoral indolence, he has his idle shepherd-boys occupy themselves, not just with sun-bathing and pipe-playing, but with dressing-up:

> Or with that plant which in our dale
> We call Stag-horn, or Fox's Tail
> Their rusty Hats they trim:
> And thus as happy as the Day,
> Those Shepherds wear the time away.

> ('The Idle Shepherd-Boys, or
> Dungeon-Gill Force, Pastoral', ll.18–22)

Coombe and Coleridge identify the trimming as *Lycopodium clavatum* or 'club-moss' – or, as Withering has it, '*Wolf's-claw*'[56] – though the common names Wordsworth uses are closer to either 'Stag's-horn Cup Lichen' or 'Fox-tail Feather-moss'.[57] All three plants, as it happens, belong to a class called *cryptogamia*, whose sexual activity is cryptic, hidden, invisible to all but prying or botanical eyes: as Darwin puts it in the 'Preface' to *The Loves of the Plants*, 'the word "*secret.*" expresses the Class of Clandestine Marriage'[58] – this marital arrangement being his transliteration of the Latin. Named by Linnaeus, but for obvious reasons not much attended to in his system, the *cryptogamia* are given a great deal of house room in Withering.[59] Discreet and unobtrusive, these 'clandestine' plants suggest the ways in which Wordsworth is beginning to conceive his own, and others', ideal place in the Lakes. And it is in the fourth of his 'Poems on the Naming of Places' that another member of the 'clandestine' class turns up: among many 'Fair ferns and flowers', the poet singles out

> that tall plant
> So stately, of the Queen Osmunda nam'd,
> Plant lovelier in its own retir'd abode

On Grasmere's beach, than Naid by the side
Of Grecian brook, or Lady of the Mere
Sole-sitting by the shores of old Romance.

('A narrow girdle of rough stones and
crags', ll.35–40)

This example of the native 'Royal Fern', *Osmunda regalis*, is growing, as it should, in a shady spot beside the water – where it could have been as much as eight feet 'tall'. Such botanical exactitude sits slightly oddly alongside the poetic fancy that is suggested by the fern's 'stately' appearance. Wordsworth's naming and placing is offered as a tender corrective to the lure of 'old Romance': his local specimen is 'lovelier ... than Naid ... or Lady of the Mere'. But 'the Queen Osmunda' is herself, apparently, an invented figure; and the plant's royal namesake threatens to personify the fern[60] in ways that risk comparison with the fanciful–scientific method of *The Loves of the Plants*: Darwin, too, does 'The fair OSMUNDA', but as an unchaste anchorite, who 'seeks the silent dell, / The ivy canopy, and dripping cell; / There hid in shades *clandestine* rites approves, / Till the green progeny betrays her loves' (I, ll.93–6). Darwin's Osmunda cannot help but 'betray' her sexual meaning, yet, as his note reveals, the fern is as near to privacy as the Linnaean system gets: 'This plant grows on moist rocks; the parts of its flower or its seeds are scarce discernible; whence Linneus has given the name of clandestine marriage to this class. The younger plants are of a beautiful vivid green' (I, l.93n.). Wordsworth's interest in the *cryptogamia* suggests a muting or privatizing of the sexual content so blatantly on display in the era of 'Ruth' and 'Nutting'.

It also suggests that, in its slighter versions at least, the new Wordsworthian pastoral makes for a novel, and partly awkward, hybridization of the realistic programme that is advanced in the 'Preface' to *Lyrical Ballads*. Southey singled out the hat-trimming in 'The Idle Shepherd-Boys' as a contradiction of Wordsworth's wish 'to be considered a faithful painter of rural manners'; but, even as he did so, events triumphantly conspired to prove him wrong: 'Just as the words had passed his lips two boys appeared with the very plant entwined round their hats' (Fenwick Note; *LBB*, p. 303). The subtler objection is not to the falsification of local customs, but to the artifice of the poetic diction; and it is raised by Coleridge in *Biographia* – where however the poem is celebrated precisely for its elevating departure from the 'ordinary language' theory of the 'Preface' (*BL*, ii.105). And Coleridge was right about this divergence of theory from practice: even where they are genuine, the poet's local habitations and names may be literary imports rather than rural idioms. Undoubtedly, the strength and seriousness of the 1800 collection emerges when Wordsworth changes these pastoral notes to tragic: the homecoming, and mourning, that go unrecognized in 'The Brothers', and, in 'Michael', the heartbreak that is mutely yet eloquently traced in the brokenness of the rural architecture. Despite the differences in tone, however, the kinds of attentiveness those poems give to the 'human heart' share with the more fanciful pastorals the dream of a home where the heart is. What the lighter poems show, and the tragic masterpieces work against, is that Wordsworth's homecoming can be a humorous and slightly edgy affair; and that both these qualities gather around a literary language, and manner, that are not always quite at home with 'the manners of rural life' and 'the real language of men' (*WPrW*, i.124, 150). In this sense, then, the works of 1800 recall the pattern established by the sacred-*cum*-sexual nature-poetry of 1798–9, when the 'lyrical ballad' acted as a kind of commentary upon the lofty aspirations of the philosophical verse.

Throughout the period in which the new *Lyrical Ballads* are written, the recurrent tension between Wordsworth's 'faithful[ness]' to nature, and his 'faith' in her – the rival paths, as it were, of 'Preface' and *The Recluse* – is registered, as we have seen, in his poetry of the 'loves of the plants'. In 1799, the 'inarticulate language' of sacred nature had been challenged by the 'dangerous food' of natural sexuality. In 1800, the language of plants has once again become 'inarticulate', but now it is their sexualization that has been subdued.

Notes

1   'There is an active principle ...', ll.1, 9–11; 'Not useless do I deem ...', ll.93–5 (Gill, pp. 676; 680).

2   There is an important sense in which *The Recluse* itself arose out of and responded to such testing: see Kenneth R. Johnston, *Wordsworth and* The Recluse (New Haven, Conn./London: Yale University Press, 1984), chapter 1.

3   Robert Burns, *Poems in Scots and English*, ed. Donald A. Low (London: Dent (Everyman), 1993; repr., 1996), p. 88.

4   'Not useless do I deem ...', ll.39–41 (Gill, p. 679).

5   'There is an active principle ...', l.22 (Gill, p. 677).

6   Richard E. Matlak, *The Poetry of Relationship: Wordsworth and Coleridge, 1797–1800* (Basingstoke/London: Macmillan, 1997), p. 120.

7   See Matlak, *Poetry of Relationship*, pp. 111–12, citing James H. Averill, *Wordsworth and the Poetry of Human Suffering* (Ithaca, NY: Cornell University Press, 1980). See also Averill's 'Wordsworth and "Natural Science"': The Poetry of 1798', *JEGP* 77 (1978) 232–46, pp. 239–44.

8   See *The Economy of Vegetation*, Canto IV, 'Additional Notes', no.XXXVII (pp. 101–5); and 'Notes Omitted' (pp. 124–5); and *The Loves of the Plants*, IV, l.388n. (p. 164). *The Economy of Vegetation* and *The Loves of the Plants* are (the separately paginated) Parts I and II, respectively, of Darwin's *The Botanic Garden; A Poem, in Two Parts* (London: Johnson, 1791; facsimile reprint, Menston, Yorkshire: Scolar Press, 1973). Originally published anonymously, he acknowledged authorship in *Zoonomia; or, The Laws of Organic Life* (2 vols; London: Johnson, 1794–6).

9   See the 'Proem' to Darwin, *The Loves of the Plants*, p. vi, on the 'original animality' of plants; and see also *Zoonomia*, i.101–7, 507.

10 Philip C. Ritterbush, *Overtures to Biology: The Speculations of Eighteenth-Century Naturalists* (New Haven, Conn./London: Yale University Press, 1964), pp. 109–200, writes about 'The Triumph of Botanical Analogy' from Linnaeus through Darwin, and its subsequent rejection by Lamarck, Davy, and Hunter. According to Janet Browne, in 'Botany for Gentlemen: Erasmus Darwin and *The Loves of the Plants*', *Isis* 80 (1989), pp. 593–621, the 'analogy with animal processes' was the deciding factor in the development of botanical theory (p. 596).

11 Bruce Bigley offers a fine discussion of 'Multiple Voices in "Nutting": The Urbane Wordsworth', *PQ* 70 (1991), pp. 433–52.

12 In *Paradise Lost*, Satan as the serpent addresses the Tree of Knowledge, 'O sacred, wise, and wisdom-giving plant, / Mother of science' (an apostrophe echoed by Eve as she eats); but his delay, earlier in Book IX, was purely involuntary (IX, ll.679–80, 795–7, 463–5; *The Poems of Milton*, ed. John Carey and Alistair Fowler (London: Longman, 1968; corr. repr., 1980), pp. 896, 903, 884). For further Miltonic echoes, see Roberts W. French, 'Wordsworth's *Paradise Lost*: A Note on "Nutting"', *Studies in the Humanities* 5 (1976), pp. 42–5.

13 Citing Milton's use of the same phrase in the sonnet 'On the late Massacre in Piedmont' (l. 4; *Poems of Milton*, p. 411), Anthony John Harding observes connotations of 'crude paganism', and hence of 'destroying the groves of idols': *The Reception of Myth in English Romanticism* (Columbia/London: University of Missouri Press, 1995), p. 106.

14 The key verbal links are 'vacancy'/'vacant' and 'kindred'/'kindliness', 'Lines left', ll.7, 38; 'Nutting', ll.41–2.

15 *Don Juan*, I, ll.713, 743–4; *Byron*, ed. Jerome J. McGann (Oxford: Oxford University Press, 1986), pp. 400, 401.

16 See Coleridge's concise history of the subject in *The Friend*, ed. Barbara E. Rooke (2 vols; London/Princeton, NJ: Routledge & Kegan Paul/Princeton University Press, 1969), i.466–70. Plant sex was a relatively new theory, starting in the 1690s, and generally accepted by the 1720s: see Alan Bewell, '"Jacobin Plants": Botany as Social Theory in the 1790s', *TWC* 20 (Summer 1989) 132–9, p. 133. Linnaeus's major works were being published from the 1730s. His *Genera Plantarum* and *Mantissæ Plantarum*, supplemented by work done by his son, were translated 'By a Botanical Society at Lichfield'

(that is, chiefly, Erasmus Darwin), as *The Families of Plants, with their natural characters, according to the number, figure, situation, and proportion of all the parts of fructification* (2 vols; Lichfield/London: Jackson/Johnson, 1787): the 'Key of the Sexual System' is found in the 'Account of the Work' (i.lxxvii). Linnaeus's Latin treatise on plant reproduction, which was the prize-winning entry in a competition set up by the Imperial Academy of Saint Petersburg in 1759, and which was published the following year, was translated as *A Dissertation on the Sexes of Plants* (1786) by James Edward Smith, the founder, in 1788, of the English Linnaean Society: see Browne, 'Botany for Gentlemen', pp. 596–7, and Bewell, '"Jacobin Plants"', p. 133. According to Raymond Southall ('Botany into Poetry: Erasmus Darwin, Coleridge, & Wordsworth', *ELN* 33 (1995) 20–2, p. 22n.1): 'In 1783 Smith bought Linnaeus's collection of plants, insects, shells, coral, minerals, books and letters from the widow of the Swedish botanist ... upon the advice of Sir Joseph Banks', which 'remains with the Linnean Society'.

17 Browne, 'Botany for Gentlemen', p. 597. Ritterbush, *Overtures to Biology*, pp.111–15, states that, from 1738 (in *Classes Plantarum*) to 1751, Linnaeus tried, and failed, to place all plants in a linear series corresponding to a scale of nature. At its simplest, the arrangement meant that plants were organized into classes by number of stamens ('male' parts: the first of twenty-four classes was monandria, the second diandria, and so on), and then into orders by number of pistils ('female' parts: monogynia, digynia, etc.). Thus, a monandria monogynia and monandria digynia would belong to Class 1; a diandria monogynia to Class 2, and so forth.

18 Bewell, '"Jacobin Plants"', p. 133.

19 For the gender issues in botany, and the history of women botanists, see Londa Schiebinger, *Nature's Body: Gender in the Making of Modern Science* (Boston: Beacon Press, 1993), chapter 1, and Ann B. Shteir, *Cultivating Women: Cultivating Science* (Baltimore/London: Johns Hopkins University Press, 1996), chapters 1–3.

20 Hugh Rose, *The Elements of Botany* (London: Cadell, *etc.*, 1775), p. 151; quoted, Browne, 'Botany for Gentlemen', p. 600.

21 For the Linnaean basis of the poem, see the 'Preface'; its model in Darwin's own eight-acre botanical garden outside Lichfield appears in the 'Proem' (pp. v–vi), inviting the 'GENTLE READER' to 'view the wonders of my INCHANTED GARDEN'.

22 Tim Fulford, 'Coleridge, Darwin, Linnaeus: The Sexual Politics of Botany', *TWC* 28 (1997) 124–30, p. 126. Linnaeus himself 'humorously personifies plant reproduction in terms of human sexual relations' in *A Dissertation on the Sexes of Plants* (Fulford, 'Coleridge, Darwin, Linnaeus', p. 129).

23 Catalogued by William Withering, in *An Arrangement of British Plants, according to The Latest Improvements of the Linnæan System; with an easy Introduction to the Study of Botany* (6 edn, rev.; 4 vols; London: Scholey, 1818), ii.1, 9, 18.

24 The phrase was readily assimilated: see, e.g., 'the Sexual System of LINNÆUS', in letter to the editor, *The Anti-Jacobin; or, Weekly Examiner* 34 (2 July, 1798), p. 270; and 'the study of the sexual system of plants', in [Richard Polwhele], *The Unsex'd Females: A Poem, Addressed to the Author of The Pursuits of Literature* (London: Cadell and Davies, 1798; facsimile

reprint, NY/London: Garland, 1974), p. 8n. Other British objectors are quoted, by Bewell, '"Jacobin Plants"', p. 133; and French and British examples cited, by Browne, 'Botany for Gentlemen', pp. 597–8.

25   Cf. Polwhele, *The Unsex'd Females*, p. 8n.: 'I have, several times, seen boys and girls botanizing together.'

26   The caricature combines the professions of 'Physician' and 'Philosopher'. The latter is glossed as 'scientist' (i.e. natural philosopher) in both Gill, p. 694, and *LBM*, p. 318, while Averill, 'Wordsworth and "Natural Science"', pp. 245–6, reasonably identifies Darwin as the target; but the context also suggests the irreverant anatomizing of domestic relationships with which Wordsworth has come to associate Godwin: specifically, the 'Epitaph' may be glancing at the notorious 'fire cause' in *Political Justice*, where Godwin argues that even one's mother should not be exempt from death, should her life conflict with the greater good of mankind.

27   In chapter 7 of *A Vindication of the Rights of Woman*.

28   Polwhele, *Unsex'd Females*, pp. 8–9.

29   Polwhele (p. 8n.) failed to supply the page number in citing a 'note from Darwin's Botanic Garden, at p.', but probably meant to refer to *The Economy of Vegetation*, IV, l.456, and the 'Additional Note' number XXXVIII, on 'Vegetable Impregnation' (pp. 105–7). His subsequent note (on p. 9), '"The prolific dust" – of the botanist', quotes Darwin, *Economy of Vegetation*, IV, l.454 ('prolific dust').

30   'A Philosophical Apology for the Ladies', published *Morning Post* 22 June, 1801; in S.T. Coleridge, *Essays on His Times*, ed. David V. Erdman (3 vols; London/Princeton, NJ: Routledge & Kegan Paul/Princeton University Press, 1978), iii.303–4.

31   As the May-tree, the hawthorn is however very much connected with sexuality and fertility.

32   See Robert Burns Neveldine, 'Wordsworth's "Nutting" and the Violent End of Reading', *ELH* 63 (1996), pp. 657–80; Rachel Crawford, 'The Structure of the Sororal in Wordsworth's "Nutting"', *SiR* 31 (1992), pp. 197–212; Gregory Jones, '"Rude Intercourse": Uncensoring Wordsworth's "Nutting"', *SiR* 35 (1996), pp. 213–43; M.W. Rowe, 'The Underthought in Wordsworth's "Nutting"', *English* 44 (1995), pp. 17–23.

33   *Paradise Lost*, IV, ll.132–7; *Poems of Milton*, pp. 615–16.

34   Geoffrey Grigson, *The Englishman's Flora* (1955), Foreword by Jane Grigson, Introduction by William T. Stearn (London: Dent, 1987), pp. 247–8. My thanks to Seamus Perry for directing me to Grigson's splendid work.

35   *The Seasons*, III, ll.610–21; James Thomson, *Poetical Works*, ed. J. Logie Robertson (London: Oxford University Press, 1908; repr., 1971), pp. 154–5.

36   *Othello*, I, iii, l.168; William Shakespeare, *Othello*, ed. M.R. Ridley (London: Methuen (Arden Shakespeare), 1958), p. 31.

37   *Paradise Lost*, I, l.742–3; *Poems of Milton*, p. 505.

38   A possible mythological rationale for the phallic female is offered by Darwin, *Economy of Vegetation*, II, l.586n.: 'the cypress groves in the antient greek writers, as in Theocritus, were dedicated to Venus; and afterwards became funereal emblems', because of 'the annual processions, in which she was supposed to lament over the funeral of Adonis'.

39   William Bartram's *Travels through North and South Carolina, Georgia, East*

and West Florida... (London: Johnson, 1792). John, Bartram's father, was 'botanist to the king of Great Britain, and fellow of the Royal Society' ('Introduction', p. viii); Bartram junior set sail from Philadelphia in 1773, 'At the request of Dr. Fothergill, of London ... for the discovery of rare and useful productions of nature, chiefly in the vegetable kingdom' (p. 1). For the virgin land, cf. p. 3: 'the amplitude and magnificence of these scenes ... present to the imagination, an idea of the first appearance of the earth to man at the creation'. For specific links with 'Ruth', see John Livingston Lowes, *The Road to Xanadu: A Study in the Ways of the Imagination* (London: Constable, n.d.), p. 455n.28.

40 Polwhele, *Unsex'd Females*, pp. 25–6, and n.

41 Bartram, *Travels*, pp. 218/219.

42 The 'Apology' to *The Economy of Vegetation* states (p. vii) that the 'operations of Nature ... allegorized in the heathen mythology' are 'ingeniously explained in the works of Bacon, Vol. V. p. 47. 4th Edit. London, 1778'. Marilyn Butler, *Romantics, Rebels, and Reactionaries: English Literature and its Background 1760–1830* (Oxford: Oxford University Press, 1982), pp. 129–30, observes that for Darwin 'the loves of gods and goddesses were anthropomorphic representations of general truths about nature', a nature that was 'driven by sex'; and adduces the fertility cults uncovered by excavations at Pompeii and Herculaneum, and the priapic studies of Sir William Hamilton and Richard Payne Knight.

43 Rousseau's *Letters on the Elements of Botany, addressed to a lady*, trans. Thomas Martyn, Regius Professor of Botany at Cambridge, and dedicated 'To The Ladies of Great Britain' (2nd edn, rev.; London: White, 1787). Rousseau's 'Second Letter on Botany' is referred to in *The Anti-Jacobin* 34 (2 July, 1798), pp. 270–1.

44 Still more damagingly, Ruth herself is betrayed: 'The engines of her grief' are 'rocks and pools, / And airs that gently stir / The vernal leaves' (ll.193–6).

45 Bartram, *Travels*, pp. 487–9.

46 *Shelley's Poetry and Prose*, ed. Donald H. Reiman and Sharon B. Powers (NY: Norton, 1977), p. 335.

47 A.G. Morton, *History of Botanical Science: An Account of the Development of Botany from Ancient Times to the Present Day* (London/NY: Academic Press, 1981), p. 272; quoted, Bewell, '"Jacobin Plants"', p. 139n.5. Cf. the 'Account of the Work' in Linnaeus, *The Families of Plants*, trans. the Lichfield Botanical Society, i.lxi: 'it has pleased Infinite Wisdom to distinguish the Genera of Plants by their FRUCTIFICATION'.

48 *Paradise Lost*, IV, ll.269–72; *Poems of Milton*, p. 629. See Harding, *Reception of Myth in English Romanticism*, pp. 110–15.

49 'Apology', in *Economy of Vegetation*, p. vii. (See n.42 above.)

50 Wordsworth's copy was the 4-volume third edition (Birmingham: for the author, 1796): see D.E. Coombe, 'The Wordsworths and Botany', *N&Q* 197 (July, 1952) 298–9, p. 298; and Duncan Wu, *Wordsworth's Reading 1800–1815* (Cambridge: Cambridge University Press, 1995), pp. 245–6.

51 See Jonathan Bate's reading, out of Geoffrey Hartman, of the qualified self-consciousness of these poems, in *Romantic Ecology: Wordsworth and the Environmental Tradition* (London/NY: Routledge, 1991), pp. 87–8, 90–102.

52 Mary Moorman, *William Wordsworth: A Biography. The Early Years 1770–1803* (Oxford: Clarendon Press, 1957), pp. 101n., 480.

53 See, in *The Poetical Works of John Langhorne* (2 vols; London: Mawman, 1804), Fable IV, 'The Garden Rose and the Wild Rose', and Fable X, 'The Wilding and the Broom' (which also offers an example of idle shepherds: stanza 1, ii.37).

54 Langhorne, *Poetical Works*, ii.18–20.

55 Darwin to Withering, giving publishing advice, 13 May, 1775: *The Letters of Erasmus Darwin*, ed. Desmond King-Hele (Cambridge: Cambridge University Press, 1981), p. 74.

56 Coombe, 'The Wordsworths and Botany', p. 299; *BL*, ii.105; Withering, *Arrangement of British Plants*, iii.984.

57 Withering, *Arrangement of British Plants*, iv.43, iii.1104.

58 Darwin, *Loves of the Plants*, p. [v].

59 See Withering, *Arrangement of British Plants*, i.346.

60 The fern's stately retirement echoes the Lucy of both 'Three years she grew' (l.32) and 'She dwelt among th' untrodden ways'. Attributing royalty to flowers has a venerable tradition: cf. Fanshawe's *Ode on His Majesty's Proclamation*: 'The lily, queen, the royal rose ...'. I am grateful to Robert Cummings for suggesting this comparison.

8
Coleridge and Wordsworth: Imagination, Accidence, and Inevitability

Seamus Perry

> We need to turn our attention away from the consoling dream necessity of Romanticism ... Too much contingency of course may turn art into journalism. But since reality is incomplete, art must not be too much afraid of incompleteness.
>
> Iris Murdoch[1]

(i)

Critics often identify the earliest stirrings of Coleridge's *Biographia* in a notebook entry of autumn, 1803: 'Seem to have made up my mind to write my metaphysical works, as *my Life*, & *in* my Life – intermixed with all the other events / or history of the mind & fortunes of S.T. Coleridge' (*NB*, i.1515). Certainly, that fragment is the first glimpse of the final work's generic peculiarity; but the dispute with Wordsworth that ultimately provoked the literary chapters of *Biographia* can be dated a little further back still – firstly, to the troubling sense of divergence from Wordsworth's aims that Coleridge discovers in the summer of 1802, and, beyond even that, as I shall argue here, to the 'moment' of 1800. By 'moment' I mean the span a year or two either side of that date, when Wordsworth was beginning to practise the startling kind of lyricism that appeared, most prominently, in the second volume of *Lyrical Ballads*, and which his new 'Preface' sought to describe in more general terms.

Coleridge's complaint in *Biographia* is that Wordsworth has misled his own art: naturally equipped to achieve the visionary epic successes of a modern-day Milton, he has thwarted his own vocation with a muddling theory – the programme that is vehemently, if

169

paradoxically, announced in the 1800 'Preface'. In volume two of *Biographia*, Coleridge wastes no time in addressing the discrepancy between the true greatness of Wordsworth and the 'many parts of this preface' to which he 'objected ... as erroneous in principle' (*BL*, ii.9), a divergence between theory and practice which underlies the Wordsworthian chapters to follow. But while no poem could bring itself to fulfil the precepts of the 'Preface' (as Coleridge argued) it is nevertheless true that the imperatives announced in the great essay maintain a genuine, if sometimes obscure, parallel with the audacious experiments and successes of Wordsworth's lyric poems of the same time – that is, in (and either side of) 1800. Still, even though Wordsworth often declines the visionary excellences, and thrives poetically when disappointing Coleridge's expectations, yet he continues to hold, quite devoutly, conceptions of poetic excellence that he has learnt from his friend; so the relationship between Wordsworthian achievement and Coleridgean standard is an especially tangled one (which doubtless made it all the more provoking for Coleridge).

Several critics have recently described the way that Coleridge's persisting sense of a *'radical* Difference' (*CL*, ii.812) from Wordsworth animates the literary chapters of *Biographia*; my approach to the matter is not at all opposed, but comes at it a little obliquely: for what I want particularly to tease out is a curious feature of Coleridge's critical vocabulary. At a crucial moment during the Wordsworth pages of *Biographia*, Coleridge criticizes his friend's misled art by invoking the unusual attribute of *accidentality* to describe its failing: having described the *'matter-of-factness'* that mars certain Wordsworth poems, Coleridge goes on to announce a critical principle – 'To this *accidentality*, I object, as contravening the essence of poetry, which Aristotle pronounces to be σπουδαιότατον καὶ φιλοσοφώτατον λένος, the most intense, weighty and philosophical product of human art'. This, in turn, takes us back to the Aristotelian credo invoked several chapters before: 'I adopt with full faith the principle of Aristotle, that poetry as poetry is essentially *ideal*, that it avoids and excludes all *accident*' (*BL*, ii.126, 45–6). If a failure of poetic ideality is a fall into accidents, then, presumably, the positive criterion of excellence is the avoidance or elimination of accidence – inevitability, that is to say, or necessity. As it happens, history records that inevitability was a lasting Wordsworthian credential too: Matthew Arnold remembered 'hearing him say that "Goethe's poetry was not inevitable enough"'.[2] And Charles Lamb, as so often, reworks Coleridgean principles in the mode of comedy: faced with the manuscript of 'Lycidas' he recoils in horror at its evidence of Milton's second or third thoughts: 'I had thought of the Lycidas as of a full-grown beauty – as springing up with all its parts absolute ... How it staggered me to see the fine things in their ore! ... as if they might have been otherwise, and just as good!'[3]

Part of Coleridge's intention in invoking Aristotle was a pointed act of correction. Wordsworth had written in the 1802 additions to the 'Preface': 'Aristotle, I have been told, hath said, that Poetry is the most philosophic of all writing: it is so: its object is truth, not individual and local, but general, and operative' (*WPrW*, i.139, with 1802 variant);[4] but it was (at least as Coleridge came to see it) precisely those Aristotelian excellences that the tenets of the muddlesome 'Preface' had inspired Wordsworth to abandon. On a more public level, citing Aristotle invokes authority against wilful innovation: as at other moments in *Biographia*, Coleridge's criticism seems to have an unexpectedly neo-classical flavour. It was Sir Joshua Reynolds, after all, who had stipulated in his *Discourses* that 'Nature herself is not to be too closely copied', and that the object of art was properly the beauty that 'is general and intellectual ... an idea that subsists only in the mind'. Such beauty, says Reynolds, arises from the elimination of 'accidental deviation', the sort of thing Dutch artists kept in: the proper artist's discriminating eye was 'enabled to distinguish the accidental deficiencies' and so purge them to form 'the Ideal Beauty'.[5] Coleridge thought Reynolds a happy example of the Platonic tradition tenaciously hanging on in an empiricist age, which is a coat-trailing piece of misreading,[6] but one that may give us a clue to the true nature of *Biographia*'s apparent appeals to classical authority. For much of its neo-classicism is a sort of craftily cultivated optical illusion;[7] the noises sound much the same, and eminently respectable, but they are really animated by imaginative impulses from a different source: Coleridge's concept of aesthetic inevitability has its deepest roots in more idiosyncratic ground than the general ideas of Reynolds's aesthetics.

Worrying at the secret Coleridgean history of inevitability as a criterion of poetic excellence, and accidence as a mark of poetic failure, discovers an important background for the extraordinary lyrical experiments that Wordsworth was making in the last years of the eighteenth and first years of the nineteenth century, and casts some light on the evasive but vital relationship which they have with Coleridgean precept. A 'dream necessity' may well be a key ingredient in 'Romanticism', as Iris Murdoch brilliantly diagnosed in 'Against

Dryness' (the epigraph to this chapter); but 'Romanticism' might already offer its own contingent counter-voice, challenging such aesthetic inevitability in the name of an undreaming 'reality'.

(ii)

Tracking inevitability in Coleridge takes us back to his theological-*cum*-political thought of the 1790s, when he entertains a particular *idea of history* – an idea that he shares with Wordsworth and, indeed, with many friends of liberty (before and since). The belief is a doctrine of *historical inevitability* – the idea that history has a pre-ordained shape and destiny, before which individual human wills are helpless, and into which their apparently free actions are entirely subsumed, as into a world-spirit or *Zeitgeist*. The pervasive millennialism that marked radical thought in the 1790s placed a doctrine of historical inevitability at its heart. Inevitability, rather than millennialism, is what is at issue here, though the two are hard to disentangle, but strictly historical inevitability need not be millennial: the inescapable trend of necessity need not take you to a new Jerusalem; it might as well take you, as it took Anna Karenina, no matter how Tolstoy tried to re-write her story, to an irresistible destiny beneath the wheels of a train. But such pessimistic determinism is rare, for obvious enough reasons of psychological self-preservation, the same reasons that make most Calvinists believe that they are part of the elect (the terrible case of Cowper, who believed the opposite, makes the point).

Coleridge's necessitarianism, repeatedly announced throughout the mid-1790s, draws its courage from a redeemed inevitablism: 'I would ardently, that you were a Necessitarian,' Coleridge tells Southey, '– and (believing in an all-loving Omnipotence) an Optimist' (*CL*, i.145). 'The Destiny of Nations' hymns God as 'All-conscious Presence of the Universe! / Nature's vast ever-acting Energy! / In will, in deed, Impulse of All to All!', and relates a millennial destiny: the warrior maid of France, at the depth of her woes, feels that Impulse in the local form of her tutelary spirit, 'an inevitable Presence' (ll.460–2, 271; *CPW*, i.146–7, 140). The 'Argument' to Coleridge's departing ode to 1796 reiterated a millennial confidence, addressing 'the Divine Providence that regulates into one vast harmony all the events of time, however calamitous some of them may appear to mortals' (*CPW*, i.160): metaphors of harmony and universal music are extremely common in Coleridge's early verse, and often carry the Providential ambience of that sense of history announced by the 'Argument'. It was a belief in the ubiquity of God (an all-loving Omnipotence) that took young Coleridge to the optimistic extremes of necessity – and Coleridge was not alone in considering himself a 'compleat Necessitarian' (*CL*, i.137): his fellow Unitarian, Lamb, was also pleased to name himself 'a Necessarian', as he told Coleridge while enthusing about 'Religious Musings'.[8] If the only activity in the life of the universe comes from the omnipresent energy of God, then there can be no autonomous, volitional contribution from individual humans – a doctrine which, as Basil Willey once gently remarked, had a fatal attraction for someone with as wobbly a sense of obligation as STC.[9] You can pick up a certain anxiety about free-agency in several of his 1790s poems, which worry at the obligations declined by retirement, or cast Coleridge in one way or another as incapacitated or disabled – 'Lam'd by the scathe of fire', for instance – or invent narratives that mythologize a similar incapacity, as though finding dramatic equivalents for the philosophical passivity described by the theology. Coleridge was honest enough to admit that the doctrine was not easy to apply to the bleak contemporary scene: 'In my calmer moments I have the firmest Faith that all things work together for Good. But alas! it seems a long and a dark Process'.[10] Nevertheless, the world-view retained its radical capacity to inspire. '[B]y having no will but the will of Heaven,' as he wrote in an early Notebook, 'we call in Omnipotence to fight our battles!' (*CN*, i.22).

Young Wordsworth was quite as excited by the prospect of inevitability, and at least in part caught his excitement from his always-contagious friend: he singled out for special praise some apocalyptic lines from 'Religious Musings' (see *CL*, i.216). (The desire for the inevitable is one aspect of the needy tendency of Wordsworth's imagination long ago diagnosed by David Perkins in *The Quest for Permanence*)[11]. Later in life, Coleridge confided to Poole, as though entrusting something scandalous, 'W, you know, was even to Extravagance a Necessitarian' (*CL*, ii.1037); and a draft for *The Prelude* (written around February, 1799) shows what sort of thing he may have had in mind:

> I seemed to learn
> That what we see of forms and images
> Which float along our minds, and what we feel
> Of active or recognizable thought,
> Prospectiveness, or intellect, or will,
> Not only is not worthy to be deemed

> Our being, to be prized as what we are,
> But is the very littleness of life.
> Such consciousness I deem but accidents,
> Relapses from that one interior life
> That lives in all things, sacred from the touch
> Of that false secondary power by which
> In weakness we create distinctions, then
> Believe that all our puny boundaries are things
> Which we perceive, and not which we have made –
> In which all beings live with God, themselves
> Are God, existing in one mighty whole,
> As undistinguishable as the cloudless east
> At noon is from the cloudless west, when all
> The hemisphere is one cerulean blue.

>   (From 'Peter Bell MS. 2'; *Norton Prelude*, p. 496)

One imagines Coleridge's startled response at so starkly unguarded an expression of sentiments that he himself had originated – sentiments which he entertained just as exuberantly by instinct, but typically couched more circumspectly when required to come up with a statement of his position. (The palinodic form of 'The Eolian Harp' describes an exemplarily Coleridgean pattern.) What Wordsworth dismisses as but 'accidents, / Relapses from that one interior life / That lives in all things' is nothing less than independent human consciousness itself, which makes the necessitarian implications of Coleridge's One Life rather too clear for comfort. It is also illogical: if you can slip out of the side of an otherwise inclusive necessity to discover the littleness of accidence, then it can hardly have been strict *necessity* you were involved with in the first place. But that kind of illogic is familiar from other poems of the period, by both men – the Ancient Mariner, for instance, by some readings anyway, learns about the inclusive power of the One Life by disastrously swerving outwith its properly comprehensive control.

But what matters is not the logical conundrum of the position so much as the poetic delight that it inspires in the idea of the inevitable or necessary – things happening that are *meant* to happen – and the corresponding disparagement that it incites towards mere 'accident' – 'what happened to happen', in Larkin's disabused phrase.[12] 'The moving accident is not my trade', as Wordsworth grandly announced at the beginning of Part Second of 'Hart-Leap Well' (first published in the 1800 *Lyrical Ballads*), so belittling a creative life devoted to the world of mere outward contingency, and advocating instead an imaginative vocation devoted to the deeply inward and sheerly necessary. The masterwork of this vision was to be *The Recluse* – the great philosophical epic that Coleridge had effectively commissioned his friend to write in the Spring of 1798 – which, as Jonathan Wordsworth has argued, was to be an explicitly millennial work.[13] Most of *The Recluse* never materialized, but, given its Coleridgean pedigree, it is not surprising that the bits and pieces that did emerge show clear traces of the idiosyncratic inevitabilist rhetoric that was set to govern the poem at large. Long stretches of *The Prelude* seek to persuade their author of the providential design and destined propriety of what happened to happen – a long sequence (despite appearances) of inevitable rectitude. The golden age of his Lakeland childhood, for instance, he pictures as a place of 'simplicity, / And beauty, and inevitable grace'; and he prides himself elsewhere that 'less / Than other minds I had been used to owe / The pleasure which I found in place or thing / To extrinsic transitory accidents' (*Prelude*, VIII, ll.157–8, 777–80). Approaching the end of the poem, Wordsworth pauses to review his story, exultantly imagining himself 'As if on wings, and saw beneath me stretched / Vast prospect of the world which I had been, / And was', and roundly proclaims 'All gratulant if rightly understood' (*Prelude*, XIII, ll.378–80, 385). Such Panglossian confidence gathers strength from the looming redemptive presence of *The Recluse*, meant to follow a few lines later, once the preliminaries of *The Prelude* have ended with their promise of 'redemption, surely yet to come' (*Prelude*, XIII, l.441). 'Home at Grasmere', written for *The Recluse* (and begun in 1800), similarly imagines a millennial future: 'the blessedness which love / And knowledge will, we trust, hereafter give / To all the Vales of earth and all mankind', and begins to find something already like it in the complete 'self-sufficing world' of Grasmere, 'A Whole without dependence or defect' (ll.254–6, 204, 168). And curiously, as though drawing strength from an inspiring millennial precedent, Wordsworth drafted 'Home at Grasmere' in an interleaved copy of Coleridge's 1796 *Poems*, literally around – and sometimes between the very lines of – the inevitabilist excitements of 'Religious Musings'.[14]

(iii)

The physical proximity that 'Home at Grasmere' enjoyed with Coleridge's poem might well have struck Wordsworth as a greater and greater irony, something Jonathan Wordsworth has nicely observed: 'As Coleridge mounted to his triumphant millenarian conclusion, Wordsworth's own poem – though grander still in its aspirations – faltered to a halt'.[15] This failure was symptomatic, though Coleridge does not seem to have regarded it in that way at the time. In April 1800, just as 'Home at Grasmere' was petering out, Coleridge reported to Southey Wordsworth's plans for the new *Lyrical Ballads* (as well as the unlikely prospect of a Wordsworthian novel), and his tone sounds fairly dispassionate, even though he had protested to Wordsworth the previous October that 'of nothing but "The Recluse" can I hear patiently', and it is difficult to imagine his pressing sense of urgency abating that much so quickly (*CL*, i.585, 538). Perhaps, on the contrary, it was a settled conviction of Wordsworth's deep certainty of purpose that allowed him to watch the new *Lyrical Ballads* occupying such valuable time without too much anxiety.

Several critics have described the distinctive place that *The Recluse* held in the psychological dynamics of Wordsworth's writing life, and they identify a characteristic pattern:[16] bursts of creativity, periodically displaced from the impossible millennial epic into other projects, often into the successive revisions of *The Prelude*, but also into shorter poems. Many of the most striking new poems of the 1800 *Lyrical Ballads* were written during the 1798–9 winter, when early attempts at *The Recluse* were already failing (and the first shoots of *The Prelude* were appearing in its place); similarly, as 'Home at Grasmere' began to fail in the spring of 1800, energy was diverted into preparing the second edition of *Lyrical Ballads*, and then on into the protracted burst of lyric poetry that lasts until 1803. The pattern recurs throughout Wordsworth's writing life: the 1804–5 revisions of *The Prelude* were succeeded, not by an assault on the colossal task for which the autobiography was a self-confirming preparation, but instead by work on *Poems, in Two Volumes* (1807); just as *The Excursion* was followed, not by a final turn to the great epic, but instead by the business of publishing *Poems* (1815); and as late as 1833, 'tiresome small Poems' that still weren't *The Recluse* were emerging in its place to irritate Mary Wordsworth.[17] Wordsworth himself drew an unforgiving contrast between his epic ambition and his different, smaller lyric achievement: 'I have great things in meditation,' he told Wrangham in 1804, 'but as yet I have only been doing little ones' (*EY*, p. 436).

So, although no-one could have known it at the time, the moment of 1800 set a precedent, at once ominous and promising, for an entire career; and, in the subtle pattern of imaginative displacement which characterizes the work of that moment, hindsight might discover a distinctively Wordsworthian state of mind. Wordsworth's activity (and his inactivity) around 1800 comes to seem something crucial or defining, because it was then that his unacknowledged but instinctive divergence from the Coleridgean template for genius began to grow unignorably clear. In retrospect, that is to say, the definitive attribute of Wordsworth's 1800 *Lyrical Ballads* for Coleridge came to be, simply but suggestively, that they were not *The Recluse*. And not only not *The Recluse*, but implicitly antithetical to it – written in a countering poetic voice, and evidence of an imagination profoundly at odds with the kind of creativity that *The Recluse* would require. The poems Wordsworth writes in the first years of the new century emerge from a failure to write a millennialist epic; and I think they can often be seen, on their smaller scale, in implicit or metaphorical ways, to be registering an embarrassment of inevitabilist expectation. The millennial confidence that Coleridge had hoped to enjoy vicariously through his friend's epic was fraying into a new kind of lyric art which explored instead the counter-forces of accidence, contingency, and circumstance – poems that embraced the quite private associations of individual fancy, and occasionally delighted in a mundanely opulent redundance of narrative or descriptive detail.

Of course, this was not, from Wordsworth's point of view, simply a sad, less still an unwitting, defeat. Wordsworth was certainly excited by inevitability, as we have seen, but he was stirred by the idea of accidence too, in a way that Coleridge was scarcely prepared openly to acknowledge in himself.[18] 'I might advert / To numerous accidents in flood or field, / Quarry or moor, or 'mid the winter snows, / Distresses and disasters, tragic facts / Of rural history' (*Prelude* (1799), I, ll.279–83), he writes promisingly in the first version of *The Prelude*, borrowing a flavour of the positive exoticism of accidents from Othello. It is a sense of the saving *innocence* of diverse accidents – their happy freedom from a tyrannically systematic mindset – that Wordsworth cherishes when deploring the French Revolutionary period as a time when 'all the accidents of life, were pressed / Into one service'; and in a similar spirit (some lines later in *The Prelude*), when satirizing the grandiose egotism of Godwinian rationalism, he mocks its pretensions to 'a resolute mastery shaking off / The accidents of nature, time, and place' (*Prelude*, X, ll.325–6, 821–2). ('Resolution and Independence' (1802), one of the greatest masterpieces to emerge from the period of Wordsworth's writing life that I am concerned with here, has the leechgatherer arriving with all the force of a providential destiny – 'a peculiar grace, / A leading from above, a something given' (ll.50–1); but an important part of the poem's total effect comes from the admitted coincidence of the encounter ('Yet it befel . . .').)

Several of the most impressive new *Lyrical Ballads* of 1800 show the distinctive kind of unfulfilled effect, a worrying at the promises and frustrations of inevitability, that grew, as by reaction, from within the failed inevitabilities of *The Recluse*. Their art frequently concentrates its energies on teasingly odd or somehow aborted endings, on imaginative connections that do not quite connect, morals that do not relate properly to the narratives they are meant to cap – in all such cases, the poetic mind resigns its God-like powers, as though distracted by duties owed to varieties of experience that lie outside art. In the 'Elegiac Stanzas', written some years later, Wordsworth nobly rationalizes this recurrent impulse to abdicate poetry, casting it as a broken submission, the spirit knuckling under to the unyielding demands of the non-imaginary and starkly true: 'A power is gone, which nothing can restore; / A deep distress hath humanized my Soul' (ll.35–6). But the poems of the 1800 moment rarely experience such brave despair, and do not embrace the ethical obligations of the humanized imagination with such bleakly self-conscious duty: indeed, their artful self-consciousness is never far away from comedy, even if it is of a dark or sorry kind. Despite the extreme difference in tone, Wordsworth may well have drawn inspiration for his kind of writing from *Tristram Shandy*, one of the books he had enjoyed as a young man (*EY*, pp. 56–7): the whole texture of Sterne's masterpiece is a repeated interruption of the expected formulae of art by the contingency of what happens to happen. At a more profound level, it is an effect which Wordsworth might well have learnt from Shakespeare too: by implicitly delineating a region within the world of the play which openly acknowledges its own art, Shakespeare allows the events which occur outside that magic circle a kind of freedom, as though somehow replete with the accidence of ordinary lives without art (with which we are more familiar). The ending of *Love's Labours Lost* illustrates the technique at its most primitive: just as the play is moving seamlessly toward the inevitable endings of romantic comedy (multiple marriages), news unexpectedly arrives of a father's death, and plans are postponed for a year and a day. 'Our wooing doth not end like an old play; / Jack hath not Jill: these ladies' courtesy / Might well have made our sport a comedy', says Berowne, drawing attention artfully to the comedy's artless and (to him) unwelcome divergence from its apparent destiny as a comedy. 'Come, sir', counters his friend and fellow suitor, the more sanguine king, 'it wants a twelvemonth and a day / And then 'twill end.' 'That's too long for a play', answers Berowne tartly.[19]

Something very like that Shakespearean, realist comedy of disruptive inconsequence provokes several of the sprightlier ballads of 1798: 'What more I have to say is short, / I hope you'll kindly take it; / It is no tale; but should you think, / Perhaps a tale you'll make it' ('Simon Lee', ll.77–80), as though the poem were raw material preparatory to a poem and not a finished work itself. This very characteristic sense of poetry giving up, or running out, crops up in 'The Idiot Boy' too, in a nice parody of neo-classical invocation, a forerunner of Byron's celebrated 'Hail, Muse! *et cetera*':[20] 'Oh gentle muses! is this kind? / Why will ye thus my suit repel? / Why of your further aid bereave me? / And can ye thus unfriended leave me?' (ll.352–5). The spirits there are high and gamesome and jokey, though they are already working in an instinctive way towards the more meditative and quietly audacious achievements of the second edition. There, the vivacious, even mannerist, self-consciousness that Wordsworth had discovered in the happy confidence of the Alfoxden spring took on a more weighty quality. 'Strange fits of passion I have known' exemplifies the sort of effect I have in mind. As a piece of story-telling, the poem seems to be moving solidly in one direction (towards Lucy's home), and its atmosphere matches that apparent certainty of purpose, the whole suffused with a sense of mysterious but unmissable destiny, an ominousness that gathers round the symbol of the dogging moon. But while the moon apparently accumulates significance with each repetition, yet the poem ends parodically for an omen-poem; its seemingly inevitable, steady and reliable course, confirmed by the trudging of the horse, is suddenly disrupted by a most unexpected, 'wayward' turn, as the poet discovers something quite different has been going on in his head all along:

> What fond and wayward thoughts will slide
> Into a Lover's head –
> 'O mercy!' to myself I cried,
> 'If Lucy should be dead!'

> (ll.25–8)

To find that you were not thinking what you thought you were thinking is a Shandyan revelation, though Wordsworth's poem is more puzzled than amused by the frustration of its firm sense of artistic destination, and stumbles to an inconsequential stop: a poetry of not-arriving, it stops still out on the road, ending in an abrupt narrative collapse.

'Strange fits' suggests the experimentalism – an uneasiness or hesitancy about aesthetic finality and narrative closing, an imaginative openness to the wayward and simply fortuitous, or to the spoiling or distracting detail – which distinguishes many of the poems of the 1800 moment. In the note to 'The Ancient Mariner' added to the 1800 *Ballads*, Wordsworth criticized, among other 'great defects', 'the events having no necessary connection' (*LBB*, p. 276); but the sense of evading apparently necessary connections is at the heart of many of his own most successful poems of the same period. The way that Wordsworth's art pulls off this effect, cultivating moments that decline art, is difficult to grasp in criticism (for really it is all art), which risks making the effect seem more witty and contrived than it is: the paradoxes are much more implicit, or deeply submerged, than the fully self-advertizing exhibitions of wit. Instead, a kind of bafflement and inconsequence shapes the most memorable poems in the 1800 *Ballads*, replacing the optimistic schedules of *The Recluse* with the unmeaning occurences and frustrations of mundane existence.

The most emphatic case of the *Recluse*-vision inverted is 'Nutting', which is effectively a parodic reversal of the worshipful immersion in nature's benign processes that Coleridge's optimistic monism was supposed to describe. Unsurprisingly, the poet sounds frankly astonished at his own behaviour and its sudden, apparently quite unmotivated, violence ('Then up I rose...'): his actions are related in disconnected and unexplained sequence, rather like the Mariner's in Coleridge's cognate poem of nature abused. The three-line conclusion that rounds the poem off has an unmistakable though uneasy comedy about it, making the right noises of pedagogic consequentiality ('Then, dearest Maiden!...') but without the slightest justification. It has an improvisatory feel, aided by that practically Sternean dash, as though an orthographical mark for the act of thinking on one's feet: '— for there is a Spirit in the woods' (l.55). No doubt that is what the 'philosophy' says; but it is something imported, hardly something that the poem has shown us. Such abrupt terminations, sprung upon us, register a sense of interruption or way-laidness, as does (in very different temper) the last stanza of that bizarrely winning little poem, 'The Waterfall and the Eglantine', which (literally) ends in a rush, the whole donné of the verses simply washed away without warning, and the poem with it, in the accident of a sudden flood, leaving the luckless briar silenced for good, midway through his loquacious case for survival: 'Those accents were his last' (l.56).

That makes something like a joke of a death, in a way which only emphasizes the poet's private dismay (an effect reminiscent of Gray's publicly amused, but personally devastated, 'Ode on the Death of a Favourite Cat'). Death often has a peculiar resonance in the baffled art of the 1800 poems, which it enters more as a disturbing intrusion than an inevitable culmination. The abrupt ending of 'There was a Boy', for instance, mishandles news of the boy's demise in an adeptly maladroit way, Wordsworth carelessly letting slip the detail of the boy's grave, and then rapidly trying to cover the gap in the story which he has inadvertently uncovered:

> And there along that bank when I have pass'd
> At evening, I believe, that near his grave
> A full half-hour together I have stood,
> Mute – for he died when he was ten years old.

> (ll.29–32)

A beautifully contrived recreation of sad human speech's incompetence, the lines enact the confidence of artistry shaken by the unspeakable subject of death: again, the dash has a kind of real-time drama about it, like one of Sterne's, though of course in a wholly different mode. The more polished *Prelude* version of these lines (*Prelude*, V, ll.389–422) has the boy's death announced where a more controlled exposition would insist: at the start of the second verse paragraph and before the reader sights the grave ('This boy was taken from his mates, and died / In childhood ere he was full ten years old'); but the sure gain in poetic professionalism means a loss in the dejected inconsequence which the 1800 version so brilliantly pulls off.

This sense of art running out haunts even 'Michael', where the grand determinism of a tragic destiny might have ensured a greater sense of poetic self-possession. The revelation of Luke's ruin, the poem's turning-point, seems, not only to disprove the upbeat *Recluse*-necessity of a more confident Wordsworth ('Knowing that Nature never did betray / The heart that loved her': 'Lines written ... above Tintern Abbey', ll.123–4), but to describe the fall away from natural piety with an almost throw-away, wholly non-explanatory abruptness, as though broaching properly unmentionable things, or braving such inconceivable failure by a show of negligence, almost a steely nonchalance, and so leaving an insoluble puzzle at the heart of the poem:

> ... Meantime Luke began
> To slacken in his duty, and at length
> He in the dissolute city gave himself
> To evil courses: ignominy and shame
> Fell on him, so that he was driven at last
> To seek a hiding-place beyond the seas.

(ll.451–6)

As befits a poem written out of a struggling faith in the optimism of inevitability, 'Michael' casts tragedy as inexplicable accidence. Thwarting the classical expectations, the poem accepts instead the sheer ill fortune of things working out wrong, rather than anything more grandly predestined; and this was a type of tragic vision that Wordsworth might have learned, again, from Shakespeare, whose tragic endings are often comedies undone by meaningless bad luck – as when the truth about gulled Othello emerges at last, but only after Desdemona is already dead. (Nearer the case of 'Michael', perhaps, would be the unanswerable misfortune recognized by Miranda: 'Good wombs have borne bad sons'.[21])

'The Brothers', similarly, fails to fulfil the expectations of its art, faltering as though distracted by an unspeakable sadness that lies without its expected compass. The poem works patiently towards a revelatory climax that never happens: unlike, say, 'The Ruined Cottage', its story-teller, the Priest, does not arrive at anything like a full consciousness of the situation in which he is repeating his narrative, and the listener cannot bring himself to enlighten him until the episode is over (when he writes him a letter). It is a triumph of frustrated or denied emotion (as is that miniature masterpiece 'The Childless Father'), and refuses us the dramatic satisfaction or emotional release of anything approaching a denouement. Appropriately, then, the poem's close repeatedly describes actions and events that do not occur: 'The Stranger would have thank'd him, but he felt / Tears rushing in'; 'looking at the grave, he said, "My Brother". / The Vicar did not hear the words ...' (ll.421–2, 425–6). And, finally, the poem concludes with a studied randomness of detail, as though deliberately declining the totalizing ambitions of a more orthodox conclusion, such as a moral reflection or a psychological observation, or even a counsel not to despair, might allow:

> This done, he went on shipboard, and is now
> A Seaman, a grey headed Mariner.
>
> (ll.448–9)

'[N]ow' is inspired, shifting us away from the poem and leaving us, in the final line, in the alternative, contingent immediacy of what is occurring as we read. 'A slumber did my spirit seal' also works marvellously on the readerly time of a 'now', which it plays off against the imaginative time of the past tense. It offers two stanzas in mysterious sequence: if the first contains a miniature act of prophecy, made while the spirit lies sealed within itself, then the outcome in the world, 'now' (l.5), that the second describes, juxtaposes with its prediction obscurely. It is not at all clear whether the second stanza is the inevitable realization of the first stanza's prophetic dream, or whether it is merely an unforgivingly juxtaposed account of what happened to turn out. True, the poem retains a muted feel of before-and-after, of prognosis and realization ('Now Lucy *is* what she *seemed* to be', remarks Hartman[22]); and yet one is hardly sure whether the final stillness and passivity is the happy achievement of an inevitable fate, or a terrible twist on the wonder of the dream-vision, a cruel piece of punning like a bad magician's in a fairy tale. The poem is devastatingly gentle in describing a seemingly inevitable but wholly inscrutable relationship between expectation and experience, thoroughly confusing (but not destroying altogether) any sense of poetic logic or narrative consequence.

The 1800 poems sometimes show Wordsworth testing the boundary where poetry runs out, and the accidental and unpoetical external world takes over, by including himself in his poems, an extraneous figure, as if incidental to the stories he relates: someone who happened to be passing. This is a poignant effect in 'Ruth' ('I, too, have pass'd her on the hills': l.217), and in 'Lucy Gray' ('I chanc'd to see at break of day / The solitary Child': ll.3–4), partly thanks to what Coleridge once called the 'credibilizing effect' of the eye-witness, but also for its odd implication that Wordsworth himself is somehow to one side of his own poetry, as though his encounters with it are a matter of the purest fortune. (The poignancy I have in mind is caught in a phrase of Larkin's: 'Something is pushing them / To the side of their own lives'.[23]) 'The Idle Shepherd-Boys' replays the same kind of effect, but more whimsically: here, the poet himself is again the representative of the world without ('A Poet, one who loves the brooks / Far better than the sages' books': ll.84–5), and, chancing to be wandering by, he rescues the stranded lamb ('An unexpected sight!': l.92); but then stops to offer gratuitous ethical injunctions, effectively short-circuiting a poem of high spirits and youthfulness with which his moralism is wholly at odds, somewhere he is not really at home. (A century before Beerbohm's celebrated cartoon, Wordsworth seems to be parodying the intrusively sermonizing persona that he adopts in some of his most notorious poems, who often brings those works to an abrupt halt.) This really is close to Sternean ground, and I must not present too sombre a picture of the new volume: the effects are very various. Some of the more vivacious poems tease poetic expectation by bringing themselves to closes of a deliciously pat kind, as though parodying (or nearly so) poetic fulfilment and its coarser pleasures. The 'Inscription' for St Herbert's hermitage is delightfully deadpan or matter-of-fact, apparently quite unstirred by the astonishing fulfil-ment of prayerful expectation which it is describing – 'as our Chronicles report, / Though here the Hermit number'd his last days, / Far from St. Cuthbert his beloved friend, / Those holy men both died in the same hour' (ll.18–22) – and certainly not moved to high eloquence: the deflating redundance of the tautology ('both … in the same') implies as much. The conclusion to 'Ellen Irwin', meanwhile, has a practically farcical kind of completeness, as though a mock-completeness, like something facetious by Hilaire Belloc: 'And, for the stone upon his head, / May no rude hand deface it, / And its forlorn Hic jacet' (ll.54–6).

But the prevailing tone, or undertone, is more chastened, or trou-bled. The vigorous descriptive powers of 'A whirl-blast from behind the hill', for instance, work toward some resounding reflection that does not emerge, leaving a stirring exemplum that has lost its expli-cation: it is as though any symbolical potential Wordsworth might once have found in the natural scene has failed; and in its place, the poet merely hopes that he may never cease to find 'Even in appear-ances like these / Enough to nourish and to stir my mind!' (ll.26–7). Such a diminished or disenchanted perspective – that you might only hope to find '[e]nough', at least, to 'stir' you – haunts many of the 1800 poems (a matter of 'finding / What will suffice', in Stevens's phrase); and creates a peculiar atmosphere of emptiness, as though poetry has already run out, or cannot get started properly, or somehow lies beyond present resources. 'Song for the Wandering Jew', a most un-Wordsworthian sort of production, puts this tenacious spirit of negation at its most legendary: 'Never nearer to the goal, / Night and day' (ll.18–19); but other poems evoke the same kind of stalled or disabled feeling more characteristically. 'Poor Susan' is an exemplary anti-story, in which nothing happens; 'Lines written with a Slate-pencil' advises its passer-by to do nothing. In retrospect, one can see that 'Strange fits of passion' begins, as it were, by cancelling itself out: the poet promises not to tell any but the 'lover' the strange fit upon which he has already embarked. Most adventurously, the whole structure of the evasively riddling 'Song' ('She dwelt among th' untrodden ways') is a kind of nothing, working by a sort of self-cancelling: having established Lucy's precarious sort of being, the poem does not embark on the narrative business the reader might expect, but rather empties itself out all of a sudden into the blank absence of a sheer, incommunicable, 'difference', poetry running out in a wordless 'Oh!' (ll.12, 11). Nothingness haunts even the ecological ebullience of the 'Poems on the Naming of Places', which for all their celebration, it seems to me, find themselves subtly undercut by an under-sense of vacancy, a redundancy or arbitariness that the several naming-acts cannot successfully disguise. The namings seem to present themselves with the confident ambition of a new Adam nomi-nating a local habitation; but that feeling is undercut by the implicit contrast which the poems persistently evoke between the heedless durability of the landscape and the undisguisable contingency of the namings, dependent as they are on purely personal associations ('a private and peculiar interest': *LBB*, p. 217): 'And, therefore, my sweet MARY, this still nook / With all its beeches we have named from You' (V, ll.23–4). As it happens, Coleridge was writing enthusiastically to Godwin in 1800, urging him philosophically 'to destroy the old antithesis of *Words* & *Things*, elevating, as it were, words into Things, & living Things too' (*CL*, i.626); but Wordsworth's poems about words and things quietly insist on just such an antithesis: between the private language of the family circle and the oblivious permanance of the mountains' external 'truth'.

>   ... 'Tis in truth
> The loneliest place we have among the clouds.
> And She who dwells with me, whom I have lov'd
> With such communion, that no place on earth
> Can ever be a solitude to me,
> Hath said, this lonesome Peak shall bear my Name.
>
>   (III, ll.12–17)

A first impression of celebratory confidence gives way to something less consolatory (though no less tender): their names adhere to their landscape by the most precarious threads – 'two or three, perhaps, / Years after we are gone and in our graves, / When they have cause to speak of this wild place, / May call it by the name of EMMA'S DELL' (I, ll.44–7). Only two or three, and only 'perhaps' – and, even then, only when they chance to talk about the spot – *may* use the name: it is very far from the organicist Cratylian confidence that Coleridge was dreaming about.

Many more examples of Wordsworth's art-declining, or art-deferring, art might be offered; but perhaps I have said enough to imply the range and capacity of the idiom, and its insistent, self-checking exploration of interruption, accidence and narrative errancy. All of which would seem to imply the most essentially idiosyncratic of imaginations; but there is a parallel of a kind in Hardy, whose most striking lyric poems frequently explore the arbitrariness and inconsequentiality that his official 'philosophy' sought to refine into the implacable processes of 'the Great Will'.[24] Unlike Wordsworth, Hardy actually managed to produce a philosophical epic of a kind (though *The Dynasts*, rather like *The Excursion*, worked the philosophy through the encouraging medium of dramatised narrative); but it is the anecdotal, curious but uncertain idiom, which flourishes in the unsystematized occasions of his smaller poems, that strikes the most characteristic Hardy note, as in the second, and last, stanza of 'The Caged Goldfinch':

> There was inquiry in its wistful eye,
> 　　And once it tried to sing;
> Of him or her who placed it there, and why,
> 　　No one knew anything.[25]

The parallel between poet and bird is a little more clearly deliberated than Wordsworth usually is, its air of accepting puzzlement and its cultivation of circumstantial satire more emphatic; but it draws on something like the same repertoire of feeling.

(iv)

Hardy is an especially useful parallel to bear in mind, because the bone of contention in most discussions of his poetry leads us to what is most pointedly at issue in Coleridge's response to Wordsworth in

Biographia: the question of a proper poetic diction; and this takes us firmly back, once again, to the moment of 1800. The poet and critic John Powell Ward once placed Hardy prominently in a 'line' descending from Wordsworth, a tradition which he labelled (following Mill's description of Wordsworth as 'the poet of unpoetical natures') a 'poetry of the unpoetic';[26] and that puzzling phrase might be taken happily to summarize exactly what most worries Coleridge about Wordsworth. Coleridge locates the root of the problem as the muddlesome 'theory' in the 'Preface' of 1800, which cannot help but encourage *'prosaisms'* (*BL*, ii.79). And, to be sure, the 'Preface' might be taken as *the* manifesto for an 'unpoetic' poetry. '[T]here is no necessity to trick out or to elevate nature,' Wordsworth announces there, declaring his wish instead 'to keep my Reader in the company of flesh and blood', and warily defending the virtues of 'nakedness and simplicity' (*WPrW*, i.139 (part of the 1802 additions), 130, 146): the whole piece breathes a distrust of art. Hardy's kinship with Wordsworth is not surprising, since he adopted, as 'the Wordsworthian dictum', the realist principle that 'the more perfectly the natural object is reproduced, the more truly poetic the picture' – a conviction which seems naturally to tally with his declared ambition 'to see the beauty in ugliness', a willed expansion of the range of poetic subject which clearly echoes the ambitions of the *Lyrical Ballads*.[27]

The paradoxical kind of imagination discovered in the new *Lyrical Ballads*, devoted as it is to running up against the ends of art, finds a small-scale opportunity to prove itself at the level of diction. Wordsworth's audacious exploration of the imaginative power of disappointment plays itself out in the sometimes startling movements of his verse, between an established 'poetic' elevation and 'ordinary' language. The lure of the ordinary in language, naturally enough, accompanies a renewed interest in the imaginative legitimacy of the quotidian and mundane; and it is this belief that the 'Preface' repeatedly asserts, implicitly declining the high task of visionary epic ('Poetry sheds no tears "such as Angels weep"': *WPrW*, i.134) and announcing instead the merits of a vigorously realist kind of imagination, insisting on the precedence of 'nature' over artifice, and denying the distinction and specialness of the aesthetic. Wordsworth's poems will utilize 'the very language of men' and forsake 'the common inheritance of Poets' (*WPrW*, i.130, 132). It is not hard to see that this hostility to art involves a paradox, which, as Coleridge quickly demonstrated when he teased at the theory in

Biographia, proves wholly self-undoing if you try to make it system-atic. Wordsworth claims that his poems in *Lyrical Ballads* utilize an ordinary idiom (which he confusingly identifies with the language of 'prose') and appeals to the real language of men as a criterion by which to rule out personification and the other tricks of poetic diction. By the time of *Biographia*, Coleridge had come to value the differentness and peculiarity of poetic language, not its kinship with ordinary speech, or with prose, and he has no trouble showing that Wordsworth's language is frequently quite extra-ordinary (*BL*, ii.105–6). But perhaps this misses the important point about ordinar-iness in Wordsworth's verse: the clue to that might be glimpsed when Coleridge disputes Wordsworth's analysis of Gray's sonnet on the death of West (*BL*, ii.63–4, 73–5), intent on showing the unworkable nature of Wordsworth's distinction between an artifical and a natural idiom. Wordsworth had quoted the sonnet in his 'Preface', italicizing the lines which he saw breaking the artful rule of Gray's own neo-clas-sical prejudice and stooping instead to the true voice of the real language of men.

> In vain to me the smiling mornings shine,
> And reddening Phœbus lifts his golden fire:
> The birds in vain their amorous descant join,
> Or chearful fields resume their green attire:
> These ears, alas! for other notes repine;
> *A different object do these ears require;*
> *My lonely anguish melts no heart but mine;*
> *And in my breast the imperfect joys expire;*
> Yet Morning smiles the busy race to cheer,
> And new-born pleasure brings to happier men;
> The fields to all their wonted tribute bear;
> To warm their little loves the birds complain.
> *I fruitless mourn to him that cannot hear*
> *And weep the more because I weep in vain.*
>
> (*WPrW*, i.132–4)

Wordsworth says it is obvious that the only parts of the sonnet of any value are the italicized bits, which are redeeming resorts to the ordi-nary: 'the language of these lines does in no respect differ from that of prose' (*WPrW*, i.134); while Coleridge disagrees, finding most of them quite as remote from normal language as the rest of the poem (*BL*, ii.74).

The subtler point suggested by Wordsworth's method of quoting is that the chosen lines acquire their sense of suddenly felt truth (if they do) because of the contrast their register strikes with the surrounding, artful lines: ordinariness is contextual, and emerges thanks to the poem's *diversity* of idioms. I gratefully borrow this point from Michael O'Neill;[28] and it calls to mind, in a general way, the discussion of poetic diction in Donald Davie's *Purity of Diction in English Verse*. Davie there pointed out that the great effect made possible by the apparently restrictive expectations of dictional propriety is their calculated violation, so that (for instance) a poem may appear to lapse momentarily from the regions of artistry and into, as it were, a lived immediacy without art. Pope satirized such descents as 'sinking in poetry', and Coleridge borrowed the derogatory term 'sinkings' in *Biographia* (*BL*, ii.52); but a renovated form of such bathos, might be seen as lying at the heart of many of Wordsworth's most distinctive poems, a version on the small scale of diction of the kinds of frustration of art, the staged lapsing into the 'unpoetic', that I have been describing his poems enacting on the larger scales of narrative and subject-matter.

Coleridge evidently watched the dissipation of the great philosophical poem into little poems with concern and exasperation. He sounds keen enough about the 1800 *Ballads* in letters (*CL*, ii.707–8, 714); but his remarks to Southey about the poems Wordsworth had written by the summer of 1802 are more openly sceptical, though still anxious to retain the faith, and single out the determinedly unpoetic lapses of Wordsworth's diction as the problem: 'here & there a daring Humbleness of Language & Versification, and a strict adherence to matter of fact, even to prolixity, that startled me'. The letter links these doubts directly with Coleridge's hesitations over the tenets of the 'Preface' of 1800 – 'the Preface as it stood in the second Volume', he calls it, presumably meaning 'edition' – which, evidently, have led Wordsworth astray (*CL*, ii.830). Years later, in *Biographia*, his complaint is the same. There, pointedly, Coleridge borrows Wordsworth's method of quoting, and turns it back on his friend's own work: he italicizes to much the same effect as Wordsworth had Gray; but now these 'sinkings' away from the language of art are condemned, and the italics exasperated, marking lapses from poetry – lapses from an idiom of aesthetic 'vision' to one merely of circumstantial sight, and so forgoing the self-sufficing aesthetic value of 'pleasure' for the contingent and worldly attribute of 'truth' (*BL*, ii.130). The star exhibits in Coleridge's chapter of complaints were mostly products of 1802, but they were chosen for manifesting the adventurous use of 'incongruity' (*BL*, ii.124) that had been sponsored by the contaminating realist impulses of the 1800 'Preface' (as Coleridge saw it). 'Resolution and Independence', in particular, exemplified the way that Wordsworth's art dwells distractingly on the 'accidental circumstances ... the full explanation of his living characters' (*BL*, ii.126).

Coleridge's way with 'I wandered lonely as a cloud' represents his technique most clearly. Having praised warmly Wordsworth's description of 'the *inward* eye ... which is indeed *"the bliss of solitude"'*, he goes on to complain (resorting to emphatic italics),

> Assuredly we seem to sink most abruptly, not to say burlesquely, and almost as in a *medly* from this couplet to –

> > And then my heart with pleasure fills,
> > And dances with the *daffodils*.

> > (*BL*, ii.137)

A sinking 'prosaism' out of the poetic, like this, occurs when the poem's aesthetic destiny is interrupted by a truth too ordinary, too locally occasional. Wordsworth's imagination clearly thrived upon such truths, often in an illicit kind of way, and upon the realist recalcitrance they offered to the would-be absolute authority of the poet's sublime ego. Still, he remained sensitive to possible attack, and defended himself warily in the 1800 'Preface' against those critics who 'when they stumble upon these prosaisms as they call them, imagine that they have made a notable discovery, and exult over the Poet as over a man ignorant of his own profession' (*WPrW*, i.132): my prosaisms are witting ones, he seems to say; my arts lapses into its sinkings with my permission. Wordsworth can hardly have predicted that his partner in *Lyrical Ballads* would turn out to be one of those hostile critics – although, with hindsight, he might have recognized that signs of dissent were always there. Despite the disapproval of poetic diction that young Coleridge shared with Wordsworth,[29] he had already begun to suspect a literary 'affectation of unaffectedness' (*CL*, i.357); so the criticisms in *Biographia* were, in part, acts of belated self-criticism. (Wordsworth often found himself occupying the unwelcome role of a surrogate for an aspect of Coleridge's own earlier self in *Biographia*, which may help explain his impatient response to the book.)

(v)

Coleridge's increasing distaste for the contingent, accidental and ordinary, and his consequent distaste for Wordsworth's art of the 1800
moment, which sought so resourcefully to include them, marks a decisive shift in his theological views, away from the optimistic
necessitarianism which had prompted *The Recluse* in the first place,
and towards a philosophy that, instead, elevated the sovereign mind
above the unmeaning and diverse contingencies of its worldly circumstances. Consciousness, in this view, far from being itself an
'accident', is the only place where a necessary unity might inhere; and
poetry exemplifies the sorts of ideal order that the mind is uniquely
empowered to achieve: poets are 'Bridlers by Delight, the Purifiers ...
the true Protoplasts, Gods of Love who tame the Chaos' (*CN*, ii.2355).
Wordsworth worked assiduously to keep up with the changing
Coleridgean scene, and included some powerful passages in the
revised versions of *The Prelude*, and elsewhere, confirming the new
position; but one senses that he was much less compelled than
Coleridge to resolve the conflicting ingredients of his thought, and
the poems he had written when inspired under a quite different
dispensation, and the 'Preface' to *Lyrical Ballads*, stood, revised but
unretracted, in successive editions.

   Still, if the theology that prompted the inevitabilism had waned, its
emotive appeal, and even its rhetoric, persisted in the writings of both
men. The metaphor in Coleridge's complaint about Wordsworth's
'*disharmony* in style' (*BL*, ii.123) might already lead us back to the
symphonic rhetoric of necessity of the 1790s. And less figuratively,
when *Biographia* attacks Wordsworth's lapses into the unpoetic, it
does so (as I have already said) by lamenting a poetry that declines a
properly inevitable destiny. In doing so, it repeats Coleridge's objections when (years before) he had lamented Wordsworth's small poems
not being the millennial success of *The Recluse*. Now, however, that
inevitability is not a theme for philosophical epic – an attribute of
history or of the good life – but has been conjured into a purely
aesthetic criterion: what Coleridge once called, in a pregnant phrase,
'the necessity of poetry'.[30] The fully developed teleological aesthetic –
which *Biographia* deploys, rather unforgivingly, upon the cultivated
errancy of Wordsworth's lyrics – does not find expression until the
middle part of Coleridge's career, in the idea of a perfectly self-neces-
sitating poem, which 'contain[s] in itself the reason why it is so, and
not otherwise' (*BL*, ii.12), like a textual version of the inevitable grace

Wordsworth wishfully found in Grasmere, 'A Whole without dependence or defect'. The poem, in this displaced millennial vision, grows under the implacable influence of its own mini-'*Natur-geist*', every aspect of its completed existence an expression of its 'indwelling Power', 'acting creatively under laws of its own origination'.[31]

All that sounds thoroughly German; but the seeds of the position, I am arguing, lie in the inevitabilist thought that Coleridge shared with Wordsworth in the 1790s. (I am following Abrams, then, who describes the translation of concepts from theological historicism to aesthetic doctrine in *Natural Supernaturalism* and elsewhere.) The parallel that Coleridge will habitually draw, in his later aesthetics, between God in His Universe and the genius in the micro-cosmos of his poems, grants each great poem a mini-Providence of its own: 'what the Globe is in Geography, *miniaturing* in order to *manifest* the Truth', Coleridge told Cottle, 'such is a Poem to that Image of God, which we were created into, and which still seeks that Unity, or Revelation of the *One* in and by the *Many*' (*CL*, iv.545). Imagination becomes a way of redeeming the world, momentarily, idealizing nature to the nonce-heaven of the poem: like God in the necessitarian universe that Coleridge had once espoused, imagination in the poem is 'a subtle Spirit, all in each part, reconciling & unifying all' (*CL*, iii.361). And like that discarded image of a providential universe, poetic works possess an ideal inevitability: 'each Line, each word almost, begets the following – and the Will of the writer is an interfusion, a continuous agency'[32] – and talk of the 'interfusion' of the ineluctable but undetected author–God takes us swiftly back to the inevitabilist 1790s rhetoric of 'Religious Musings' and 'Lines written … above Tintern Abbey'. 'Wordsworth's poetry', said Arnold, after quoting the master on the shortcomings of Goethe, 'when he is at his best, is inevitable, as inevitable as Nature herself';[33] and Coleridge would doubtless have agreed. But, unlike Arnold, he chose to invoke the concept mostly when regretting those poems that lacked it by their reckless and accidental admission of the 'unpoetic'. The incidental detail with which Wordsworth is drawn to surround his characters – like the proliferating and extraneous data included in his long 1800 note to 'The Thorn' (*LBB*, pp. 287–9) – belongs properly with the contingencies of biography ('It is for the Biographer, not the Poet, to give the *accidents* of *individual* Life': *CL*, iv.572), or with the pseudo-histories of Defoe (*BL*, ii.133), not, certainly, in the idealizing realm of poetry.

After *Biographia*, Wordsworth dutifully corrected some of the prosaisms that Coleridge had identified, like the famous lines from

'The Thorn', replacing them with something killingly decorous. That implies some hesitation on his own part; and indeed Wordsworth seems always to have been less than wholly secure in his medley-art. No wonder: since the disapproval that its heterogeneity earns at some points in *Biographia* is secretly very close to the warm praise the poetic imagination receives at others for bringing together discordant elements. When wanting poetry to be ideal and inevitable, Coleridge deplores Wordsworth's hybrid imagination, which admits the inconsequence of the actual; but this heterogeneity of ideal and real is, during the more generous moments of *Biographia*, precisely Coleridge's grounds for maintaining his friend's genius, which is held triumphantly to reconcile opposites, uniting the idealizing power of the mind's eye with the steady eye of a nature poet. Wordsworth, at these moments, might seem to emulate Shakespeare, whom Coleridge once praised for his ability to give 'reality, individual Life, by the introduction of *Accidents*'.[34] '[A] poem of any length neither can be, *or ought to be*, all poetry', Coleridge declares in *Biographia* (*BL*, ii.15, emphasis added), as though responding more enthusiastically to the hybrid art, of poetic and unpoetic together, that he elsewhere deplored.[35]

(vi)

Perhaps the central question about Coleridge's literary career is that of its continuity, or discontinuity; but investigating the possibility of an intellectual or imaginative continuity is complicated by another difficulty, which is where to look for it. Quite diverse kinds of Coleridgean thought are often shaped by the same fundamental conception or impulse: what Richard Haven called long ago, in a suggestive phrase, 'patterns of consciousness';[36] and, as they appear in one area of Coleridge's thought, and then in another, they create a distinctive spectacle: styles of thinking which reflection has proven beyond the pale in their original contexts – political or theological contexts, say – often persist in other areas of his capacious genius. The inevitabilism of Coleridge's criticism of Wordsworth is such a phenomenon: Coleridge continuing, in a quite diverse area of his thought, patterns of consciousness that, in their original conceptual home, have long since been officially surpassed – patterns which, in this particular case, he had originally shared with the object of criticism upon whom he is now directing their displaced version.[37]

Notes

1 Iris Murdoch, *Existentialists and Mystics. Writings on Philosophy and Literature* (London: Chatto and Windus, 1997), pp. 294–5.

2 Matthew Arnold, *Essays on English Literature*, ed. F.W. Bateson (London: Longman, 1965), p. 104.

3 *London Magazine* (October, 1820); quoted in *The Romantics on Milton. Formal Essays and Critical Asides*, ed. Joseph Antony Wittreich, Jr. (Cleveland, Ohio: Case Western Reserve University Press, 1970), p. 298.

4 Not quite what Aristotle said, in fact: see *WPrW*, i.179, note to l.378.

5 Joshua Reynolds, *Fifteen Discourses Delivered at the Royal Academy* (London: Dent (Everyman), [n.d.]), pp. 27, 155, 107, 30.

6 *The Philosophical Lectures of Samuel Taylor Coleridge, Hitherto Unpublished*, ed. Kathleen Coburn (London: Pilot Press, 1949), p. 194. For Coleridge's misreading of Reynolds, see M.H. Abrams, *The Mirror and the Lamp. Romantic Theory and the Critical Tradition* (New York: Oxford University Press, 1953), pp. 342–3n.48.

7 In the way that Coleridge's organicism, while it can claim Aristotelian precedent, has been so re-invigorated by Coleridge's speculations about life and vitality as to be practically a new doctrine.

8 *The Letters of Charles and Mary Anne Lamb*, ed. Edwin W. Marrs (3 vols to date; Ithaca, NY: Cornell University Press, 1975–), i.18.

9 Basil Willey, *Samuel Taylor Coleridge* (London: Chatto and Windus, 1972), p. 39.

10 S.T. Coleridge, *The Watchman*, ed. Lewis Patton (London/Princeton, NJ: Routledge and Kegan Paul/Princeton University Press, 1970), p. 132.

11 David Perkins, *The Quest for Permanence. The Symbolism of Wordsworth, Shelley and Keats* (Cambridge, Mass.: Harvard University Press, 1959).

12 'Send No Money'; in Philip Larkin, *Collected Poems*, ed. Anthony Thwaite (London: Marvell Press/Faber, 1988), p. 146.

13 Jonathan Wordsworth, *William Wordsworth: The Borders of Vision* (Oxford: Clarendon Press, 1982; corr. repr., 1984), p. 342. I am gratefully indebted to Jonathan Wordsworth's fine account of millennialism and *The Recluse*.

14 See William Wordsworth, *Home at Grasmere. Part First, Book First of* The Recluse, ed. Beth Darlington (Ithaca, NY: Cornell University Press, 1977), pp. 11, 139ff.

15 Wordsworth, *Borders of Vision*, p. 359.

16 Wordsworth, *Borders of Vision*, pp. 340–77; Stephen Gill, *William Wordsworth. A Life* (Oxford: Clarendon Press, 1989), pp. 163, 230–1, *etc.*; and Kenneth Johnston, *Wordsworth and* The Recluse (New Haven, Conn.: Yale University Press, 1984).

17 Quoted from a letter of Dora Wordsworth by Beth Darlington: *Home at Grasmere*, p. 30.

18 In fact, a not dissimilar divergence from the requirements of Coleridge's incipient aesthetic theory can be seen in the formal experiments of Coleridge's own poems, as I have argued elsewhere (in 'Coleridge's Millennial Embarrassments', *Essays in Criticism* 50:1 (2000), pp. 1–22).

19 V, ll.864–8; William Shakespeare, *Love's Labours Lost*, ed. Richard David (London: Methuen (Arden Shakespeare), 1951; repr., 1956), p. 193.

20   *Don Juan*, III, l.1; *Byron*, ed. Jerome J. McGann (Oxford: Oxford University Press, 1986), p. 488.

21   *The Tempest*, I, ii, l.119; William Shakespeare, *The Tempest*, ed. Frank Kermode (London: Methuen (Arden Shakespeare), 1954; repr., 1961), p. 16.

22   Geoffrey H. Hartman, *Wordsworth's Poetry 1787–1814* (New Haven, Conn.: Yale University Press, 1964; repr., 1971), p. 159.

23   'Afternoons'; in Larkin, *Collected Poems*, p. 121.

24   See the letter reproduced in Thomas Hardy, *The Life and Work of Thomas Hardy*, ed. Michael Millgate (Basingstoke/London: Macmillan, 1984; corr. repr., 1989), pp. 360–1. In fact, as this letter shows, Hardy considered his 'philosophy of life' to have reconciled freedom and determinism (rather as Coleridge came to hope his own system had); but the first plans of *The Dynasts* seem to have envisaged the dissolution of free agency as the point: 'Action mostly automatic, reflex movement, etc. Not the result of what is called *motive*, though always ostensibly so, even to the actors' own consciousness' (*Life*, p. 152).

25   'The Caged Goldfinch'; in *The Complete Poems of Thomas Hardy*, ed. James Gibson (London: Macmillan, 1976), p. 491.

26   John Powell Ward, *The English Line. Poetry of the Unpoetic from Wordsworth to Larkin* (Basingstoke/London: Macmillan, 1991).

27   Hardy, *Life*, pp. 151, 124.

28   Michael O'Neill, '*Lyrical Ballads* and "Pre-Established Codes of Decision"': above, p. 138.

29   In 1802, Coleridge told Mary Matilda Betham that he admired her 'On a Cloud', but went on (as she recalled), 'it would have been faultless if I had not used the word *Phoebus* in it, which he thought inadmissable in modern poetry' (*CPW*, i.374). 'Phoebus' is still an object of disapproval in *BL* (ii.75).

30   S.T. Coleridge, *Table Talk*, ed. Carl Woodring (2 vols; London/Princeton, NJ: Routledge/Princeton University Press, 1990), i.442. The phrase is picked out, and its implications expounded, in Paul Hamilton, *Coleridge's Poetics* (Oxford: Blackwell, 1983), pp. 135–85.

31   S.T. Coleridge, *Lectures 1808–1819 On Literature*, ed. R.A. Foakes (2 vols; London/Princeton, NJ: Routledge and Kegan Paul/Princeton University Press, 1987), ii.223; i.495.

32   S.T. Coleridge, *Marginalia*, ed. George Whalley and H.J. Jackson and George Whalley (4 vols to date; London/Princeton, NJ: Routledge and Kegan Paul/Princeton University Press, 1980–), i.401.

33   Arnold, *Essays*, p. 104.

34   Coleridge, *Lectures 1808–1819 On Literature*, i.561.

35   A lesson, incidentally, which Hardy took: 'following Coleridge in holding that a long poem should not attempt to be poetical all through' (Hardy, *Life*, p. 212).

36   Richard Haven, *Patterns of Consciousness. An Essay on Coleridge* ([n.p.]: University of Massachusetts Press, 1969).

37   I am most grateful to the participants in the 1999 Wordsworth Summer Conference at Dove Cottage (where a version of this essay was presented) for their discussion; and I owe a particular debt to the generous suggestions of Dr Jane Stabler and Professor Nicholas Roe.

9
Reading Aloud: An 'Ambiguous Accompaniment'

Lucy Newlyn

(i) Hazlitt on preaching, chanting, and speaking

'It seemed to me, who was then young, as if the sounds had echoed from the bottom of the human heart, and as if that prayer might have floated in solemn silence through the universe' (Hazlitt, xvii.108). The year of writing is 1823. Hazlitt (at forty-five the most distinguished journalist and critic in Britain) is recalling his first encounter with Coleridge, which took place in the small Unitarian chapel at Shrewsbury, one Sunday morning in 1798. It was a year he retrospectively associated with youthful idealism, the birth of a new poetic spirit, and, crucially, the emergence of his own creative voice. Preaching a Unitarian sermon, Coleridge had the 'long pendulous hair ... peculiar to enthusiasts', and in the dim light of the chapel, 'a strange wildness in his aspect, a dusky obscurity'. Passionate with the eloquence of gratitude, Hazlitt remembers listening to him as the experience of a lifetime:

> my heart, shut up in the prison-house of this rude clay, has never found, nor will it ever find, a heart to speak to; but that my understanding also did not remain dumb and brutish, or at length found a language to express itself, I owe to Coleridge. (Hazlitt, xvii.107)

In his many regretful and angry reproaches against this genius who deserted the radical cause, Coleridge the Unitarian preacher – a larger-than-life, more magnetic version of his own father – haunted Hazlitt's imagination in a form reminiscent of Milton's republican hero, the damaged archangel of *Paradise Lost*. 'The figures that composed' the date 1798 were etched in his memory as clearly as 'the dreaded name of Demogorgon'. Associatively recalling the momentous year of 1789, they conjured up the spirit of millennarian optimism, embodied in Coleridge, which first inspired him to write. Accompanying his tribute to the poet's 'strange power of speech', there was a longing that history might reverse itself (like the two last figures of 1798); that the shadows of a personal, political, and spiritual betrayal might be removed, and the 'primitive spirit of Christianity', with its progressive power, restored.

'My First Acquaintance with Poets' is a deeply affectionate and elegiac essay, but not an uncritical one. It discloses the depth of Hazlitt's anger with respect to Coleridge's apostasy, and his regret that the political impetus behind *Lyrical Ballads* could not be sustained. Hazlitt's reception of *The Statesman's Manual* and *A Lay Sermon*, which can be traced in a sequence of reviews in *The Examiner* and the *Edinburgh Review* in 1816–17, is a key to understanding its allusive implications. In the infamous 'review by anticipation' published anonymously among the 'Literary Notices' in *The Examiner* on September 8, 1816, Coleridge had been accused of haunting the public imagination 'with obscure noises', keeping up 'the importance of his oracular communications, by letting them remain a profound secret both to himself and the world' (Hazlitt, vii.114). In the *Edinburgh Review* article which appeared in December of the same year, he was reprimanded for muttering 'all unintelligible, and all impertinent things'; for speaking rhapsodically from a pulpit or rostrum that was 'high enthroned above all height' like the Satanic seat of Dullness in Pope's *Dunciad* (Hazlitt, xvi.113). In his spoof-letter to the editor of *The Examiner*, dated January 12, 1817, Hazlitt adopted the persona of his own earlier self to eulogise Coleridge's sermon-delivery in 1798 ('Poetry and Philosophy had met together, Truth and Genius had embraced, under the eye and with the sanction of Religion'), then asked truculently how there came to be such a mismatch between the Coleridge he remembered and the Coleridge whose 'Lay Sermon' had recently been reviewed:

> what I have to complain of is this, that from reading your account of the 'Lay-Sermon,' I begin to suspect that my notions formerly must have been little better than a deception. ... Again, Sir, I ask Mr Coleridge, why, having preached such a sermon as I have described, he has published such a sermon as you have described? What right, Sir, has he or any man to make a fool of me or any man? (Hazlitt, vii.129)

This letter formed the germ of 'My First Acquaintance', and when Hazlitt requisitioned it in 1823, he was tacitly recalling two very different contexts in which Coleridge had delivered sermons. In 1798, he had talked on 'peace and war; upon church and state – not [as in 1816] their alliance, but their separation' (Hazlitt, xvii. 108). A contemporary audience would have been more immediately aware than we are of the troubled reception-history packed into that single, glancing remark.

The same holds true of ironies further on in the narrative of 'My First Acquaintance'. Soon after his description of the encounter with Coleridge in Shrewsbury chapel, Hazlitt moves to a scene of reading that is altogether more homely. Describing his first visit to see the Wordsworths at Alfoxden, he remembers how 'Coleridge read aloud with a sonorous and musical voice, the ballad of *Betty Foy*' (Hazlitt, xvii.117). The full resonance of those words 'sonorous and musical' comes from their double associations – with the charged eloquence of Coleridge's earlier sermon-delivery, and with the bardic orality recently celebrated by such writers as Macpherson and Blair, and revived in the collaborative venture of *Lyrical Ballads*. There is a touch of bathos in the conjunction between registers, the idiomatic sounds of Wordsworth's 'Betty Foy' becoming slightly muffled in Coleridge's elevated recital. Hazlitt hints, here, with the benefit of hindsight, at the 'radical Difference' (*CL*, ii.830) between two theories of poetic language. It was a difference that had emerged implicitly in the 1798 collaboration, and it became discernible in the 'Preface' to *Lyrical Ballads* (1800). In subsequent statements by Coleridge in 1802 it was openly recognized, and by the time *Biographia Literaria* was published it had become the focus for sustained theoretical discussion.[1] It centred on whether poetry was or was not inevitably more elevated than spoken language. Wordsworth in 1798 had wanted to take poetry as close as possible to the rhythms and register of ordinary speech, while Coleridge by 1816 had concluded that poetic language was by definition extraordinary. This difference with respect to language was confirmed by other differences of poetic temperament and subject-matter. Summarizing these in *Biographia Literaria*, Coleridge hit upon a shorthand formula: there was, he argued, a division of labour between the two poets, Wordsworth dealing with everyday concerns, while he himself focused on the supernatural. This *post hoc* rationalization of their divergence helped to minimize the pain and mess to which it had given rise.

Hazlitt's hint that differences were already apparent in 1798 is amplified two pages later in 'My First Acquaintance' when he describes how Wordsworth 'sat down and talked very naturally and freely, with a mixture of clear gushing accents in his voice, a deep gutteral intonation, and a strong tincture of the northern *burr*, like the crust on wine' (Hazlitt, xvii.118). The Rousseauian associations of 'naturally and freely' (implicitly contrasted with 'sonorous and musical') combine here with an enjoyment of regional accent and personal idiolect, themselves redolent of the vernacular liberties celebrated in *Lyrical Ballads*. Wordsworth's voice acquires what Hazlitt elsewhere calls 'gusto': its intensity and immediacy are those of 'manly' prose.[2] Familial and domestic, the meal around the kitchen-table at Alfoxden both complements and contrasts with the dark chapel at Shrewsbury, where Coleridge had disclosed his affinities with seventeenth-century enthusiasm. There was, Hazlitt implies, a powerful convergence of eloquence and oratory on the one hand with idiomatic spontaneity on the other, which made the *Lyrical Ballads* a rich experiment in progressive discourse. But at the same time, this hybrid venture was shadowed from the outset by its bifurcation.

If the ironies and equivocations in Hazlitt's narrative show him to be retrospectively alert to subtle incompatibilities between Wordsworth and Coleridge, pulling their linguistic theories in opposite directions, they also point to more troubling affinities in the two poets' attitudes to audience, which had complicated the reception of *Lyrical Ballads* and hampered their subsequent careers. A passing resemblance between Wordsworth's northern burr and the 'burr burr' of the idiot boy (unlikely to be accidental) at once celebrates and ironizes an aesthetic grounded in the sympathetic identification between a poet and his subject-matter. Hazlitt's irony, directed at the poet's lack of critical detachment, is confirmed a page further on, when he tells how

> Wordsworth read us the story of Peter Bell in the open air; and the comment upon it by his face and voice was very different from that of some later critics! Whatever might be thought of the poem, 'his face was as a book where men may read strange matters'. (Hazlitt, xvii.118)

As the focus of attention moves from the poet's performance of his poem among friends to its public reception by critics and reviewers, Hazlitt's sympathy gives way to sarcasm:

There is a *chaunt* in the recitation both of Coleridge and Wordsworth, which acts as a spell upon the hearer, and disarms the judgment. Perhaps they have deceived themselves by making habitual use of this ambiguous accompaniment. (Hazlitt, xvii.118)

The aside is brief but telling. Hazlitt plays on the phonetic and etymological links between 'chant' and 'enchantment' to drive home a critique of the poetics underpinning *Lyrical Ballads*. He suggests that, despite their underlying difference of opinion with respect to language and the supernatural, Coleridge and Wordsworth shared a desire to awaken in their readers a sense of mystery – to bring them under a spell. For Hazlitt, whose dissenting origins put him on the side of rational enlightenment, this component of poetic language was suspect. It was this that made poetry 'fall in with the language of power' (Hazlitt, iv.214–15), sometimes against its own intentions.

In showing how the two poets enchanted each other, Hazlitt begins to adumbrate the story of withdrawal and political apostasy which was to unfold in their subsequent careers. He seems to hold their collaboration responsible for each poet's relinquishment of an authentic radical voice. The 'chaunt' in which he remembers hearing them read their poems aloud sounds a hollow note after the passionate commitment of Coleridge's sermon and the rugged homeliness of Wordsworth's spoken idiom. It recalls a mode of delivery which flattened and homogenized their distinctive energies into a monotonous unity. Hazlitt's choice of the obsolete, poetic variant of the word 'chant' is redolent of 'The Ancient Mariner's archaic diction. 'Chaunt' was the word with which Wordsworth chose to replace 'speak' when he revised the passage in *The Prelude* Book XIII in which he nostalgically re-lived the 1798 collaboration: 'Thou in bewitching words, with happy heart, / Didst chaunt the vision of that Ancient Man, / The bright-eyed Mariner' (*Prelude* (1850), XIV, ll.400–2). And when Coleridge composed 'To William Wordsworth', 'on the night after his recitation of a poem on the growth of an individual mind', he returned Wordsworth's compliment with an apposite allusion. *The Prelude*, he wrote, was 'An Orphic tale indeed, / A song divine of high and passionate thoughts / *To their own music chaunted!*' ('To William Wordsworth', ll.45–7; *CPW*, i.406; emphasis added). The association of 'chaunting' with the highest of poetic registers (epic, heroic, traditional) is confirmed by Hazlitt himself in his *Spirit of the Age* essay on Byron, where it is used to describe the 'solemn measures' in which *Childe Harold* 'chaunts a hymn to fame', rekindling 'the earliest aspirations of the mind after greatness and true glory' (Hazlitt, xi.73). The Oxford English Dictionary gives as its second and fourth definitions of the word, 'to sing, utter musically' (often with notion of 'prolonged or drawling intonation'); and 'to recite musically, intone; to sing a chant, as the Psalms, etc. in public worship'. If the dimension of 'public worship' implied in chanting was out of place in the safety and privacy of Alfoxden, so too the democratic agenda of the *Lyrical Ballads* volume (the 'levelling muse' discerned by Hazlitt) was at odds with an elevated and mystifying delivery.

Hazlitt's critique extends beyond the politics of style, into the politics of reception. Mischievously applying Coleridge's idea of the 'suspension of disbelief' to this private scene of reading, he suggests that the *Biographia*'s distinction between illusion and delusion is shaky, and that this casts doubt on the quality of the material delivered.[3] Hearers who succumb to a spell may 'chuse to be deceived', but if their judgement is disarmed in the process, how is it possible to distinguish between 'enchantment' and what Hugh Blair calls 'blind, implicit veneration'?[4] Once again, the shadow-context of December 1816 provides a key to Hazlitt's meaning. 'In this state of voluntary self-delusion', he laments, in his review of the *Lay Sermon*, Coleridge 'mistakes hallucinations for truths ... It is [in] this sort of waking dream, this giddy maze of opinions, started, and left, and resumed ... that Mr Coleridge's pleasure lies' (Hazlitt, xvi.101). Implied in Hazlitt's comments on reading aloud was a critique which reflected more widely on coterie reading-circles, systems of private patronage, and mutual 'puffing', as they prevailed in late eighteenth-century Britain. Just as the magic exerted over an audience by the sing-song voice of a poet disarmed the judgement of both poets and listeners, so the mutual congratulation of poets who were each others' ideal audience was in danger of preempting the criticism poetry needed and deserved. 'Chaunting', in this context, began to take on associations with the vanity of Chaucer's Chaunticleer.

(ii) The orator's speaking body: from Sheridan to Thelwall

To understand the full implications of Hazlitt's allusion to 'chaunting' in this late essay, we need to put it in the wider context of issues concerning the politics of language – and specifically of performative utterance – which had been actively debated in Britain from the mid-eighteenth century onward. Our knowledge of how reading aloud was understood both inside and outside the dissenting tradition helps us to make clear discriminations between a bodily eloquence whose rhythms were those of everyday prose and an elevated, chanting delivery whose affiliations were to poetry. In practice, however, as we shall see, ideas that travelled down different conduits of influence could cross over and merge. When Hazlitt identified Wordsworth's and Coleridge's manner in reading aloud as 'an ambiguous accompaniment', he nicely caught the sense in which the *Lyrical Ballads* project straddled discursive preferences. Chanting had a complex linguistic significance, disclosing a range of possible inflections for oral discourse at this time. Its musicality could claim kinship with the ballad tradition, and with a distinctly progressive notion of primitivism. But it could also attach itself to the more oracular authority of the Anglican church. Symbolically, the doubleness of these associations, as retrospectively detected by Hazlitt, accounts for the later divergence of Wordsworth's 'natural conversation of men under the influence of natural feelings' (*BL*, ii.42) from Coleridge's Aristotelian belief that 'poetry is essentially *ideal*' (*BL*, ii.45).

Hazlitt's preference for the spoken idiom of prose over the sung idiom of poetry had its roots in an oratorical tradition, germane to the collaboration of 1798, in which chanting was condemned. The key contributors to this tradition were the Irish orator, Thomas Sheridan (father of Richard Sheridan), who gave lecture courses all over Britain in the 1760s; James Burgh, who published a cheap and popular instruction manual, *The Art of Speaking* in 1763; Hugh Blair, whose *Lectures on Rhetoric and Belles Lettres* were delivered over a period of twenty-four years in Edinburgh; and Joseph Priestley, whose *Lectures on Oratory and Criticism*, given at the Dissenting Academy of Warrington, were published in 1777.

'Some of our greatest men have been trying to do that with the pen, which can only be performed by the the tongue; to produce effects by the dead letter, which can never be produced but by the living voice, with its accompaniments'.[5] These words are taken from the 'Preface' to Sheridan's *Lectures on Elocution*, the single most important contribution to elocutionary theory in the eighteenth century. Published in 1762 with a subscription-list of 1700 names, 600 of them 'taken down at the door of the several places where the lectures had been delivered',[6] this book represented the summation of a decade's thought, as it had been tried and tested on numerous audiences in Bristol, Oxford, Cambridge and Edinburgh. W. Benzie, in his learned monograph, *The Dublin Orator*, informs us that Sheridan learnt the art of oral expression from Swift, his godfather, who made him read aloud two to three hours a day – a tradition later upheld, in the 'Attic Mornings' in Bath beginning in 1763, where Sheridan recited select passages from great authors.[7]

At the centre of Sheridan's theory of language was a belief that there were two kinds of language, spoken and written – 'one ... the gift of God, the other, the invention of man' – and that the power which words acquired, 'when forcibly uttered by the living voice', was a power for good, creating sympathy between human beings through a universal language.[8] In drawing attention to the gap between speaking and writing, Sheridan's focus narrowed on the act of reading, which 'must fall short of the power of speaking, in all articles which depend upon feeling'. He lamented what he called 'a certain tone or chant in reading or reciting'. This, he claimed, was produced by the modern art of punctuation, 'not taken from the art of speaking' but from 'grammatical construction, often without reference to the pauses used in discourse'. If punctuation had never been invented, there would have been no such thing as the 'reading tones' or 'false pauses and rests of the voice':[9]

> Here then is to be found the true source of the bad manner of reading and speaking in public, that so generally prevails: which is, that we are taught to read in a different way, with different tones and cadences, from those which we use in speaking; and this artificial manner, is used instead of the natural one, in all recitals and repetitions at school, as well as in reading.[10]

Sheridan's solution to the gap between the spoken and the written discourse was twofold: first, he advocated a vocal eloquence, reinforced by 'expressive looks and significant gestures' – in short, a body-language of transparent feeling; and, secondly, he designed a new form of notation, directing the vocal emphases and pauses of the speaker in oral delivery by accents placed over the relevant words. In *The Art of Reading*, published in 1775, this notation was used 'to serve as Lessons to practice on',[11] and introduced so as to coincide with the political climax of Sheridan's argument – the moment at which a claim for eloquence became a claim for constitutional stability. In keeping with what Peter De Bolla calls 'the consensus politics of liberal humanism, the balanced economy of civic politesse',[12] Sheridan here made the commonplace link between the state of the language and the health of the nation:

> Now if the minds of the inhabitants of this country were formed by a suitable education correspondent to the nature of the constitution ... it would produce subjects worthy of so noble a form of government and capable of supporting it.[13]

The full force of Sheridan's vocal emphasis can be felt by comparing his pages with those from an exactly contemporary publication by the Cumbrian schoolmaster William Cockin, *The Art of Delivering Written Language; or, an Essay on Reading*, which was dedicated to the actor David Garrick. Cockin also advocated naturalness of spoken utterance in reading aloud; but his notation was graphocentric rather than phonocentric. In his text, all the emphases and modulations of the speaker's voice were directed by changes in font, paradoxically reinforcing the bondage of eye to text. Sheridan's was as near as one might get to a manual for reading aloud; Cockin's remained a visual representation of the voice reading.

James Burgh's *The Art of Speaking*, published in 1763, was associated with the 'mechanical' school of elocution, to which John Walker (author of three later works on elocution) also belonged. Burgh was of Scottish descent: the son of a Presbyterian minister in Perthshire, he abandoned his training for the ministry to become a businessman, but later set up an academy at Stoke Newington. From here, he published a number of important and strongly reformist works, including *Thoughts on Education* (1747) and *Political Disquisitions* (1774), a book that Hazlitt admired. Burgh's *The Art of Speaking* was designed 'to offer a help toward the improvement of youth in the useful and ornamental accomplishment of speaking properly their mother tongue', and its 'easy expence' and readable format made it one of the most popular instruction-manuals of its kind.[14] Wordsworth, who (like many other schoolboys) owned a copy, would have been familiar with its words of warning against monotonous delivery in reading aloud:

> Young readers are apt to get into a *rehearsing* kind of *monotony*; of which it is very difficult to break them. Monotony is holding one *uniform* humming sound through the whole discourse, without rising or falling. Cant is, in speaking, as psalmody and ballad in music, a strain consisting of a few notes *rising* and *falling* without variation, like a peal of bells, let the *matter* change how it will. The chaunt, with which the prose psalms are half-sung, half-said, in cathedrals, is the same kind of absurdity.[15]

Burgh's dismissal of three kinds of monotony – 'chaunting in cathedrals, psalmody in parish churches, ballad-music put to a number of verses' – is intriguing in the light of the various registers discussed in 'My First Acquaintance with Poets'; as is the etymological connection between 'chaunt' and 'cant'.[16]

Sheridan and Burgh were not alone in stressing the superiority of the living voice over the printed word. By the mid-eighteenth century, this preference had emerged as a distinctive feature of the primitivist poetic widely advocated in Britain and on the Continent. Hugh Blair (appointed to the newly created Chair in Rhetoric and Belles Lettres at Edinburgh University in 1760), was Scotland's counterpart to Rousseau in his commitment to what Derrida calls 'the metaphysics of presence'. As Fiona Stafford has argued, Blair saw 'the continuing value of speech even in modern society where written discourse had long been the medium of authority, and was becoming the main channel for intellectual traffic'.[17] His belief in the power of spoken utterance informed his enthusiasm about the discovery of Ossian, in whom he found his views on the connection between passion, primitive society and great poetry confirmed. Blair mentioned Sheridan in the published text of his *Lectures* in 1783. His preference for spoken over written communication was grounded in a conviction that 'the voice of the living speaker makes an impression on the mind, much stronger than can be made by the perusal of any writing'.[18] Voice precedes writing, in the same way that a natural language of gestures precedes sophisticated linguistic communication:

> The tones of voice, the looks and gesture, which accompany discourse, and which no Writing can convey, render discourse, when it is well-managed, infinitely more clear, and more expressive, than the most accurate Writing. For tones, looks, and gestures, are natural interpreters of the sentiments of the mind. They remove ambiguities; they enforce impressions, they operate on us by means of sympathy, which is one of the most powerful instruments of persuasion. Our sympathy is always awakened more, by hearing the Speaker, than by reading his works in our closet.[19]

In his extensive discussion of eloquence, Blair underlined the distinction between voice as the vehicle of sympathy and the printed word as its empty signifier: 'a discourse that is read moves us less than one that is spoken, as having less the appearance of coming warm from the heart' he says; and again: 'a discourse read, is far inferior to an oration spoken. It leads to a different sort of composition, as well as of delivery; and can never have an equal effect upon any audience'.[20] The habit of sing-song delivery was condemned by him, as it was by Sheridan, for its suppression of the sense behind the words spoken:

> If any one, in Public Speaking, shall have formed to himself a certain melody or tune, which requires rests and pauses of its own distinct from those of the sense, he has, for certain, contracted one of the worst habits into which a Public Speaker can fall.[21]

The relation of print to voice was also important to Joseph Priestley, who acknowledged the influence of Sheridan in his *Lectures on Oratory and Criticism* published in 1777. For Priestley, the art of oratory was the art of persuasion. It did not consist in elevated diction and delivery, but rather in the use of 'an *unpremeditated discourse*, in which the sentiments are supposed to be natural and sincere, proceeding directly from the heart'.[22] Priestley used the history of the dissenting tradition as proof of the power of extempore speaking: 'Can we imagine it possible that the primitive Christians, the first reformers, and, I may add, the founders of our modern sects ... could ever have attained to so great a degree of popularity, without the talent of haranguing extempore?' His elocutionary ideal was modelled on enthusiasm, its communicative power consisting in an expressive immediacy which was universally legible. Oratory was persuasive in so far as it was egalitarian: just as pauses, hesitations, consulting the interlocutor, created a bond of sympathy, on which the speaker's efficacy relied; so it was the informality of the spoken voice that rendered feelings powerfully: 'when the mind is agitated, the voice is interrupted, and the man expresses himself in short and broken sentences'. [23]

Priestley's discursive allegiances are summarized in a passage which was deeply germane to the concerns of Wordsworth and Coleridge in 1798–1800, but even more so to Hazlitt, educated at the Dissenting Academy in Hackney where Priestley taught after the Warrington Academy was dissolved in 1783:

> Anciently, I believe, in all nations, mankind were so captivated with the charms of verse, that, in reciting poetry, no regard was paid to anything but the metrical pause; which made the pronunciation of verse a kind of *singing* or *chanting*: and accordingly we never read of *poems* being *read*, but always of their being *sung* by them. Nor shall we wonder at this, if we consider that, even in our

own age, all persons who have not been instructed in the true art of pronunciation (which is governed wholly by the *sense*) naturally pronounce verse in the same manner, and quite differently from their manner of pronouncing prose; so that it generally requires a good deal of pains to correct that vicious habit.[24]

For Priestley, then, the art of correct pronunciation was one that disaffiliated 'reading aloud' from the poetic and musical end of the discursive spectrum, moving it securely into the domain of plain speaking. 'Let your primary regards be always to the *sense* and *perspicuity*', he advised, 'and in every competition between harmony and these more valuable objects ... let the harmony be sacrificed without hesitation'.[25]

Priestley's preference for reading aloud that is governed by a spoken rather than a written discourse was symptomatic of his loyalty to the clear-thinking tradition of enlightenment dissent. That preference was however complicated by his acknowledgement that writing was permanent, speech transient, and that print made ideas accessible in ways that voice could not. This explains the occasional equivocations in his text as he weighed up the advantages and disadvantages of both media. For Peter De Bolla, these equivocations have a sharply political resonance: Priestley, he says, had

> a more complex view of the interaction between speech and writing than Sheridan, one-time friend of Johnson and recipient of a state pension, [because] his own experience of the distribution of 'free speech' was marked by a profound recognition of the inequality perpetrated in its name'.[26]

The inference one might draw from this – that important connections exist between dissent, literacy, progress and print culture – has ramifications, both for the chronological plot I am tracing, and for Hazlitt's role within it. We should remember, though, that there was no equivocation in Priestley's belief that poetry is a less transparent medium of communication than prose.

The combined influence of Sheridan's and Priestley's elocutionary ideas on an entire generation of writer–readers cannot be overstated. Sheridan's was the wider audience: more diffuse as well as more diverse in its political and social complexion than the dissenters who heard and perpetuated Priestley's teachings; and, as De Bolla reminds us, Sheridan was 'far from clear about the political ramifications' of his role, which wavered between 'democratic populist philosopher and speech master to the aspiring ruling classes'.[27] It was, however, Sheridan who made explicit the possibilities that might open up for women, as vernacular discourse gained in importance, edging out the primacy of the classics:

> let the men take care of themselves for should they continue to rely on their old weapon the pen to the neglect of speech and on their skill in the dead languages without cultivating their own they would find themselves overmatched in all topics of conversation and 'victory declare itself on the side of the ladies'.[28]

It is interesting, in this context, to think that the young Hannah More, who heard Sheridan lecturing in Bristol in 1761 (and dared to show him a copy of her poems) may have had his lectures in mind when writing her poem 'The Bas Bleu; or Conversation' in 1787; and that in this respect she was linked by a strong affinity with Anna Barbauld – educated at the Warrington Academy, friend of Priestley, and the author of a poem which famously celebrated the prattle of women.[29] It was Barbauld who provided the epigraph for William Enfield's *The Speaker* (1774), a volume underpinned by Priestley's ideas, in which 'miscellaneous pieces selected from the best English writers' were 'dispersed under proper heads, with a view to facilitate the improvement of youth in reading and speaking'. Her poem on the 'Warrington Academy', included further on in the body of the anthology, contains a moving tribute to Priestley's influence, celebrating a generation of dissenters who, 'Love in their heart, persuasion in their tongue, / With words of praise shall charm the list'ning throng'.[30]

Enfield's translation of Priestleyan ideas into an instruction-manual, designed to teach the art of reading aloud, had an important parallel in the educational theory and practice of the radical writer John Thelwall – member of the London Corresponding Society, associate of Wordsworth and Coleridge, who was tried for sedition in 1794. Thelwall delivered lectures on 'The Science and Practice of Elocution' in 1796, and supposedly withdrew from politics in 1798; but found in his speech-therapy and his lecture-tours an alternative form of radical expression. At the Institution for the Correction of Speech Defects, which he set up and ran, his 'plan and object' was 'the removal of those defects, usually considered under the denomination of Impediments: but also ... the correction of Feebleness or Dissonance of Voice; Foreign and Provincial Accents, and every offensive peculiarity of Tone and Enunciation'.[31] Thelwall aimed to restore 'a completely intelligible distinctness' to speech-patterns by encouraging 'the habits of clear and energetic enunciation' and the use of 'physical and harmonic rhythmus.'[32] In doing so, he drew consciously, not just on his own experience (the *Dictionary of National Biography* informs us that he himself had suffered originally from 'a marked hesitation of speech and even a slight lisp') but on a well-known classical precedent. The Athenian orator, Demosthenes, had suffered a speech-defect which he cured by declaiming with pebbles in his mouth, and he was often referred to by eighteenth-century elocutionists as a role-model. Late eighteenth-century experiments, of the kind undertaken by Thelwall, derived much of their optimism from this famous instance of education triumphing over circumstance to produce a model of oratorical perfection. Extensive documentary evidence, in the form of case-histories, proved that Thelwall's own methods brought about a correspondingly dramatic improvement in his pupils' speech. What this signified was nothing less than that discourse was capable of progress; that individuals might empower themselves through the discovery of eloquence. In the process, they would contribute to what Thelwall called 'the expanding undulations of virtuous sympathy' which characterized a truly progressive society.[33]

(iii) The politics of reading aloud

Not only, as we have seen, was the practice of 'reading aloud' a thriving one at the end of the eighteenth century, but the debates surrounding it were deeply implicated in the politics of language. For Blair, Sheridan, Priestley, and Thelwall, there was a clear perceived connection between extempore delivery and enthusiasm: 'The sectaries and fanatics, before the Restoration', Blair argued, 'adopted a warm, zealous and popular manner of preaching; and those who adhered to them, in after-times, continued to distinguish themselves by somewhat of the same manner'. It was, he complained, the odium of these sects that 'drove the established church from the warmth which they were judged to have carried too far, into the opposite extreme, of a studied coolness of manner'.[34] The political point was driven home by Blair in a way that bore directly on the practice of reading aloud:

> The practice of reading Sermons, is one of the greatest obstacles to the Eloquence of the Pulpit in Great Britain, where alone this

practice prevails. No discourse, which is intended to be persuasive, can have the same force when read, as when spoken. The common people all feel this, and their prejudice against this practice is not without foundation in nature.[35]

This was a point later confirmed by Thelwall, who complained, in his *Selections and Original Articles ... on the Science and Practice of Elocution* (1806), that 'the Dulness and Indolence of modern Elocutionists' had reduced 'almost all public speaking, but that of the stage, to one sympathetic monotony of tone and look and attitude'; and that a hue and cry had been raised against 'all expression of attitude and feature'. But 'what is Oratory', he asked, 'if it does not awaken and influence and impel?'

> when really actuated by any strong or genuine emotion, the tones become affected; the physiognomy assumes a sympathetic expression; and, bursting thro' the boundaries of fashion and chains of unnatural torpor, each limb and muscle seems to swell and struggle with inspiring passion.[36]

In figuring the natural eloquence of the body in direct antithesis to the artificiality of a 'churchy' voice, Thelwall drew on the long tradition I have been tracing here, in which monotonous delivery was condemned. To understand the implications of that tradition for all forms of reading aloud – from sermon-delivery to schoolroom learning – we have only to glance back at John Mason's *Essay on the Action proper for the Pulpit*, published fifty years earlier, in which the author had inveighed against the 'entirely uniform and ever-returning Tune or Cadence, employed alike on all occasions, for all purposes whatsoever', which he likened to 'a *Chime* of Bells, that clink continually upon the Ear, in one wearisome, unvaried, uninterrupted Tenour'.[37]

The damaging effect of 'singsong' habits, as practiced in the pulpit and encouraged in the schoolroom, later proved important in the dispute which took place between Andrew Bell and Joseph Lancaster over the respective merits of chanting and speaking. Bell was the author of *An Experiment in Education* (1797), an influential tract which outlined the advantages of the 'monitorial' system he had piloted while working as superintendent of an understaffed orphanage asylum in Madras. This serviceable and economical system involved the older children in teaching the younger ones (thus reducing the need for trained staff), and was swiftly adopted with modifications by

Joseph Lancaster for use at a large Quaker school in Southwark. As the editors of the *Biographia* have noted,

> Lancaster was given such enthusiastic support by the Nonconformists that the Church of England asked Bell to organise some schools in a similar way. Thereafter, especially because religious differences framed it, the men were thrown into the position of rivals. (*BL* ii.60n.3)

Their competition centred on who had first patented or practised the monitorial system, and which version of that system was preferable, especially in respect of its attitudes to discipline and punishment. Coleridge and Southey, who both entered the debate, came down decisively on the side of Bell; one of their reasons for doing so being that they disliked the punishments allegedly used by Lancaster to correct 'singsong' habits of recitation. In his essay on *The Origin, Nature, and Object of the New System of Education* (1812), Southey complained about the contempt and risibility that Lancaster's punishments provoked:

> When a boy gets into a singing tone in reading, he is hung round with matches, ballads, or dying speeches, and marched round the school with some boys before him, crying 'matches, last dying speech, &c. – exactly imitating the dismal tones with which such things are hawked about the streets in London'.[38]

Southey's objections were echoed, a year later, in a lecture delivered by Coleridge in Bristol, when he protested that 'to load a boy with fetters ... to expose him to the sneers and insults of his peers, because forsooth he reads his lessons in a singsong tone, was a pitiful mockery of human nature'.[39] Later, when he wrote in his *Biographia* footnote about the practice of reading aloud in the schoolroom, his preference was for an incantatory mode of delivery. Alluding to the Bell-Lancaster controversy, he again sided with Bell:

> It is no less an error in teachers, than a torment to the poor children, to inforce the necessity of reading as they would talk. In order to cure them of *singing* as it is called; that is, of too great a difference, the child is made to repeat the words with his eyes from off the book ... But as soon as the eye is again directed to the printed page, the spell begins anew ... (*BL* ii.60n.)

In its context, the footnote reinforced his more general point, that poetry was distinct from prose, and that 'prose itself, at least in all argumentative and consecutive works, differs, or ought to differ, from the language of conversation; even as reading ought to differ from talking' (*BL*, ii.60–1). The anti-democratic implications of his thinking are underlined in Coleridge's reference to the author as 'one far wiser' than the child himself, whose superiority is acknowledged in the elevated register he elicits from his spellbound readers. The idealizing properties of poetry are ascribed not only to their musical effects, but to the easy transference of their authorial spirit from powerful source to submissive recipient. Just as the argument as a whole bears out the truth of Hazlitt's claim, that 'the language of poetry naturally falls in with the language of power' (Hazlitt, iv.214–15); so it can be seen that Coleridge's model of sympathetic reciprocity between author and reader is poetic rather than prosaic. Enacted, here, is a set of preferences which indicate how far he had travelled from the radical affiliations he shared for a time with Priestley.

The Bell–Lancaster debate crystallized around the opposition between Anglican and dissenting traditions of eloquence – an opposition which helps to explain the underlying differences between Coleridge and Hazlitt. Although still a Unitarian when he preached his sermon at Shrewsbury, Coleridge's later career had been marked by a steady movement towards the Anglican church. But Hazlitt hints in 'My First Acquaintance' at the possibility that Coleridge's dissent had always been compromised by a tendency towards mystification. Whereas he himself had remained democratically attuned to his audience, Coleridge had from the first been destined to write in an abstact and elevated register, which most readers would find daunting.

It came as no surprise to Hazlitt that Coleridge sided with Bell not Lancaster, and he highlighted their difference in this respect. In his *Examiner* review of *The Statesman's Manual*, where Coleridge's views on education are discussed, he protested against the conservative repudiation of Lancaster's reforms which Coleridge shared with Southey. 'Learning', he wrote sarcastically, 'is an old University mistress, that [Coleridge] is not willing to part with, except for the use of the church of England; and he is sadly afraid she should be debauched by the "liberal ideas" of Joseph Lancaster!' (Hazlitt, vii.126). This comment, which appeared in a paragraph addressed to the theory and practice of reading, meshed Hazlitt's political loyalties with his discursive tastes. In the same way, when Thelwall, in his 1806

Selections, contrasted a transparent body-language of enthusiasm with 'the usual Pedantic and Bell-man Styles of reading', he was using 'Bell' as shorthand for orthodox Anglicanism.[40] Implicitly, he thus expressed his preference for the conversational register in recitation advocated by Lancaster over the 'singsong' delivery which Bell leaves unpunished. The very name 'Bell' was fortuitously connected with churchiness, with the 'entirely uniform and ever-returning Tune or cadence' condemned by writers such as Mason; and Thelwall played wittily on the associations provided by this pun. Similarly, when he wrote about monotony in its various forms – the *'Barking or Schoolboy Style'*; the *'Monotonous Level'* style, the *'Clerical Drawl'*, and the *'Cathedral Chant'*[41] – he gave them an orthodox, Anglican inflection which contrasted with his own enthusiasm.

(iv) Speech/writing, prose/poetry, public/private

There were, as we have seen, important connections between 'reading aloud' and the progressive model of vocal and bodily eloquence to which Hazlitt claimed allegiance. These are celebrated both in 'My First Acquaintance' and elsewhere in his writings:

> Horne Tooke, among other paradoxes, used to maintain, that no one could relish a good style who was not in the habit of talking and hearing his own voice. He might as well have said that no one could relish a good style without reading it aloud, as we find common people do to assist their apprehension. ... I agree that no style is good, that is not fit to be spoken or read aloud with effect. This holds true not only of emphasis and cadence, but also with regard to natural idiom and colloquial freedom. ('On the Conversation of Authors'; Hazlitt, xii.40)

But there were also some special features of reading aloud in the Wordsworth–Coleridge circle, which had more troubling implications. At a time when literature was establishing itself in the market-place, and the reading-public was emerging as the final arbiter of its merit, writers were obliged either to welcome or to resist the transition from a culture based on oral delivery and manuscript-circulation into a culture centred on print. Hazlitt's observation of the coterie-practice of 'chaunting' shows his awareness that a Romantic aesthetic grounded in orality might camouflage a hostility to the public sphere. That awareness helps bring into sharper focus the political animus which lies behind his attacks on Coleridge, even as it discloses an ambivalence in his own response to orality.

Something of this ambivalence (is the erosion of orality a gain or a loss?) was discernible in the preface which Hazlitt attached in 1807 to his *Eloquence of the British Senate*: a memorial to the great parliamentary addresses delivered by 'those celebrated men of the last age ... who filled the columns of the newspapers with their speeches, and every pot-house with their fame'. These men, Hazlitt wrote, who were 'the wisdom of the wise, and the strength of the strong, whose praises were inscribed on every window-shutter or brick-wall, or floated through the busy air, upborne by the shouts and huzzahs of a giddy multitude' were now, like their orations, 'silent and forgotten; all that remains of them is consigned to oblivion in the misty records of Parliament, and lives only in the shadow of a name' (Hazlitt, i.139–40). Hazlitt's noble ambition was 'to revive what was forgotten, and embody what was permanent' (Hazlitt, i.140), but this was no easy task. He sensed that what was precious in these speeches could not be recovered, because each was a single, irreplaceable *performance*; but equally, that these irrecoverable elements might have deserved their ephemerality, since the tastes of the 'giddy multitude' were not always to be trusted.

Hazlitt was consistently ambivalent about the craving for publicity which linked popular literature and demagoguery with what he diagnosed as personality disorders of the Coleridgean variety. In his essay 'On Novelty and Familiarity' he associated the desire for popularity with addiction: actors, he claimed, 'live on applause, and drag on a laborious artificial existence by the administration of perpetual provocatives to their sympathy with the public gratification ... The excitement of public applause at last becomes a painful habit, and either in indolent or over-active temperaments produces a craving after privacy and leisure' (Hazlitt, xii.299–300). Similarly, 'On the Difference between Writing and Speaking' gives us the flip-side of his concern to arrest the passage of time and restore the vanishing power of orality:

> The orator's vehemence of gesture, the loudness of the voice, the speaking eye, the conscious attitude, the inexplicable dumb shew and noise, – all 'those brave sublunary things that made his raptures clear', – are no longer there, and without these, he is nothing. (Hazlitt, xii.265)

In this essay, loquacity is figured as the obverse of profundity. Hazlitt identified, not with the great speakers of the day, who court popularity, but with the silent thinkers, who 'in revenge for being tongue-tyed' poured 'a torrent of words from their pens': 'What they would say (if they could) does not lie at the orifices of the mouth ready for delivery, but is wrapped in the folds of the heart and registered in the chambers of the brain'(Hazlitt, xii.278–9). For these deep-thinking *writers*, Hazlitt reserved his highest stylistic lexicon. There is something De Quinceyan, even Piranesian, in the spatial metaphors he used to describe their hidden but durable profundity:

> The whole of a man's thoughts and feelings cannot lie upon the surface, made up for use, but the whole must be a greater quantity, a mightier power, if they could be got at, layer under layer, and brought into play by the levers of imagination and reflection. (Hazlitt, xii.279)

By comparison, *The Eloquence of the British Senate* was an act of loving restitution towards transient speech. But it still reflected Hazlitt's anxiety that oratory was superficial, stimulus-driven, habit-forming, as well as his longing that something might survive, beyond the ephemeral speech-act, of lasting value.

The complexity of Hazlitt's observations on speech and writing is everywhere apparent, and nowhere more so than in his many scattered comments on Coleridge, who became the symbolic focus for his mistrust of voice as the signifier of thoughts and feelings. This mistrust is not what one might expect of the Hazlitt who had emerged from the dissenting tradition, which placed its faith in elocution as a passport to intellectual and social standing; and believed that speech, in and of itself, had a progressive power. But it does tally with what we know about Hazlitt's temperament, and with what he sensed was a deep underlying difference between Coleridge and himself. Tongue-tied, as an adolescent, in the presence of his intellectual hero, Hazlitt was diffident always. Drawing on Crabb Robinson's *Diary*, Stanley Jones gives a mortifying account of his first lecture, on Tuesday 14 January, 1812, recited 'calamitously, despite the loyal encouragement of his friends' to a blur of faces:

> He had never before stood at a lecturer's rostrum. He delivered himself in a low, monotonous, half-audible voice, kept his eyes

glued to the manuscript, not once daring to look at his hearers, and read so rapidly that no-one could follow.[42]

The next week, asked to repeat the first lecture, he 'stopped abruptly half way through' and 'could not be persuaded to continue'. This anecdote carries a special charge of irony in the light of Coleridge's legendary eloquence, recorded by Hazlitt over an entire writing career.
    'He talked far above singing', recalls the younger man, in 'On Going a Journey' (from *Table Talk* (1821)): 'If I could so clothe my ideas in sounding and flowing words, I might perhaps wish to have some one with me to admire the swelling theme; or I could be more content, were it possible for me still to hear his echoing voice in the woods at All-Foxden' (Hazlitt, viii.183). The envy is as transparent in his touching generosity here as it is beneath his frustration and rage against wasted talent elsewhere. 'If Mr Coleridge had not been the most impressive talker of his age, he would probably have been the finest writer' he remarked acidly in *The Spirit of the Age* (1825), 'but he lays down his pen to make sure of an auditor, and mortgages the admiration of posterity for the stare of an idler' (Hazlitt, xi.30). More painful in its bleakness of loss is this close-up of Coleridge's drugged face, twenty years on from the Shrewsbury sermon recollected in 'My first Acquaintance with Poets':

> Look in C—'s face while he is talking. His words are such as might 'create a soul under the ribs of death'. His face is a blank. Which are we to consider as the true index of his mind? Pain, languor, shadowy remembrances are the uneasy inmates there: his lips move mechanically! ('On the Knowledge of Character'; Hazlitt, viii.305)

We have, I think, to be aware of what Tom Paulin has called the 'density of associative reference' in Hazlitt's writings, their 'self-allusive and autotelic' richness, if we are fully to understand the complexity of significance he invested in the figure of Coleridge the Talker.[43] As if suffering a bereavement that could not be accepted, he never entirely gave up on the memory of Coleridge the radical – or, for that matter, on the hope that Coleridge's gift for extempore enthusiasm might be made durable in writing. In his essay 'On Effeminacy of Character', the poet's dormant revolutionary spirit is reawakened and activated by this impassioned plea:

> Oh thou! who didst lend me speech when I was dumb, to whom I

owe it that I have not crept on my belly all the days of my life like the serpent, but sometimes lift my forked crest or tread the empyrean, wake thou out of thy mid-day slumbers! (Hazlitt, viii.251)

Hazlitt's allusive language is charged with personal, poetic, and political significance. Lamenting the decline of all that had once seemed heroic in Coleridge, he remembers two equally momentous passages in Milton, both concerned with the public accountability of heroes. He reassures Coleridge that his creative power will return to him, after its apparent stagnation, much as Milton reassures the English nation that, at the end of a long period of political quietism, freedom will be achieved. But this regeneration can only occur, Hazlitt warns, if Coleridge is prepared to exchange the transient, untrustworthy mobility of speech for the durable medium of writing:

Shake off the heavy honey-dew of thy soul, no longer lulled with that Circean cup, drinking thy own thoughts with thy own ears, but start up in thy promised likeness, and shake the pillared rottenness of the world! Leave not thy sounding words in air, write them in marble, and teach the coming age heroic truths! Up, and wake the echoes of Time! (Hazlitt, viii.251)

Coleridge is here associated with *Samson Agonistes*, stirring himself out of his temporary lethargy into the courageous act of heroism that will liberate his people. But he is also linked – through a cognate Miltonic echo that Blake would have approved – with 'that noble and puissant nation' in *Areopagitica*, 'rousing herself like a strong man after sleep and shaking her invincible locks'.[44] This reference to the most famous of publications on the freedom of the press works tacitly as a rebuke to Coleridge for his stance against reviewers, periodicals, and the reading-public – a stance that Hazlitt had denounced openly on several occasions: 'For what have we been labouring for the last three hundred years?' he asked in 1816:

Would Mr Coleridge, with impious hand, turn the world 'twice ten degrees askance', and carry us back to the dark ages? Would he punish the *reading public* for their bad taste in reading periodical publications he does not like, by suppressing the freedom of the press altogether, or destroying the art of printing? (Hazlitt, xvi.106)

Angry reproaches such as this one remind us of the intractable differ-ence of ideology which persisted between these two writers. Coleridge the conservative poet–critic, embattled and beleaguered in relation to the reading-public, is presented as a loquacious performer. Hazlitt the radical journalist, tongue-tied when it comes to speaking, is seen as welcoming and eagerly entering the world of publication. But although both writers recurred constantly to these public-private, speech-writing oppositions, neither in the end believed them to be valid, except as symbolic shorthand for more complex emotions and ideas.

1816 ought to have been a momentous year for Coleridge's recu-peration, in that it saw the poet's sudden re-emergence, after a long period of silence, into the world of print. But in Hazlitt's view Coleridge had signally failed to 'rouze [him]self like a strong man after sleep, and shake [his] invincible locks.' Hazlitt did not write the with-ering review which appeared anonymously in the *Edinburgh Review* in September 1816; but he might just as well have done. 'Forth steps Mr Coleridge, like a giant refreshed with sleep', sneers the reviewer, slip-ping in sideways the apposite and topical allusion to *Areopagitica*:

> and as if to redeem his character after so long a silence (his poetic powers having been, he says, from 1808 till very lately, in a state of suspended animation) ... breaks out in these precise words – ''Tis the middle of the night by the castle clock'.[45]

As a judgement on the quality of Coleridge's writing, this bathetic quotation is left to speak for itself. The charge pressed home by the reviewer is that 'Christabel' has come to be *over-valued* as a result of its private circulation and oral delivery, but above all, as a result of its having been praised and advocated by Lord Byron:

> we are a little inclined to doubt the value of the praise which one poet lends another. It seems nowadays to be the practice of that once invisible race to laud each other without bounds; and one can hardly avoid suspecting, that what is thus lavishly advanced may be laid out with a view to being repaid with interest. Mr Coleridge, however, must be judged by his own merits.[46]

In this acid remark, one hears an anticipation of the charge implicitly levelled in 'My First Acquaintance' at another pair of writers, who back in 1798 had read their poems aloud in a chaunting voice. Were they not also in danger of 'lauding each other without bounds'? Did their dependence on coterie admiration not signify a defensive adherence to systems of patronage and puffing, which Hazlitt abhorred? The case for considering Hazlitt as the author of this review has long been closed. But it's not hard to see why Coleridge should have made the attribution. Connecting the *Edinburgh Review* article, the cluster of reviews of the *Lay Sermons*, the essay on 'Patronage and Puffing', and (more subtly) 'My First Acquaintance with Poets', was a consistent thread of criticism. Coleridge stood accused of a cowardly refusal to embrace the modernity and progress associated with print culture – a refusal which disguised itself as a commitment to the sociable diffusion associated with oral discourse. In his use of the practice and figure of 'reading aloud' – alluded to in the Preface to 'Christabel' and later in *Biographia* – he protected himself from the candid, disinterested criticism likely to be levelled at his published writings.

The politics of reception are inescapably linked to the politics of language and style. Even as early as 1798, Hazlitt seems to suggest in 'My First Acquaintance with Poets', Coleridge's defensive conservatism was symbolized by the ambiguous accompaniment, the fake orality, of 'chaunting'. Wordsworth too – for all his affinity with Blair, his professed allegiance in 1800 to the 'natural conversation of men', and his northern burr – was drawn under an Anglican spell when it came to reciting poetry. Hazlitt does not go so far as to say that this was a spell cast by Coleridge over his friend; but he does hint that of the two writers Coleridge had always been more inclined to reverence the act of enchantment that can take place between a poet and his listeners. The linkage between incantation and enchantment revealed what in Hazlitt's eyes seemed to be an attraction on Coleridge's part towards the elevated, mystificatory potential of all discourse, including conversation. In Wordsworth's case, it appeared indicative, rather, of the special category into which he placed poetry – his own in particular – despite all his assertions to the contrary in the 1800 'Preface' to *Lyrical Ballads*. The carefully poised ironies of Hazlitt's essay accuse both poets of an incipient political apostasy, apparent from the outset of their careers in their manner of reading poetry aloud. The 1798 collaboration, even as it is recognized for the inauguration of a new kind of poetry, is retrospectively seen as instigating their withdrawal into a private and self-protective world of mutual enchantment. From this safe haven, Hazlitt implies, the two poets went on in later life to consolidate their reputations as conservative members of the Anglican Church, addressing their readers in an increasingly exclusive language. Hazlitt, meanwhile, true to his dissenting origins, continued to champion the cause of 'colloquial freedom' in the unambiguously public forum of the periodical press. His abiding commitment was to a republic of letters, founded on the principles of meritocracy; and his medium was always prose.

Notes

1 See, in particular, *BL*, chapters 17–19.

2 See Tom Paulin, *The Day-Star of Liberty: William Hazlitt's Radical Prose-Style* (London: Faber and Faber, 1998).

3 See *BL*, ii.134; and also S.T. Coleridge, *Lectures 1808–1819 On Literature*, ed. R.A. Foakes (2 vols; London/Princeton, NJ: Routledge and Kegan Paul/ Princeton University Press, 1987), i.134, and ii.266. See my discussion of this issue in 'Coleridge and the Anxiety of Reception', *Romanticism* 1 (1995) 206–38, pp. 225–6.

4 Blair argues that the true function of criticism is to help us to guard against 'blind implicit veneration', and to teach us 'to admire and to blame with judgement, and not to follow the crowd blindly': *Lectures on Rhetoric and Belles Lettres* (2 vols; London: Strahan and Cadell, 1783), i.8.

5 Thomas Sheridan, A.M., *A Course of Lectures on Elocution: together with two Dissertations on Language, and some other Tracts relative to those Subjects* (London: Strahan, 1762), p. xii.

6 Sheridan, *A Course of Lectures*, p. xix.

7 W. Benzie, *The Dublin Orator* (Leeds: Scolar Press, 1972), pp. viii, 54. See also Linda Kelly, *Richard Brinsley Sheridan: A Life* (London: Sinclair Stevenson, 1988), p. 5, who argues that 'it was from Swift that [Tom Sheridan] first acquired his passionate interest in oratory and the correct pronunciation of English – the task of establishing a general standard of pronunciation, along the lines laid down by the French Academy, was one that Swift had always hoped to carry out'. Sheridan in his turn, taught grammar and oratory to his sons, carrying on the tradition of reading aloud which he had learned from Swift (Kelly, *Sheridan*, pp. 22–3).

8 Sheridan, *A Course of Lectures*, p. xiii.

9 Sheridan, *A Course of Lectures*, p. 80.

10 Sheridan, *A Course of Lectures*, p. 4. This complaint is repeated in his *Rhetorical Grammar*, where Sheridan claims that 'the usual fault of introducing sing-song notes, or a species of chanting, into poetical numbers, is disagreeable to every ear but that of the chanter himself'; quoted by Gilbert Austin, *Chironomia, or a Treatise on Rhetorical Delivery* (London: Cadell and Davies, 1806), p. 55.

11 Thomas Sheridan, *Lectures on the Art of Reading; First Part: Containing the Art of Reading Prose* (London: Dodsley, *etc.*, 1775), p. 286.

12 Peter De Bolla, *The Discourse of the Sublime: Readings in History, Aesthetics and the Subject* (Oxford: Blackwell, 1989), p. 172.

13 Sheridan, *Art of Reading*, i.296–7.

14 James Burgh, *The Art of Speaking* (2nd edn; London: Longman and Buckland, 1768), p. 3.

15 Burgh, *The Art of Speaking*, p. 8.
16 For Hazlitt, as for Byron, the word 'cant' has entirely negative associations when used in its figurative sense: 'Of all the cants that ever were canted in this canting world, this is the worst!' he protests, in his *Examiner* review of *The Statesman's Manual* (Hazlitt, vii.121). Cant is also the word used in the eighteenth century to describe private languages, dialects, or idiolects. Hazlitt may be playing on this sense of the word 'cant' to suggest that Wordsworth and Coleridge speak to each other in a vocabulary that is inaccessible to those outside their circle. Compare his observation, in the first of his two essays 'On the Conversation of Authors', that

> There is a Free-masonry in all things. You can only speak to be under-stood, but this you cannot be, except by those who are in the secret ... C— is the only person who can talk to all sorts of people, on all sorts of subjects, without caring a farthing for their understanding a word of what he says – and *he* talks only for admiration and to be listened to, and accordingly the least interruption puts him out. (Hazlitt, xii.35)

17 Fiona Stafford, 'Hugh Blair's Ossian, Romanticism and the Teaching of Literature'; in Robert Crawford (ed.), *The Scottish Invention of English Literature* (Cambridge: Cambridge University Press, 1998) 68–88, p. 76.
18 Blair, *Lectures on Rhetoric and Belles Lettres*, i.126.
19 Blair, *Lectures on Rhetoric and Belles Lettres*, i.136.
20 Blair, *Lectures on Rhetoric and Belles Lettres*, ii.7, ii.43.
21 Blair, *Lectures on Rhetoric and Belles Lettres*, ii.214.
22 Joseph Priestley, *A Course of Lectures on Oratory and Criticism* (London: Johnson, 1777), p. 111.
23 Priestley, *A Course of Lectures*, pp. 112, 293.
24 Priestley, *A Course of Lectures*, p. 300.
25 Priestley, *A Course of Lectures*, p. 313.
26 De Bolla, *Discourse of the Sublime*, p. 176.
27 De Bolla, *Discourse of the Sublime*, p. 163.
28 Sheridan, *The Art of Reading*, p. 329.
29 See Barbauld's poem 'Washing Day' (which begins: 'The muses have turned gossips ...').
30 Included in William Enfield, *The Speaker: Or, Miscellaneous Pieces, Selected from the Best English Writers, and Disposed under Proper Heads, with a View to Facilitate the Improvement of Youth in Reading and Speaking. To which is Prefixed an Essay on Elocution* (London: Johnson, 1774), p. 271.
31 *Plan and Objects of Mr Thelwall's Institution* (London: Lincoln's Inn Fields, 1813) p. 1. In the Bodleian Library copy, the pamphlet is bound with *Results of Experience* (see next note).
32 *Plan and Objects*, p. 2; *Results of Experience in the Treatment of cases of Defective Utterance, from Deficiencies in the Roof of the Mouth, & other Imperfections & Mal-conformations of the Organs of Speech; with Observations on Cases of Amentia, and tardy & imperfect Development of the Faculties* (London: McCreery, 1814), pp. 2, 43.
33 John Thelwall, *Selections and Original Articles for Mr Thelwall's Lectures on the Science and Practice of Elocution: together with the Introductory Discourse and Outlines* (Birmingham: Belcher, 1806), p. 16.
34 Blair, *Lectures on Rhetoric and Belles Lettres*, ii.43.

35   Blair, *Lectures on Rhetoric and Belles Lettres*, ii.118.

36   Thelwall, *Selections*, pp. 11, 27. Thelwall had earlier made comments on the connection between eloquence and animated oral delivery in a series of lectures whose content was clearly political, albeit in an ironically camouflaged way:

> the grand charm of oral eloquence consists not only in the correspondence of the tone of voice with the subject matter, but in that powerful harmony of feature and gesticulation – that electric animation of the eye, which, varying its expression with every transition of rising passion, prepares the audience for the sentiments about to be delivered.

See *Prospectus of a Course of Lectures to be delivered every Monday, Wednesday, and Friday, during the ensuing Lent, in strict conformity with the restrictions of Mr Pitt's Convention Act* (London: sold at the lecture room, 1796), p. 3.

37   John Mason, *An Essay on the Action proper for the Pulpit* (London: Dodsley, 1753), p. 42.

38   Robert Southey, *The Origin, Nature, and Object of the New System of Education* (London: Murray, 1812), p. 89. Southey is quoting from Lancaster's *Improvements in Education* (London: Lancaster, 1808), pp. 86–7:

> When a boy gets into a singing tone in reading, the best cure that I have hitherto found effectual, is by *force* of ridicule. – Decorate the offender with matches, ballads; (dying-speeches, *if needful;*) and, in this garb send him round the school, with some boys before him, crying matches, &c. exactly imitating the dismal tones with which such things are hawked about the streets in London.

39   Coleridge, *Lectures 1808–1819 On Literature*, ii.588. (See also ii.286n.3).

40   Thelwall, *Selections*, pp. 25–6.

41   Thelwall, *Selections*, pp. 27–8.

42   Stanley Jones, *Hazlitt: A Life, from Winterslow to Frith Street* (Oxford: Clarendon Press, 1989), p. 66.

43   Paulin, *Day-Star of Liberty*, p. 184. For a discussion of Hazlitt on speech and writing, see also Timothy Clark, *The Theory of Inspiration: Composition as a Crisis of Subjectivity in Romantic and post-Romantic Writing* (Manchester: Manchester University Press, 1997), pp. 84–6; and Uttara Natarajan, *Hazlitt and the Reach of Sense: Criticism, Morals, and the Metaphysics of Power* (Oxford: Clarendon Press, 1998).

44   The full passage runs:

> Methinks I see in my mind a noble and puissant Nation rousing herself like a strong man after sleep, and shaking her invincible locks; and Methinks I see her as an Eagle muing her mighty youth, and kindling her undazl'd eyes at the full midday beam; purging and unsealing her long abused sight at the fountain it self of heav'nly radiance. (*Complete Prose Works of John Milton* (New Haven, Conn.: Yale University Press, 1959), ii.558)

45   *The Collected Works of William Hazlitt*, ed. A.R. Waller and Arnold Glover (13 vols; London/NY: Dent, 1902–6), x.412. Waller and Glover include the *Edinburgh Review* article of September 1816, but relegate it to the 'Notes' because of its doubtful provenance. It has since been attributed to Tom Moore and Francis Jeffrey.

46 Hazlitt, *Collected Works*, ed. Glover, x.412. The review ends with an even stronger condemnation of private patronage, including the following: 'Must we then be doomed to hear such a mixture of raving and driv'ling, extolled as the work of a *wild and original* genius, simply because Mr Coleridge has now and then written fine Verses, and a brother poet chooses, in his milder mood, to laud him from courtesy or interest?' (x.418.)

10
Renewing *Lyrical Ballads*
Nicholas Roe

> Efforts may be made by surviving friends to prolong his fame;
> but in fifty years hence it will scarcely be known that such a
> man has lived.
>
> John Wright, *The Genius of Wordsworth Harmonized with the*
> *Wisdom and Integrity of his Reviewers*[1]

In the 1800 'Preface' to *Lyrical Ballads* Wordsworth reminded readers
that the 1798 volume had been 'published, as an experiment', and
that the collection contained poems 'materially different from those,
upon which general approbation is at present bestowed' (*WPrW*,
i.118, 120). Exactly how the poems 'materially differed' has been a
subject for debate from their first publication. In *Romantics, Rebels,*
and Reactionaries (1981) Marilyn Butler argued that, since *Lyrical*
Ballads represented the 'tail end' of an eighteenth-century tradition
of 'popular' poetry, '[w]e should dismiss ... the belief, still widely
held, that Wordsworth's contributions to the *Lyrical Ballads* of 1798
represent an altogether new kind of poetry'. Six pages later she made
the point again: 'Of course it is an irony', Butler wrote, 'that later
critics have persisted in seeing the *Lyrical Ballads* as heralding a
new kind of poetry – when the ablest contemporary critics saw them
as being the epitome of an older, if recent and short-lived kind'.[2]
Some years ago Robert Mayo presented evidence showing how
closely Wordsworth's lyrical ballads resembled contemporary magazine verse, although his survey does not wholly account for the
paradoxical situation which Marilyn Butler describes.[3] Wordsworth's
lyrical ballad 'The Thorn' revived an older kind of ballad poetry
that could indeed be found in magazines in the 1790s but in doing
so, William Hazlitt thought, it awakened 'the sense of a new style and

a new spirit in poetry' (Hazlitt, xvii.117).

The 1798 and 1800 editions of *Lyrical Ballads* appeared at the turn of the century, when revolutions in America and France had intensified conservative and progressive currents of opinion in England. *Lyrical Ballads* might be thought of as bringing together contrary movements of the age so that tradition *or* experiment in Wordsworth's poems may not be a choice we are obliged to make. In her book *Tradition and Experiment in Wordsworth's 'Lyrical Ballads' (1798)*, Mary Jacobus pointed out that in the poems '[i]ndebtedness to the past coexists with the independence of a pioneer'.[4] *Coexists* is apparently the key word here, denoting the significance of *Lyrical Ballads* as transitional, a 'cultural turning point' or 'carrying forward of literary traditions established in previous decades'.[5] The historical moment at which the poems appeared was one of political and cultural unsettlement, and the circumstances of the book's publication in September 1798 were – and are – far from clear. The book's *fin de siècle* publication (at 'the gate of the new century . . . the date of the "Lyrical Ballads"'[6]) has encouraged readers to respond to it as a pivotal text, a threshold between 'old' and 'new', a meeting point of tradition and experiment. In a similar way the 'obscurity' from which the book allegedly emerged gave space for controversy and an extraordinary diversity of interpretations.

Robert Burns had grounded his authenticity as a poet in vernacular originality and regional 'obscurity', and contemporary and nineteenth-century commentators echoed and endorsed this self-estimate.[7] Curiosity about the 'obscure beginnings' of literary genius dated from the mid-eighteenth century, and Edward Young's influential *Conjectures on Original Composition* (1759). Published a quarter of a century afterwards, Robert Burns's *Poems Chiefly in the Scottish Dialect* (1786) brilliantly packaged 'an obscure, nameless Bard' for a readership that was now primed and eager for the original, 'native language' of his poetry.[8] Wordsworth 'read . . . and admired' Burns's *Poems* shortly after they were published; his debt to Burns is obvious, and was acknowledged by the poet himself.[9] But some critics have invented an 'obscure, nameless' Wordsworth by way of asserting his overriding claim to poetic novelty. C.T. Winchester, writing in 1916, identified Burns's poetry as a precedent for *Lyrical Ballads*, then shifted the national frame and assigned the obscure origin of 'the new poetry' to England:

And thus, just twelve years after Robert Burns had issued his first edition, the new poetry began in England with a small anonymous volume of verse, published by an obscure Bristol bookseller, and bearing the title *Lyrical Ballads*.[10]

The beginning of 'the new poetry in England' was, from the first, definitively belated and associated with a cultural margin comparable to but overlaying Burns's debut. The volume of 'new poetry ... bearing the title *Lyrical Ballads*' is physically diminutive, its authoring anonymous, and its publisher provincial, westerly, obscure. Paradoxically, the 'obscurity' of Burns had been one of his most noticeable attributes, and was made much of by Burns himself. The anonymity of *Lyrical Ballads* was – at least according to Coleridge – a prudent strategy: 'Wordsworth's name is nothing – to a large number of persons mine *stinks*' (*CL*, i.412). But for later generations the obscurity of the 'little book ... humbly put up in paper boards' and its supposedly hazardous reception were bound-up with a sublime, oracular significance: 'the visitings of a larger, purer air, and the peace of an unfathomable sky'.[11]

My concern in this essay will be with some perceptions of *Lyrical Ballads* 1798 and 1800 during the two hundred years since publication. Eminent Wordsworth scholars and editors will be heard in what follows here, although I will be attuned principally to what I call, with some esteem, the 'low' tradition of Wordsworth's reception in popular editions, commentaries, and memoirs rather than to the 'high' Wordsworthian line associated in the nineteenth century with John Stuart Mill and Matthew Arnold. I take this 'low' tradition to be the basis of Wordsworth's reputation; the ideas of Wordsworth and *Lyrical Ballads* which emanate from it are at times outlandish, even bizarre, yet these qualities are one measure of the poems' cultural vitality and their lasting popular appeal.

News of *Lyrical Ballads* and its contents was 'fairly well spread' when in September 1798 the book appeared from Cottle at Bristol and Arch in London.[12] It made a good impression in literary circles but, as Wordsworth acknowledged, there had been 'sad mismanagement in the case' (*EY*, p. 248). His proposal that the book should be published by Joseph Johnson, the dissenting publisher in St. Paul's Churchyard, had miscarried. If Johnson had indeed published *Lyrical Ballads* in September 1798, along with Coleridge's *Fears in Solitude* pamphlet, the book's presence before the public would have been significantly different. Johnson, who in 1793 had published Wordsworth's *An Evening Walk* and *Descriptive Sketches*, was the foremost publisher of liberal and dissenting pamphlets and poetry. Association with Johnson would have encouraged some readers to expect a liberal or radical bias in *Lyrical Ballads*; for others Johnson's imprint would have been sufficient warning of 'jacobin' tendencies in the poems.[13] Johnson's name, in other words, would have helped make an explicit link between the book's 'experimental' poetics and the radical and dissenting circles associated with his bookshop in St Paul's Churchyard.

Wordsworth's inquiry to Cottle in June 1799, 'Can you tell me whether the poems are likely to sell?' (*EY*, p. 263), indicates confusion and curiosity about how the book had fared. Early notices – barring Southey's and, later, Jeffrey's – had been broadly favourable,[14] yet time after time commentators have claimed that the first reception of *Lyrical Ballads* was otherwise. A history of English literature published in 1909 asserted that *Lyrical Ballads* (1798) 'attracted no attention and was practically ignored by a public that would soon go into raptures over Byron'.[15] *British Authors of the Nineteenth Century* (1936) described *Lyrical Ballads* as 'historically one of the most significant books in the line of English poetry, and which has given rise to endless discussion since ... [but] [t]he book, published by Cottle of Bristol, was a failure'.[16] This last account is paradigmatic in that it defines a gradual – and by implication, continuing – renewal from 'failure' into 'significance' through 'endless discussion', as the book invents new generations of readers as if for the first time.

One line of hostile criticism during the nineteenth century sprang from Coleridge's analysis in *Biographia* of the 'Defects of Wordsworth's Poetry'. The most prominent of these, Coleridge said, was a sinking through 'sudden and unprepared transitions' from 'lines or sentences of peculiar felicity ... to a style, not only unimpassioned but undistinguished' (*BL*, ii.121). Fifteen years after Wordsworth's death, Joseph Angus echoed Coleridge when he observed that *Lyrical Ballads* 'were not a success [and] the volume remained unsold' because 'the mixture of ludicrous images and colloquial plainness with passages of tenderness and pathos prompted ridicule which ... was too well deserved'.[17] Twenty years later Mrs. Oliphant's *Literary History of England* (1885) presented *Lyrical Ballads* as an outright swindle, a take-in, a 'serious attempt' on a reluctant nation which had drawn a 'shout of derision from all the critics'. Speaking on behalf of 'England in general', Mrs. Oliphant declared that the country 'can scarcely be said to have been less than personally offended by this serious and almost solemn attempt to impose a new poetical creed upon her. Few abortive publications have ever raised so great a ferment – for it could not at first be called anything but abortive'.[18] C.T. Winchester and Mrs. Oliphant alike regarded *Lyrical Ballads* as spurious. For Winchester it was an illegitimate publication, 'a small anonymous volume' issued 'obscurely'. To Mrs. Oliphant, though, it was only 'at first' abortive for as she concedes it raised a 'ferment' of excitement and worked as a leaven on English poetry.

James Middleton Sutherland's *William Wordsworth. The Story of his Life* (1887) shows us how one critic explained the transformation from 'abortive publication' to one generative of 'discussion' and continuously renewed 'significance'. First, Sutherland draws attention to the book's supposedly catastrophic debut: '[i]t was regarded as an outrage against common-sense', he says, 'an insult to the judgement and understanding of its readers ... [e]verybody's hand was raised against the book, but it did not for all that glide down the stream of oblivion'. Instead, '[o]ne by one, admirers were found, and a new public was created'. Sutherland acknowledged the precedence of Thomson, Cowper, Burns, and Crabbe in bringing about a 'healthy reform' of poetry, but he claimed it was Wordsworth alone who challenged readers' preconceptions about poetry, 'break[ing] away from the house of bondage'.[19] Others agreed. For Elizabeth Wordsworth, writing in 1891, *Lyrical Ballads* 'broke through the trammels of the eighteenth century'; *Lyrical Ballads* 'swept away all the cobwebs which the eighteenth century had spun', according to Laurie Magnus (1909). Walter Raleigh thought that *Lyrical Ballads* was 'a gauntlet flung in the face of public taste' (1903). Still more fantastic – or so it seems now – was the view that *Lyrical Ballads* was 'a gage [challenge] thrown down to the highly-mannered poetry of the previous century' (1936).[20]

Late nineteenth-century (pre-Raphaelite) medievalism explains the 'gauntlet' and 'gage', and Raleigh's figuring Wordsworth as a knight-at-arms ready to battle with 'the solitary word Poetry'. More persistent, it seems, is the idea of Wordsworth as a calculating jacobin who had extended the 'levelling' principles of the French Revolution to poetry. Hazlitt's account is still the best:

> [Wordsworth's poetry] is one of the innovations of the time. It partakes of, and is carried along with, the revolutionary movement of our age ... His popular, inartificial style gets rid (at a blow) of all the trappings of verse, of all the high places of poetry. (Hazlitt, xi.87)

Thomas Hutchinson, editing his centenary edition of *Lyrical Ballads* in

1898, drew attention to Wordsworth's purging of 'gaudiness and inane phraseology', but his last example here did not quite make the point:

> Why, we may suppose [Wordsworth] to ask ... why is it considered 'elegant' to speak of a cold bath as 'the gelid cistern', of the dog rose as 'cynorrhodon'? Why must Dr.Darwin, when he might say 'mother's milk', prefer to say 'nutrient streams from Beauty's orbs'? Why, alas! did I, in the days of benighted youth, prefer 'dairy produce of thrice ten summers' to 'a thirty-year-old cheese'?[21]

Why, alas, indeed: 'dairy produce ... / Of thrice ten summers' had first appeared in *Descriptive Sketches* (1793, ll. 598–9), and Wordsworth apparently thought sufficiently well of this cheesy couplet to preserve it unaltered for the next fifty-seven years! The line is unchanged in the last edition of the poems published in Wordsworth's lifetime (1849–50). Another weighty scholar and editor, Edward Dowden, interpreted Wordsworth's poems as a lyrical riddance, an 'aggressive revolt against the poetical ideas of the eighteenth century' (1897).[22] Together Hutchinson and Dowden indicate how, long after the event, *Lyrical Ballads* came to represent a 'Romantic' epoch of poetic innovation – or revolt – which was in due course assimilated to the tradition of high literary culture.

H.W. Garrod says that Christopher Wordsworth's 'dull and cautious' *Memoirs* of 1851 concentrated 'upon the dull and cautious [that is, later] period' of Wordsworth's life. But the *Memoirs* was clear – as Hazlitt had been many years before – that in *Lyrical Ballads* 'the clue to [the] *poetical* theory ... may be found in his political principles; these had been democratical, and ... were of a republican character'.[23] For the Victorians Wordsworth's revolutionary youth was a sensitive subject, and nowhere more so than in the Wordsworth family itself. Writing in 1865, half a century before the Annette Vallon affair became public knowledge, Francis Palgrave came out far enough to hint that in *Lyrical Ballads* 'something of (perhaps unconscious) republicanism was blended with the homeliness in choice of subject and simplicity in matter of words'. Towards the end of the century critics became less reticent about Wordsworth's politics: Edward Dowden in 1897 pointed to 'the Revolutionary contrast between nature, simple, beneficent, glad, and society, which so often does wrong to the life of the natural man'. Compare Thomas Hutchinson, echoing Hazlitt, in 1898: 'On this levelling, simplifying theory of poetic diction Wordsworth expended all the revolutionary ardour for which he had failed to find an outlet in public life'.[24] Here in outline is the twentieth-century view that during the 1790s political defeat, or deadlock, redirected revolutionary idealism into Romantic poetry: numerous critics have elaborated this argument, with various theoretical and ideological modifications, from Emile Legouis to E.P. Thompson to Jerome McGann and Marjorie Levinson.

Instead of following that broadly Marxist line in Wordsworth criticism, I want to glance elsewhere to suggest how responses to this now 'revolutionary' volume played an important part in the invention of English Romanticism. The *Oxford English Dictionary* dates the aesthetic senses of 'romantic', 'romanticism' and 'romanticist' to the 1820s, although Lord Byron had been aware of a new wave of 'Romantic' literature rather earlier than this. Certainly *Lyrical Ballads* and 1798 have been invoked frequently to define the Romantic period in English poetry, yet there has been little agreement on the significance of the conjunction between book and year.

On the first page of *Wordsworth. An Introduction to his Life and Works* (1907) Catharine Punch drew attention to 'that great event in the history of English literature, the publication of the "Lyrical Ballads"'. To make sure her point has registered, she reminds the reader twenty pages later that *Lyrical Ballads* was 'one of the greatest events not only of Wordsworth's life but, as has been said before, of English literary history'. And eighteen pages further on: 'in spite of its unpretentious appearance [*Lyrical Ballads*] was indeed an epoch-making book in English literature. Nothing like it had appeared before'. Still not convinced? Turn over two more pages: 'It has become a commonplace of literary criticism to say that this little volume was an epoch-making book'.[25]

A 'commonplace of literary criticism' by 1907, evidently, yet the contexts in which *Lyrical Ballads* was hailed as 'epoch-making' were strangely varied. Writing in the centenary year 1898, for example, Edmund Gosse asserted that the book marked a decisive break in literary history:

> In a little russet volume published at Bristol, and anonymously put forth by two struggling lads of extreme social obscurity, the old order of things literary was finally and completely changed. The romantic school began, the classic school disappeared, in the autumn of 1798.[26]

Gosse doesn't tell us more precisely when in the autumn of 1798 this 'complete change' occurred, but it is clear that he perceived an implicit link between 'extreme social obscurity' – which for Gosse denoted 'jacobinism' – and the sharp disjunction between 'classic' and 'romantic' schools of poetry. He comes close to admitting as much in the quaint passage that follows: '[t]he association of ... intensely brilliant and inflammatory minds at what we call the psychological moment, produced full-blown and perfect the exquisite new flower of romantic poetry'.[27] Gosse probably thought that the concept of a 'psychological moment' (meaning 'the psychologically (or rather, *psychically*) appropriate moment', *OED*) was at the cutting-edge of literary criticism, and used it to evoke the tumultuous context which had engendered romanticism. The *OED* tells us more:

> The French expression [*moment psychologique*] arose in Paris in December 1870, during the Siege, when it was asserted to have been used by the German *Kreuz Zeitung* in reference to the bombardment of the city, and explained to mean that, as the bombardment had as its aim to act upon the imagination of the Parisians, it was necessary to choose the very moment when this imagination, already shaken by famine and perhaps by civil dissension, was in the fittest state to be effectively acted upon.

If we adapt this gloss from the *OED*, we can see that the 'intensely brilliant and inflammatory minds' associated in *Lyrical Ballads* had joined together at the 'psychological moment' – September 1798? – when the English imagination, already shaken by an age of revolutions, was most susceptible to poetic 'bombardment'. Gosse was seeking to pinpoint the initiating moment of Romanticism but, as the *OED* goes on to show, his use of 'psychological moment' in that sense was

> due to an error of translation, in which the expression actually used by the German journal, *das psychologische Moment*, the psychological 'momentum', potent element, or factor, in the case ... was mistaken for *der psychologische Moment*, the psychological moment of time. The article in the *Neue Preussische* (Kreuz) *Zeitung* of 16 Dec. 1870, p. 1, col. 3, says that very cogent psychological considerations spoke against opening the bombardment before the hopes built by the Parisians upon the raising of the siege by armies of relief should be overthrown; and continued 'in all considerations the psychological momentum or factor must be allowed to play a

prominent part, for without its co-operation there is little to be hoped from the work of the artillery'. Thus attributed to German pedantry, the nonsensical *moment psychologique* was ridiculed by the Parisians, and became a jocular phrase or 'tag' for 'the fitting or proper moment'; and with this connotation it has passed equally nonsensically into English journalese.[28]

This 'pedantic' sense of 'psychological momentum' is nonetheless helpful for focusing Gosse's suggestion that Romantic poetry was uniquely associated with the historically 'final and complete' moment at which *Lyrical Ballads* appeared. More gradualist views of literary history sought to place *Lyrical Ballads* within an evolving process, as for example in the wonderfully incongruous idea of the book as 'the Magna Charta [*sic*], officially ushering in the Romantic period'.[29] The idea that *Lyrical Ballads* co-operated with and affirmed cultural changes already underway was echoed by David Rannie, who said that '[*Lyrical Ballads*] initiated the higher Romanticism in England'; by Edward Albert (1932) '[t]he volume is epoch-making, for it is the prelude to the Romantic movement proper'; and, more confidently this time, by Hamilton Thompson: 'with *Lyrical Ballads* the Romantic movement in poetry came into full existence'.[30]

   By the beginning of the twentieth century, therefore, ideas of *Lyrical Ballads* as 'epoch-making' were commonplace. Sir Arthur Quiller Couch tried to make the epochal moment reverberate once again, in this extravagant account of the book's publication:

> The two friends had launched their thunderbolt, and went off gaily. It was a real thunderbolt, too; a book to which the over-worked epithet 'epoch-making' may for once in a way be applied without stain on the truth; but for the moment England took it with her habitual phlegm.[31]

Q's 'thunderbolt' gives us *Lyrical Ballads* as a divine or supernatural intervention – albeit one that was insufficient, at first, to galvanize sluggish, phlegmatic England. A more subtle spirituality was the essence of the 'aesthetic' or Apollonian interpretation of the poems offered by Stopford Brooke: 'In the *Lyrical Ballads*', Brooke writes, 'Wordsworth and Coleridge delivered the young God of a New Poetry from his swaddling clothes; Nature was his mother, suckled him into strength and followed him with maternal love and inspiration for thirty years, till, having over-strained his manhood, he breathed his last in Keats'.[32] This seems ridiculous, but is worth taking seriously. In Brooke's nativity scene several threads are drawn together: an epoch-making, and quasi-Christian, 'New Poetry'; a benign, nurturing 'Wordsworthian' nature; a gradual decline of poetic ardour until it is extinguished by the over-exertions of phthisicky Johnny Keats. Implicit in all of this is the idea of a 'New Poetry', spiritually inspired by 'Nature' yet compatible with Christian teaching. Here too is the shape of a Romantic era in English poetry: the initiating canonical figures are Wordsworth and Coleridge, and Keats – for Brooke a poet 'with no interest in anything'[33] – represents the movement's ener-vated demise. As James Sutherland drily remarked, the extremity of Wordsworth's experiments in *Lyrical Ballads* ultimately proved fatal to English Romanticism: 'the poet [had] greatly over-ridden his hobby'.[34]

Stopford Brooke's nativity of the 'New Poetry' has a number of intriguing parallels with the descriptions of Burns's birth, repeated with little variation in Burns biographies down to our own time.[35] The appropriation of the Burns nativity motif in a Wordsworthian context suggests once again how the establishment of Wordsworth's reputa-tion required the concealing of Burns's precedence. The nativity is also intelligible as an adaptation of the 'vernal' topos in *Lyrical Ballads* criticism. Like Hazlitt's remarks on *Lyrical Ballads* in 'My First Acquaintance with Poets' ('something of the effect … of the first welcome breath of Spring': Hazlitt, xvii.117), the 'vernal' theme devel-ops from the Wordsworthian idiom (and 'Romantic' ideology) of poems like 'Lines written in early spring',

> … 'tis my faith that every flower
> Enjoys the air it breathes

– and 'Lines written at a small distance from my House':

> There is a blessing in the air,
> Which seems a sense of joy to yield[.]

By the late nineteenth century this idea of *Lyrical Ballads* had become routine: J.C. Shairp (1868): '[t]he poetic well-head, now fairly unsealed, was flowing freely'; Andrew Symington (1881): '[*Lyrical Ballads* were] the germinating spring-time of [Wordsworth's] genius'; Henry N. Hudson (1884): 'a poetry instinct with life and sparkling with dews and breathing of flowers fresh-blown and laughing out their matin joy'; Elizabeth Wordsworth (1891): '[Wordsworth's] poetical gifts seemed to be bursting into flower with all the rapidity of a kindly spring'; Catharine Punch (1907): 'a fresh living poetry in the simplest and freshest of garbs'; E. Hershey Sneath (1912): 'they come like a fresh breeze from vernal field and wood'.[36]

In commenting on *Lyrical Ballads* in 1923, H.W. Garrod tried to 'make it new' by joining the vernal motif with the southern Romanticism represented by Italy in E.M. Forster's novels. Modern technology helped do the trick. For Garrod, the swiftness of a trans-alpine train journey enabled passengers to experience the juxtaposition of the commonplace and the extraordinary that William Hazlitt had found in *Lyrical Ballads*. In reading Wordsworth, Garrod says,

> we pass ... suddenly and surprisedly, into the sunshine – by the kind of miracle which sometimes accomplishes itself for the trav-eller who travels to Italy by way of the St.Gothard tunnel: he enters it from grey and snow-laden northern skies, and, as his train leaves it twenty minutes later, it unrolls before his unprepared gaze the sun-bathed plains of Lombardy and an anomalous world of exuber-ant spring.[37]

This Italian spring also quickens in Forster's novels. 'For the first time [Lucy] felt the influence of spring', we hear in chapter six of *A Room with a View*:

> violets ran down in rivulets and streams and cataracts, irrigating the hillside with blue, eddying round the tree stems, collecting into pools in the hollows, covering the grass with spots of azure foam ... this terrace was the well-head, the primal source whence beauty gushed out to water the earth.[38]

But Forster's Italian spring doesn't flow with an ever-increasing profu-sion, '[e]ach minute sweeter than before'. In some ways it is 'anomalous', gushing with a Romantic 'exuberance' which can as swiftly drain away, as it does for Lucy Honeychurch in the Piazza Signoria, revealing '[w]hat man has made of man': 'The cries from the fountain ... rang emptily. The whole world seemed pale and void of ... meaning'.[39] Surprisingly, perhaps, Garrod's 'anomalous world of ... spring' connects with the diminished Romanticism of some late twentieth-century English poetry; his 'miracle' is accomplished by rail travel through the St. Gothard tunnel, effectively, that is, by underground, on the 'Tube'. A little further in the future this poetic line divides, heading in one direction into the suburban Romanticism of John Betjeman's Metroland and 'our lost Elysium – rural Middlesex again',[40] and in the other 'out beyond' to the more exposed vistas of Larkin's 'Dockery and Son' and 'Here'.

H.W. Garrod updates the idea that *Lyrical Ballads* was a production for which readers were 'unprepared', and in so doing he continued the process of severing the book from its original context. Although he undercuts (literally) the Romantic passion for the Alps in his journey to the Italian plains, for him Romanticism continued to be associated with miraculous revelation. In the late nineteenth and early twentieth centuries popular biographers and editors collaborated with academics like Garrod and 'Q' to exalt the miraculous powers of Wordsworth and *Lyrical Ballads* while extricating both from historical circumstances. Wordsworth the explorer, mountaineer, moral hero, seer and prophet of nature was hailed, first, by Coleridge, and subsequently by John Stuart Mill and Matthew Arnold. This is the heroic Wordsworth who, if he didn't serve at Trafalgar and Waterloo, was for W.T. Webb nevertheless 'typical of the English race at its best ... the great Cumbrian dalesman, combining, as he did, the childlike genius of Nelson with the square-hewn strength of the Iron Duke'. '[Wordsworth's] whole character, utterance, teaching, are *strong*', says Elizabeth Wordsworth, adding, with a uprush of family pride, '[t]here is no truckling to *boudoir* tastes; no cheap finery, no vulgar sentiment'. Now Wordsworth becomes the 'strong and daring pioneer of a younger day' who in *Lyrical Ballads* 'struck out for a *terra nova* in poetry ... [attaining] the highest Alpine peaks in the abiding land of song'; who like 'stout Cortez' in Keats's sonnet 'seems to brood on the extreme edge of some promontory stretching out into the ocean'. Wordsworth 'escaped into the light and air after the great disillusionment of the Revolution', says William Macneill Dixon: 'he emerged from the cloud, and, climbing higher up the mountain ... held commerce with vaster presences and the mighty shades of things to come'.[41]

This is Wordsworth as 'Prometheus Rising', the prophet–poet of the Coleridgean tradition represented in the twentieth century by Frank Kermode, Geoffrey Hartman, M.H. Abrams, and Harold Bloom – all inhabitants of the 'high places' of Romantic criticism. Yet over the same period the low tradition of Wordsworth's reception has been lost to sight, and rarely features in modern studies of him. For Hazlitt, as we've seen, it was Wordsworth's 'popular, inartificial style' that gave controversial life to *Lyrical Ballads*; correspondingly, the most lively arena of Wordsworth's reception over the last two hundred years has been popular editions, commentaries, memoirs. The dwindling of these voices accompanied Wordsworth's ascent 'higher up' to the peak of the English Romantic canon. Now that the Romantic canon has been so successfully upended, alerting us to popular writing contemporary with *Lyrical Ballads*, the debate can revive once again – renewing *Lyrical Ballads* for a third century of readers.

Notes

1 John Wright, *The Genius of Wordsworth Harmonized with the Wisdom and Integrity of his Reviewers* (London: Longman, *etc.*, 1853), p. 20.
2 Marilyn Butler, *Romantics, Rebels, and Reactionaries: English Literature and its Background 1760–1830* (Oxford: Oxford University Press, 1981), pp. 58, 64.
3 See Robert Mayo, 'The Contemporaneity of the *Lyrical Ballads*', *PMLA* 69 (1954), pp. 486–522.
4 Mary Jacobus, *Tradition and Experiment in Wordsworth's* Lyrical Ballads *(1798)* (Oxford: Clarendon Press, 1975), p. 1.
5 A.D. Harvey, *English Poetry in a Changing Society 1780–1825* (London: Allison and Busby, 1980), p. 58.
6 See Henry A. Beers, *A History of English Romanticism in the Eighteenth Century* (London: Paul, Trench, Trubner, 1899), p. 422.
7 See my 'Authenticating Robert Burns'; in *Robert Burns and Cultural Authority*, ed. Robert Crawford (Edinburgh: Edinburgh U.P., 1997), pp. 159–79.
8 Robert Burns, *Poems, Chiefly in the Scottish Dialect* (Kilmarnock: Wilson, 1786), p. iv.
9 For Wordsworth's reading of Burns, see Duncan Wu, *Wordsworth's Reading, 1770–1799* (Cambridge: Cambridge University Press, 1993), pp. 23–4.
10 C.T. Winchester, *William Wordsworth. How to Know Him* (Indianapolis: Bobbs-Merrill ('How to Know the Authors' series), 1916), p. 49.
11 *Lyrical Ballads, 1798*, ed. Thomas Hutchinson (London: Duckworth, 1898), p. ix; Walter Raleigh, *Wordsworth* (London: Arnold, 1903), p. 288.
12 See Mark L. Reed, *Wordsworth. The Chronology of the Early Years* (Cambridge, Mass., 1967), p. 247 (entry 173).
13 The best discussion of the publication of *Lyrical Ballads* (1798) is James Butler, 'Wordsworth, Cottle, and the *Lyrical Ballads*: Five Letters, 1797–1800', *JEGP* 75 (1976), pp. 139–53.
14 See, for example, 'particularly pleased' (*Analytical Review* 28 (December, 1798)); 'extremely entertained' (*Monthly Review* 2nd series, 29 (June 1799)); 'cordial approbation' (*British Critic* 14 (October 1799)): cited in 'Appendix C' to *LBB*, pp. 323–7.
15 William J. Long, *English Literature: Its History and its Significance for the Life of the English-Speaking World* (Boston/London: Ginn, 1909), p. 376.
16 *British Authors of the Nineteenth Century*, ed. S.J. Kunitz and H. Haycraft (NY: Wilson, 1936), p. 670.

17 Joseph Angus, *The Handbook of English Literature* (London: Religious Tract Society, 1865), pp. 256–7.

18 Mrs. Oliphant, *The Literary History of England in the end of the Eighteenth and Beginning of the Nineteenth Century* (3 vols; London: Macmillan, 1882), i.278.

19 James Middleton Sutherland, *William Wordsworth. The Story of his Life. With Critical Remarks on his Writings* (London: Stock, 1887), pp. 55, 205–6, 203.

20 Elizabeth Wordsworth, *William Wordsworth* (London: Percival, 1891), p. 205; Laurie Magnus, *English Literature in the Nineteenth Century: An Essay in Criticism* (London: Melrose, 1909), p. 58; Raleigh, *Wordsworth*, p. 85; *British Authors of the Nineteenth Century*, p. 671.

21 *Lyrical Ballads*, ed. Hutchinson, pp. xxxiii–xxxiv.

22 *Poems by William Wordsworth*, ed. Edward Dowden (Boston/London: Ginn ('Athenaeum Press' series), 1897), p. lxiv.

23 Christopher Wordsworth, *Memoirs of William Wordsworth* (2 vols; London: Moxon, 1851), i.125.

24 *A Selection from the Works of William Wordsworth*, selected and arranged by F.T. Palgrave (London: Moxon ('Moxon's Miniature Poets' series), 1865), p. xvii; *Poems by Wordsworth*, ed. Dowden, pp. lx–lxi; *Lyrical Ballads*, ed. Hutchinson, p. xxxv.

25 Catharine Punch, *Wordsworth. An Introduction to his Life and Works* (London: Allman, 1907), pp. 1, 20, 38, 40.

26 Edmund Gosse, *A Short History of Modern English Literature* (London: Heinemann ('Short Histories of the Literatures of the World' series), 1898), p. 279.

27 Gosse, *A Short History*, p. 279.

28 See *OED*: 'psychological', 2(b).

29 Cited from Needleman and Otis, *An Outline History of English Literature* (2nd edn, 1939); quoted in Harvey, *English Poetry in a Changing Society*, p. 64.

30 David Watson Rannie, *Wordsworth and his Circle* (London: Methuen, 1907), p. 79; Edward Albert, *A History of English Literature: A Practical Text-book* (London: Harrap, 1932), p. 310; *Selections from the Poems of William Wordsworth*, ed. A. Hamilton Thompson (Cambridge: Cambridge University Press, 1917), p. xix.

31 Sir Arthur Quiller-Couch, *Studies in Literature. First Series* (Cambridge: Cambridge University Press, 1946), pp. 211–12.

32 Stopford A. Brooke, *Naturalism in English Poetry* (London/Toronto: Dent/ Dutton, 1920), p. 3.

33 Stopford A. Brooke, *Studies in Poetry* (London: Duckworth, 1907), p. 204.

34 Sutherland, *Wordsworth*, p. 57.

35 See my 'Authenticating Robert Burns'.

36 J.C. Shairp, 'Wordsworth: The Man and the Poet'; in *Studies in Poetry and Philosophy* (Edinburgh: Edmonston and Douglas, 1868), p. 43; Andrew Symington, *William Wordsworth: A Biographical Sketch: with Selections from his Writings in Poetry and Prose* (2 vols; London: Blackie ('Men of Light and Leading' series), 1881), i.117; Henry N. Hudson, *Studies in Wordsworth …* (Boston: Little, Brown, 1884), p. 121; Elizabeth Wordsworth, *Wordsworth*,

p. 43; Punch, *Wordsworth*, pp. 41–2; E. Hershey Sneath, *Wordsworth: Poet of Nature and Poet of Man* (Boston/London: Ginn, 1912), p. 123.

37   H.W. Garrod, *Wordsworth: Lectures and Essays* (Oxford: Clarendon Press, 1923), p. 74.

38   E.M. Forster, *A Room with a View*, ed. Oliver Stallybrass (London: Arnold (Abinger Edition), 1977), pp. 67–8.

39   Forster, *A Room with a View*, p. 42.

40   'Middlesex'; in *John Betjeman's Collected Poems*, compiled and introduced by the Earl of Birkenhead (London: Murray, 1958), p. 193.

41   *Selections from Wordsworth*, ed. W.T. Webb (London: Macmillan, 1897); Elizabeth Wordsworth, *Wordsworth*, p. 199; Raleigh, *Wordsworth*, p. 227; Sutherland, *Wordsworth*, pp. 203, 225; *Wordsworth*, selected and intro-duced by William Macneill Dixon (Edinburgh: Jack ('The Golden Poets' series), 1907), pp. xxv, xxvi.

Index

Works by William Wordsworth (WW) and Samuel Taylor Coleridge (STC) appear in separate title-entries; other works are listed under authors' names, after thematic entries.